Swami
Yogeshwaranand Saraswati

The Philosophy of Self-Realisation of Swami Yogeshwaranand Saraswati

Swami Yogehswaranand Saraswati was a bold critic of the scriptures when truth was required to be established. He verified every bit of knowledge in his deep *Sāmadhi* leaving nothing to presumption. He, therefore, made some sensational departures from established concepts of Sāmkhya and Yoga philosophies in spite of being a staunch follower of these systems.

The Philosophy of Self-Realisation *of* Swami Yogeshwaranand Saraswati

DR. INDER BHAN BHASIN

New Age Books

ISBN: 978-81-7822-311-7

First Indian Edition: Delhi, 2008

Published by
NEW AGE BOOKS
A-44 Naraina Phase-I
New Delhi 110 028 (INDIA)
Email: nab@vsnl.in
Website: www.newagebooksindia.com

Printed in India
at Shri Jainendra Press
A-45 Naraina Phase-I, New Delhi-110 028

Contents

Dedication

This work is dedicated to all the Seers, Sages and Ṛṣis of yore who meditated in deep forests and crystalised the subtle truth of reality for the benefit of entire mankind.

Reminiscence

When I AM Gone.........

When tomorrow starts without me, and I'm not there to see
If the sun should rise and find your eyes all filled with tears for me
I wish so much you wouldn't cry the way you did today
While thinking of the many things, we didn't get to say
I know how much you love me, as much as I love you
And each time that you think of me, I know you'll miss me too
But when tomorrow starts without me, please try to understand
That an angel came and called my name, and took me by the hand
And said my place was ready, in heaven far above
And that I'd have to leave behind all those I dearly love
But as I turned to walk away, a tear fell from my eye
For all my life, I'd always thought, I didn't want to die
I had so much to live for, so much left yet to do
It seemed almost impossible, that I was leaving you
I thought of all the yesterdays, the good ones and the bad
I thought of all the love we shared, and all the fun we had
If I could relive yesterday, just even for a while
I'd say good-bye and kiss you and may be see you smile
But then I fully realised, that this could never be

For emptiness and memories, would take the place of me
And when I thought of worldly things, I might miss come tomorrow
I thought of you, and when I did, my heart was filled with sorrow
But when I walked through heaven's gates, I felt so much at home
When God looked down and smiled at me, from his great golden throne
He said, "This is eternity, and all I've promised you
Today your life on earth is past, but here life starts anew
I promise no tomorrow, but today will always last
And since each day's the same way there's no longing for the past
You have been so faithful, so trusting and so true
Though there were times you did some things you knew you shouldn't do
But you have been forgiven and now at last you're free
So won't you come and take my hand and share my life with me?"
So when tomorrow starts without me, don't think we're far apart
For every time you think of me, I'm right here, in your heart

(Anonymous)

Acknowledgements

My grateful thanks are due, first of all, to my spouse Lovel who prompted me to undertake the massive job of completing this work.

My thanks are also due to my son Vinay who relieved me of the responsibilities of my business and to my daughter Charu who placed at my disposal all the services of her office for my exclusive use.

I am also grateful to my mentor and guide Dr. Shubhada Joshi, an eminent scholar, who led me from darkness to light.

Lastly, I am obliged to my publishers who have brought out an impressive version of the book.

Dr. Inder Bhan Bhasin

Foreword

Swami Yogeshwaranand Saraswati was a great Yogi of his time who had attained perfect mastery over Samādhi. His knowledge of self and God is based on the intuitive experiences which he gained in deep meditation. Although he followed Sāmkhya-Yoga systems of Philosophy, yet he deviated from their concepts wherever he experienced truth differently in his meditative vision. His views about the Vrittis and Samskāras are radically different from what is believed by Sāmkhya school of Philosophy. He says that Vrittis belong to Buddhi and Samskāras belong to Citta whereas Yoga system considers Samskāras as pertaining to Citta alone. He also does not agree with Mahrishi Patāñjali that there are only five types of Vrittis which must be controlled to attain perfect Samadhi. He believes that breathing and palpitation which are necessary by-products of life, are also Vrittis and, therefore, one must control seven Vrittis instead of five. He does not accept that the Vrittis can be permanently controlled. He has come to this conclusion as a result of his ceaseless search for truth in deep Samadhi. He says that since our Samskāras cannot be completely remitted, Vrittis cannot be totally controlled. For these reasons Moksha is impossible for man to attain.

His most sensational discovery is the reality of Soul (Jīvātman). Unlike the established concept that soul is a conscious entity, which is eternal and which takes birth after birth to reap or enjoy the fruits of its past Karmas, he considers Soul to be a created entity which exists only till the time of Pralaya (the deluge). He says that Brahman pervades Prakriti and only then Prakriti commences its evolution to create the universe. According to him when Prakriti reaches the stage of cosmic Citta in the process of evolution, then Divinity which is already present in it is called soul (Jīvātman). At the time of Pralaya when every effect of Prakriti merges in its cause, cosmic Citta also merges in Mahat Sāttva which is its material cause. Thereby Divinity trapped in cosmic Citta is released and once again becomes Brahman. Thus, in his view there are only two eternal entities namely Brahman and Prakriti. For him, soul is non-permanent even though Sāmkhya considers both Purusha and Prakriti as eternal. Moreover, he does not consider soul as doer because according to him, action is an attribute of matter and not of consciousness. He, therefore, considers Citta as the doer and reaper of fruits and not soul.

With regard to Brahman also Swami Yogeshwaranand has independent views. He says that the universe has been created by the combined efforts of Brahman and Prakriti. None of the two can create the world alone. Unless Brahman pervades Prakriti the latter cannot evolve. Prakriti is the material cause of the world and Brahman is the efficient cause. Brahman's role is, therefore, restricted only to pervasion of Prakriti which proceeds, thereafter, to create the universe. God does not do anything beyond pervasion. By pervading Prakriti, Brahman transfers pseudo consciousness to Prakriti which not only creates but appears to be conscious also. He also does not believe that Brahman dispenses the fruits of Karmas of individual beings. It is the law of Karma which is responsible for dispensation of such fruits. He says that the law of Karma operates automatically and that God does not interfere in it at all. For the same reason Brahman remains unaffected whether someone praises Him or censures Him. Therefore, worship of God can have no effect whatsoever on Him.

The above are some of the most radical aspects of the Philosophy of Swami Yogeshwaranand which Dr. Inder Bhan Bhasin has analysed and discussed in this book. His approach is critical but he is also appreciative of some of the findings of Swami Yogeshwaranand which have enriched the Sāmkhya Philosophy or which have contributed to the removal of cobwebs surrounding the orthodox systems to augment the existing knowledge. He has done a commendable job of giving exposure to the philosophy of Swami Yogeshwaranand on the one hand and enlarging the scope of research and analysis of some of the fundamental characteristics of Sāmkhya thought.

Dr. Inder Bhan Bhasin has been known to me for a long time during which period I have found him to be highly dedicated to his cause. He has a philosophical bent of mind which has prompted him to many spiritual pursuits. One such pursuit is his attempt to highlight the Philosophy of Swami Yogeshwaranand whom he considers as his mentor and preceptor. He has treated the subject with utmost honesty and has been quite fair in drawing conclusion as he has done.

I give my blessings to him and wish him all success even in his future endeavours.

Om Shanti, Shanti, Shanti:

12th October, 2006

Swami Satyamitrananda Giri
Bharat Mata Mandir,
Haridwar (U. A.)

Swami Yogeshwaranand Saraswati (As I know him)

Swami Yogeshwaranand Paramhans was one of the greatest Yogis of the 20th century. He lived the life of extreme renunciation and austerity mostly in the Himalayas practicing all that is laid down in the scriptures for the realisation of soul and God and spent a lifetime in reviving the ancient science of Yoga.

Swami Yogeshwaranand Paramhans formerly known as Brahmachāri Vyasa Devaji, left the home of his well-to-do parents at a tender age of fourteen, like Buddha, in search of knowledge and self-realisation. The young Brahmachari spent the early years of his life in the study of Sanskrit language and in mastering the scriptural lore. He then followed the path of ancient rishis of Himalayas and practiced the most difficult tapasya and Yogic Sādhana while continuing the search of a real guru who could lead him to the final goal. He came across a number of ascetics about whom one reads only in the scriptures but none met with his expectation. However, his search for a real Guru was rewarded with the meeting of a great ascetic, Yogi Parmananda Avadhoot, who helped him in perfecting shunya (void) Samādhi. Later, his search for a great Yogi came to an end only when he met Avadhoot Swami Atmanand Ji (who had then returned from Tibet) in a cave near Gangotri (in Himalayas) from whom he learnt Samprajnāta Samādhi and perception of various processes of nature in the state of Samadhi, and also the ultimate divine knowledge.

The various events of his life in the Himalayas with the great ascetics and the practice of higher Yoga, are far stranger than fiction. Some of them are even unbelievable for those who are not conversant with the power of yoga. One of the events of the great yogi's life which pertain to his Swami Guru Ātmanand, is described in his own words as "He placed his gracious hands on my head, my eyes closed and I attained some unknown state. My body was illuminated as if by electric light. This light filled the entire body and revealed all its inner states of subtle processes."

By constant and dedicated practice of meditation, he experienced various types of Samādhis, some of which lasted for several weeks which culminated in his gaining knowledge of self-realisation, origin and dissolution of cosmos and the goal of human existence. Having satisfied his thirst for the ultimate divine knowledge, he spent the rest of his life imparting the valuable knowledge to hundreds of thousands of keen aspirants of all faiths from many countries of the world.

He joined the Brahman on April 23, 1985 at the age of ninety-nine.

The esoteric knowledge which used to pass from guru to disciple through personal relationship and which sometimes required not only a whole lifetime but several lives, was set down, at the behest of his guru, in his books. Some day, when the top scientists of the world pay the attention it deserves, to this subtlest sciences, these books will give all the basic material for their research and cause a stir in the world of science. At present, these books are helping keen aspirants everywhere to achieve their ultimate goal of realisation of soul and God.

Of the many books authored by Swami Yogeshwaranand Saraswati, it is worthwhile to mention the following four which deal with important subjects such as Ātman, Brahman and Prakriti.

His book "Science of Soul" deals with realisation of the self and is written in an easy, pleasing and illuminating style. In this book Swami Yogeshwaranand Paramhans has included his personal experiences gained in deep Samādhi in Himalaya. He has given a detailed method of how to pierce through three bodies and five sheaths to perceive the soul encased in the Citta in causal body and covered with five orbs.

"Science of Divinity" contains five parts and describes 35 objects which are the cause of Kaivalya. Of these objects Brahman, Prakriti and Ātman are eternal and the rest are transitory. In this book he has explained that all products that have evolved from Prakriti, have come into being because of proximity of Brahman. He has also explained how Brahman can be realised at every stage of the evolution of Prakriti from its aboriginal state to the massive universe.

God or the Absolute Brahman is Himself infinite and so is our knowledge of him. Whatever remained undealt with or escaped notice, as also such other matters which were considered by tradition as sacrosanct and were not contained in the book "Science of Divinity" were taken up for a critical examination by Swami Yogeshwaranand Paramhans in his book " The essential Colourlessness of the Absolute". He has selected twelve traditional doctrines pertaining to Brahman and fifteen such doctrines pertaining to the self which he has discussed thoroughly to determine their validity.

The fourth book namely "First Steps to Higher Yoga" is a great book which gives a learned exposition of all the eight limbs of Ashtānga Yoga of Mahrishi Patanjali. About 300 postures of Yoga along with their method and benefits are described in this book. It also describes seventy types of Prānayāmas and mentions their benefits.

All the above mentioned books are unique because all that Swami Yogeshwaranand Saraswati has written in these books, was first verified by him in his super conscious state. Because of the knowledge acquired through perception in Samādhi he differed on certain subtle aspects of the knowledge of Yoga, with many earlier seers including Patanjali himself. Any aspirant, who studies these books with devotion and dedication, will be tremendously benefited and will also find it much easier to realise the self and to perceive the presence of Brahman.

New Delhi-110023
20th July, 2007.

O. P. Raheja
President
Yoga Niketan Trust

Introduction

This book is an abridged version of my dissertation which I submitted to the University of Mumbai as my research work for the award of degree of Ph.D. The thesis was highly acclaimed by my guide as well as by my examiners who strongly recommended that the work should be published. I have, therefore, made some minor modifications in my thesis and dropped a few chapters so as to make the work easily intelligible to a common reader. I believe that the common will be as much interested in his philosophy as in Swami Yogeshwaranand himself. Accordingly, the introduction has been so designed as to give a fair idea of his life as well as of his philosophy and his works.

(1) His life

Swami Yogeshwaranand was born in an affluent family where all the comforts of life were available to him in plenty. His name, given to him by his parents, was Vyasa Deva which name he retained till he undertook Sanyas on 13th April, 1962 at the age of 75 years. Addressing a large gathering which attended the ceremony of his taking Sanyas, he said that his first teacher was one Swami Ramanand who inspired the feeling of detachment and renunciation in him. His second teacher was Parmanand Avadhut who belonged to Udasin sect from whom he learnt Sanskrit and Yoga. His third Guru was one Swami Atmanand who was a resident of Ayodhya and who had lived in Tibet for a long time. It is he who imparted complete knowledge of self (Ātman) and Brahman in a span of 17 hours by placing his thumb on the forehead of

Swami Yogeshwaranand and revealing the secrets of the whole existence. When Swami Yogeshwaranand rose from his Samādhi, tears flowed from his eyes which he kept on shedding copiously on being blessed with this wonderful knowledge. His Preceptor then said, "Get up my son. It is not the time to weep but to be happy and to experience this strange bliss and delight". His preceptor told him that what has been revealed to him was the only knowledge and there was no other knowledge beyond that. He demanded of him that he should go on perfecting the knowledge himself and impart it to others who may deserve it.

In obedience to the instructions of his Guru, Swami Yogeshwaranand set up Yoga Centres at various places such as at Rishikesh, Delhi, Uttarkashi, Pahalgam etc. where training is being given to the aspirants. With perfection attained in *Samādhi,* Swami Yogeshwaranand rose to be the greatest Yogi of his time and acquired *Siddhis* with which he cured many of his disciples and relieved many others of their hardships and miseries.

(2) His Works

Of all the works of Swami Yogeshwaranand, the following books require special attention for extremely subtle subjects dealt therein:

(1) Science of Soul;

(2) Science of Divinity;

(3) Essential Colourlessness of the absolute or the Unconditioned *Brahaman;*

In 'Science of Soul', he has dealt exclusively with the individual soul (*Jīvātman*) and has given a different exposition thereof. He has indicated the path to be followed for realising and envisioning the *Ātman*. In 'Science of Divinity', he has dealt with the subject of *Brahman*. His third book, 'Essential Colourlessness of the Absolute,' represents his investigative contemplation and his mode of thinking about *Brahman*. In fact in his earlier book, 'Science of Divinity' he has already explained in suitable details, the ways and means of realising *Brahman*. However, in this book namely "Essential Colourlessness of the Absolute," he has attempted to offer logical and reasoned conclusions after thoroughly examining many a prevalent concepts and doctrines with regard to *Brahman* and *Jīvātman*. He has given detailed explanation of how God creates the world and what all is within the purview and competence of God. This aspect assumes significance because God is universally known as *omnipotent* which means that there are no limits on the authority of *Brahman*. In the third book mentioned above, he has proved that neither *Brahman* nor *Ātman* are capable of being defined and that both are actionless. His argument is that if something has attributes, it is subject to change. But no properties subsist in *Brahman* and soul and, therefore, the two are indefinable. For this reason *Brahman* cannot be directly envisioned. Swami Yogeshwaranand says that although Brahman cannot be perceived directly, we can yet have his feel through certain media such as the subtle *Prāna*, Divine Sounds and Divine Lights. He has written a book each on the method of realisation of *Brahman* and *Ātman* through these means.

(3) Update of Knowledge

In the course of my research in the philosophy of Swami Yogeshwaranand, it is observed that he had held certain views initially, which he later on changed. For example, in this book "Science of Soul", which is one of his earliest works, he has stated that *Jīvātma* assumes the role of actor and enjoyer.[1] Again, in his book 'Science of Divinity', he says similarly that the soul is both the doer, and enjoyer.[2] However, in the book 'Essential Colourlessness of the Absoute' which was written much later, he has categorically stated that the *Jīvātman* or the living soul, cannot be treated as the doer and reaper of the fruits of its actions.[3] The reasons which prompted him to modify his earlier opinion on vital issues, are that he formed an opinion on the basis of his vision in deep meditation, at that time which he subsequently changed when he concentrated further in *Samâdhi* on the same object and realised that the earlier knowledge was not so perfect. He has stated in his works that the knowledge contained therein is not based on the study of books but on his own experience in *Samādhi*.

No Yogi, other that Swami Yogeshwaranand, is known to have maintained such record of his findings gained in his super-conscious state. He has stated that his deliberative examination of every bit of knowledge contained in each of his books, has been corroborated by his own research in the field of quiet contemplation and life-long meditation. We get mystic experiences in *Samādhi*. Mysticism aims at knowing the Reality which otherwise cannot be known by empirical sources of knowledge such as *Pramāna, Anumāna, Sabda* etc. The great mystic Sh.R.D.Ranade considers these mystic experiences as perfectly valid if such experiences are clear and vivid and also if these are objective, continuous and universal, grow step by step and finally lead to the knowledge of ultimate Reality. In the case of Swami Yogeshwaranand, the update of knowledge seems to be compatible with the criterion for mystical experiences.

The philosophy of self realisation of Swami Yogeshwaranand relates to three eternal entities namely *Brahman, Atman* and *Prakriti*. In respect of all these entities, there are certain traditionally held concepts which are widely accepted as sacrosanct. No one can dare question those truths or challenge their validity. Swami Yogeshwaranand has not accepted these concepts blindly but rejected them as untenable, if any thing was found as inconsistent with the result of his personal research in *Samādhi. These matters which are thoroughly dealt with in the book, are briefly mentioned below:*

(4) Jīvātman *(the individual Soul)*

With regard to individual soul, he has tried to establish it as absolutely free from conditioning adjuncts which dispenses with the necessity of bondage and liberation of the soul. In this view of the matter, just as *Brahman* is the indweller of the universe, the *Ātman* is the indweller of our body and both are pure, unblemished, actionless, impartible, ever free and full of knowledge.

(a) Soul Non-eternal

Although it is widely accepted that the individual soul is a conscious and eternal entity, he does not subscribe to this concept and says that the soul is neither unchanging nor eternal. This philosophy stems from his definition of the soul which is not only radical but the only of its kind. According to him when *Prakriti* proceeds to evolve, it undergoes successive stages of subsidiary creation. In the process when *Prakriti* reaches the stage of creation of cosmic *Citta*, which is the material cause of every individual *Citta*, then the Divinity which is already present in the finite *Citta*, comes to be called the living soul or *Jīvātman*. All that it means is that the soul is the created entity unlike *Brahman* and *Prakriti*. It is eternal in the sense that it lasts till the doom's day when every effect merges in its cause and, accordingly, the individual *Citta* also merges in cosmic *Citta* which in turn merges in *Mahat*– its material cause. In the state of *Pralaya*(doom), the soul reverts to its original primeval nature and once again becomes undivided *Brahman*.

(b) Bondage of the Soul

Swami Yogeshwaranand says that the soul is ever free

from bondage because bondage is for the *Citta* and not for the soul. Pure *Ātman* is not tainted by objects. *Citta* and *Buddhi* alone are tainted and the soul is the seer of the coloured *Citta* and *Buddhi*. The Soul is believed to be in bondage due to erroneously imposing bondage on the soul and this has been going on from times immemorial. This bondage is believed on account of the soul's close proximity and association with the three bodies namely gross, subtle and causal bodies. Therefore, pleasure and pain are of these bodies and not of the soul. Had the pleasure and pain belonged to the soul, they would have continued to be associated with the soul even at the time of *Pralaya* and also in the state of final liberation, being original traits of the soul. In fact bondage and release are the traits of *Citta* but the close association of consciousness imparts to *Citta* a sort of pseudo consciousness which enables *Citta* to experience pleasure and pain even though it is inert and unconscious, being a product of matter. This view of Swami Yogeshwaranand is in direct contrast with the view of *Nyāya Vaiśeṣika* school which believes that all cognitions, feelings and collations are the attributes of the soul. According to them, these qualities cannot belong to physical substance because these cannot be perceived by our external organs of perception. Therefore, they admit that these properties belong to another entity called self which is not intelligence as such but a substance having intelligence as its attribute. The self for them is not mere consciousness or knowledge but a knower and also an enjoyer.[4]

(c) *Soul as Doer*

For the same reasons as above the age old doctrine that the soul performs actions and in order to reap the fruits of its accumulated *karmas*, it takes birth again and again, falls flat. The soul is not the doer and reaper of the fruits of its actions. On the basis of the logic, mentioned in (b) above, Swami Yogeshwaranand does not regard either God or the soul to be responsible agents. His view that by dint of proximity of *Brahman* with *Prakriti* , motion and action is caused in the latter and the same effect is produced in the human body because of the soul's proximity to *Citta*, stands vindicated. According to him, for the stated reasons[5] the property of action in the soul is neither justifiable nor logically defensible. It is in the *Citta* that the tendency to action arises, once it comes into close proximity with the soul.

Therefore, being non–doer, the soul is always free and unbounded in the manner of *Brahman* and this concept of Swami Yogeshwaranand has largely widened the scope of knowledge about the soul.

(d) Multiplicity of Soul

Every one will agree, on the basis of daily experience, that there are innumerous souls in innumerous bodies. Swami Yogeshwaranand does not accept this doctrine. According to him, it is the same Supreme Soul (*Brahaman*) which is reflected in all the bodies. He says that when *Prakriti* becomes many aspected, by the manifestation of three *gunas* in the process of evolution, *Brahman* appears as manifold who was earlier only unitary at a time when *Prakriti* was in the state of re-absorption. *Brahman* and *Prakriti* are both subtle although *Brahman* is subtler than *Prakriti* so that He can pervade it and prompt it to transform. The primordial state of *Prakriti* is also its most stable state in which all the three *gunas,* namely *Satwa, Rajas* and *Tamas,* are present in equal ratio. It is also the invisible state of *Prakriti*. When the new cycle of creation is about to commence, *Brahman* pervades subtle *Prakriti* in its primeval state and disturbs it equilibrium, with the result that it starts its movement to create the universe. At that stage *Brahman* is only a single entity. It is the evolution of *Prakriti* that has apparently made *Brahman* as manifold in the innumerous individual *Cittas*. Swami Yogeshwaranand says that just as a man, standing amidst innumerable mirrors appears many, in the same way one God assumes the appearance of many souls. On this point, it has already been stated that the soul is not the doer or enjoyer of the fruits of its actions. *If we do not believe the soul as the doer and reaper, then in that case it is not necessary to believe that there are separate spirits in separate bodies.* One single supreme spirit which is all–pervasive and already abides in all the bodies, will serve the same purpose. Hence, the doctrine that so many bodies occupy so many souls in untenable.

(e) Knowledge and Action

In his book 'Science of Soul', Swami Yogeshwaranand has mentioned that after a life time of meditation, he came to the conclusion that when the soul comes to reside in the body, then two types of energies are released. One is the energy of knowledge (*Vijnāna*) and the other is the energy of action (*kriya*). These two energies combine and together they give rise to *Prāna* which energies all the three bodies and five sheaths. Thus knowledge and action go together. Where there is knowledge, there is action and *vice versa*. This is their property or *Dharma*. If we take them as also the property of consciousness, because it is consciousness which has produced these energies, then we have to accede that consciousness is result oriented and is also changeable which conflicts with the belief that consciousness is unchanging. Hence knowledge and action cannot be considered as attributes of consciousness.

The properties of action are to move up, to fall down, to contract, to expand and to walk. For obvious reasons, these qualities cannot be said to belong to consciousness. Similarly, knowledge also cannot be said to be the quality of consciousness because knowledge has action as its inner component which keeps it going. Thus knowledge cannot also be regarded as the attribute of consciousness or else we will be faced with the same problem as in the case of action. Therefore, knowledge and action both stand ruled out as attributes of consciousness. Swami Yogeshwaranand says that taking every aspect into account, we cannot escape from accepting that knowledge and action are the products of nature (matter). This is an extremely non–traditional view which is quiet contrary to the verdict of *Upanishads*. But Swami Yogeshwaranand does not consider *Upanishads* as the last world. He says that it is not correct to take whatever is written in the Upanishads or whatever is said by scholars before the advent of *Upanishads*, as gospel truth. One must inculcate the habit of independent thinking and should test every proposition on the touchstone of logic and reason.[6] According to him, it is *Prakriti* that produces results and in that process, it goes on changing.

When he says that the *Upanishads* should not be treated as the last word, he is not indulging in any blasphemy because traces of opposition against the religion of the *Vedas* are found in the *Vedas* themselves. The Indo-Aryans of yore were very bold thinkers and nothing was sacrilegious to them in their search after truth. Swami Yogeshwaranand belongs to the said class of Indo–Aryans and, therefore, his search after truth in mystic vision is quite compatible with the character of the ancient Rishis.

(5) About Brahman

With regard to *Brahman* as well, many of his conclusions, drawn in deep *Samādhi* or through common knowledge, are in stark contrast to the doctrine of long acceptance. Some such conclusions are mentioned below:

(a) Brahman as Omnipotent

There is a universal belief that God is the doer of every thing that is happening in the universe. For Swami

Yogeshwaranand this belief is untenable because, as we have already mentioned above, God is a mere spectator and witness. If we treat him as doer, then he too will be answerable for actions under the universal law of *Karma*. The soul is a minute entity compared with God and resides in a small place as the human body and yet it is called upon to render full account of its actions. Then God who occupies the whole universe cannot be absolved of the fruits of His actions.

In Yoga philosophy *Brahman* is termed as *Iśvara* who is a special *Puruṣa* and who is untainted by afflictions. This is not the occasion to go into the exact nature of *Iśvara*. However it will make our job easy if we take *Iśvara*[6] as synonymous with Brahman. In Yoga Sutra 1-23, *Patānjali* says that *Samādhi* can be obtained by devotion to *Iśvara* and, commenting on it, Vyasa says that *Iśvara* overcome by *'Pranidhāna'* which is a special kind of devotion, favours the practitioner because of his deep desire for *Samādhi*. Moreover, Yoga believes that the equilibrium of Prakriti is disturbed by the effort of *Iśvara*. Thus, this disturbance in *Prakriti* is caused by divine will of *Brahman*. According to *Bhiksu, Iśvara* has eternal aiśvarya' which is the cause of his showering grace on his devotees.[7] In view of these observations, and innumerous relevant statements in the scriptures, it is difficult to support the view of Swami Yogeshwaranand that *Brahman* is non–productive. He, However, has some point on logic which has been elaborately treated in the book.

(b) Changeability of Brahman

Swami Yogeshwaranand does not agree that *Brahman* is changeable because change is the peculiarity of inanimate *Prakriti*. Following the tradition, some scholars believe that God is variable. It only means that just as *Prakriti* creates inert and inanimate objects, *Brahman,* will create living objects. This will bring *Brahman* on par with

Prakriti which is not compatible with the views of *Brahman* in the scriptures. *Brahman* who is consciousness incarnate, ever remains unchanged. And this property of *Brahman* has been established through the personal experience of Swami Yogeshwaranand.[8] Because *Brahman* is unchangeable, knowledge and action cannot be His attributes. Otherwise He would be a mutable entity. Since *Prakriti* is also changeable, there will be no difference between *Brahman* and *Prakriti*, as both will be mutable or transformatory. There is no doubt that *Brahman* is Supra Conscious Being which implies that He is knowledge incarnate and, on that account, there is no difference between knowledge and consciousness. But this consciousness is instilled in *Prakriti* by the pervasion and close proximity of *Brahman*. This also proves that the Supreme Being is the efficient cause and not the material cause of the said knowledge. Such knowledge grows and develops and, in the course of time, it decays and perishes. Therefore, knowledge is neither a product nor an attribute of *Brahman* who is regarded as knowledge *per se* but not as Principle possessing a subservient or instrumental quality. *This view of Swami Yogeshwaranand has a sound bearing and expands, to some extent, the understanding of Brahman by way of improvement of Sāmkhya thought.* Attributes like pure knowledge or intelligence, power and initiative, do not belong to Brahman but are superimposed on Him. These are the attributes of *Prakriti* when it comes in the embrace of divinity.

(c) Perception of Brahman

According to Swami Yogeshwaranand, we can have only a feel of *Brahman* through some suitable medium. He says that we cannot directly envision Him. We require some medium, some intermediary or some means, to come face to face with *Brahman*.[9] His philosophy is that *Brahman* can be realised, or perceived, in five *Mahabhutas*, in *Tanmantras* and at every stage of creation. According to him, no other teacher has described the knowledge of self and God in this manner and that the method is the result of his own original research.[10] This can be verified only in deep *Sâmadhi* and, therefore, it will not be possible to test its truth by empirical instruments. However, the concept that *Brahman* pervades earth, fire, water, air and ether, as proclaimed by *Upanishads*, is explained for the first time by Swami Yogeshwaranand in this way in the book 'Science of Divinity'. This is a very valuable contribution to the Indian Philosophy, in general, and the philosophy of Yoga, in particular. *The basic argument is that only a thing, which has form, can be perceived but Brahman, being formless, is incapable of being directly realised. Hence, there is a need for a medium to feel His existence. He has explained that in all the objects, from Panch Mahabhutas onwards to primordial Prakriti, Brahman can be realised at every stage of creation. This is a patently new phase of realisation of Brahman based on practical experience.*

(d) Dispensation of Fruits

Brahman alone is believed to be capable of dispensing the fruits of actions of the soul because, by themselves, the actions are un-conscious and, therefore, these are incapable of giving fair reward, appropriate to the action. This notion which has received, world–wide acceptance in all systems of philosophy, fails to impress Swami Yogeshwaranand who refuses to accept its validity. His argument is that if we assign to *Brahman* the authority to decide and dispense the fruits of actions, then we have to admit in Him, the attributes of an agency. This agency could be His natural trait or an extraneous factor. In addition, He will necessarily have to keep an accurate and detailed record of actions of countless souls which will involve a mammoth effort. Even so, when *Prakriti* reverses its evolution at the time of *Pralaya*, every effect will merge in its material cause, and the record of actions will also cease to exist, with the result, that at the time of fresh creation of the world, all souls will be alike, without any distinction based on merit and demerit. Because of the similarity of souls at the commencement of a new cycle of creation, many souls might refuse to return to the world or decide not to pick up the residual *Samskāras*. This will put in jeopardy the established law of *Karma* and the transmigration of the soul. It has also to be noted that if we bestow on *Brahman* the subjective role of dispensation of fruits, then He will have to be regarded as the enjoyer of His own fruits of actions because dispensation of fruits is also an action. As a consequence of this, He will undergo the same trauma of bondage and release, as is the natural destiny of living beings. This lends support to the views of Swami Yogeshwaranand.

(e) Worship of God

God is free from such emotions as pleasure or displeasure and, therefore, He is neither pleased if some one worships him nor displeased if some one else derogates Him. If joy and sorrow are assigned to Him, He will be reduced to the level of human beings and will cease to be the Supreme Being. Traits like happiness and unhappiness are characteristics of inner organs like *Citta* and *Buddhi*. The attributes of being pleased or displeased are super-imposed on Him and, therefore, we sing praises of Him and extol his lofty virtues. Swami Yogeshwaranand rejects this concept and regards that prayers and worship cannot bring any response from God. This may give us to understand that except for the creation of the universe, *Brahman* has no role to play, so much so, that He remains unfazed even by the earnest prayers and entreaties. If this view is accepted, then God will have a status worse than an inert entity. Swami Yogeshwaranand makes it clear repeatedly that no one should consider him as an atheist but that his view of God is one of purity, piety and equity.[11] He also does not accept the most common concept that *Brahman* assumes the role of *Āvatara* (incarnation). It is believed that Rama, Krishna, Buddha, Mahavira etc. were incarnations of *Brahman* or of some deity. For him, these great personages were highly elevated souls but not incarnations of God. *There is logic in favour of this view; it is that by accepting that God incarnates, we would be limiting Him and making him finite because only then He can be supposed to be residing in a particular region of Prakriti. By incarnating, He will be shorn of His all pervasiveness. In such a case, who will direct motion and activity in the areas which are bereft of his presence?* If *Brahman* is born as an incarnation, He will be no better that a human being and, like him, become doer and reaper of the fruits of his actions, which is quite contrary to the status of God.

(6) About Prakriti (matter)

According to *Sāmkhya, Mahat* which is constituted of three *gunas*, is the first evolute while according to Swami Yogeshwaranand, *Prāna* is the first evolute. The reason is that *Prāna* is neither eternal like *Brahman* and *Prakriti* nor is there any material cause of it. Hence, *Prāna* has to be taken as the first evolute of *Prakriti* when it first comes into contract with *Brahman*. On evolution, it becomes intelligent like all other products of *Prakriti* and remains active during the states of creation and re-absorption. He feels that Kapil, the author of *Sāmkhya* Darśana, might have over looked this point and assumed the existence of only Puruṣa and *Prakriti* in the state of re-absorption, as he does not suggest the existence of *Prāna* in that state. However, according to his own experience, *Prana* is the first evolute that arises as a result of contact of *Brahman* and *Prakriti*. He says that *Prāna* is instrumental in bringing about the transformation of *Prakriti* into its triple aspect of *Sattva, Rajas* and *Tamas,* which is collectively called '*Mahat*', and which is an intelligent principle. According to *Sāmkhya* school, *Sattva, Rajas* and *Tamas* are the first evolutes of *Prakriti*. Then *Ahamkāra* is evolved and it is from *Ahamkāra* that the objects of the world are formed. Swami Yogeshwaranand does not agree with this concept of *Samkhya* school and regards *Prana* as the first evolute and says that it is *Prāna* which keeps the *Prakriti* active and dynamic. He designates as *Prāna*, the motion generated by *Brahman* in the quiescent state of *Prakriti* which is also its balanced state in which the three *gunas* are present in equal ratio. The ancient texts do not mention the existence of *Prāna* in the astral or causal bodies but on the basis of long years of research and study of the subject, Swami Yogeshwaranand accepts the presence of *Prāna* in the aforesaid bodies. His argument is that, if there are no *Prānas* in the subtle body, then how will we prove the transmigration of soul at the time of death. It is the subtle body that carries the Samskaras of our deeds. It is the *Prāna* that keeps an account of life measured in years, months and days. *Prāna* imparts movement to body and if *Prānas* are excluded, our body would be like dead wood and would be unable to keep record of our past and present Samskaras. His concept, with regard to *Prāna,* is a major improvement on the ancient views. In *Brahma Sutras, Prāna* is regarded as *Brahman.*[12] *This concept may become responsible for improvement over Sāmkhya Philosophy.*

(7) His conflict with Patānjali

Although a staunch devotee of *Patānjali*, he has severely criticized him on many important points. He boldly admits this and says, "Sage *Patānjali* was very learned, and, I have derived my inspiration from him. I have great devotion for him. But I find that I have developed analytical ability of an order that I now find fault with even *Patānjali's* exposition in some, respects."[13] He considers

Patānjali Sutra which says *Yogascittavrittinirodhah*, as confusing because it is impossible to control all the *Vrittis*. He also does not agree that *Vrittis* belong to the *Citta*. According to him *Vrittis* belong to the intellect but *Samskāras* belong to the *Citta* and has given detailed reasons for coming to this conclusion.[14] *While Swami Yogeshwaranand is justified in holding that contrary to Patānjali's version, Vrittis belong to Buddhi and not to Citta the confusion seems to have arisen, because, in Yoga school, Buddhi and Citta are taken as one. By taking them separately, Swami Yogeshwaranand has removed this confusion and made a valuable addition to the philosophy of Patānjali. In the past, no scholar has researched the philosophy of Swami Yogeshwaranand. It is for the first time that research is undertaken in his philosophy of self-realisation. That he has original views based on his super–conscious vision, has prompted us to venture into this endeavour.* In fact Swami Yogeshwaranand has brought, for the first time, the entire spiritual philosophy under a scanner and laid thread bare all its aspects through his personal knowledge. This is a valuable contribution to the subject of *Ātman*, *Brahman* and *Prakriti*. All these and many more points of controversy have been analytically discussed in the book so as to shed a new light on the age old concepts. Thinkers and scholars will surely benefit tremendously from the works of Swami Yogeshwaranand as also from the critical analysis thereof, undertaken in the book. *He has given a new direction to the spiritual philosophy which, till then, was largely a matter of belief. It will be found from the book that spiritualism has been taken beyond acknowledge boundaries.*

REFERENCES

(1) Science of Soul (pp. 144-145)
(2) Science of Divinity (pp. 49-50)
(3) Essential Colourlessness of the Absolute (p. 139)
(4) An Introduction to Indian Philosophy (p. 234)
(5) Essential Colourlessness of the Absolute (p. 129)
(6) Beads of Sermons (Pt-1 p. 113)
(7) Yoga Varttika (Pada 1, p. 13)
(8) Beads of Sermons (Pt-3 p. 22)
(9) Beads of Sermons (Pt-3 p. 23)
(10) Science of Divinity (p. 11)
(11) Beads of Sermons (Pt. 1 p. 105)
(12) Brahman Sutras (1.1.23)
(13) Beads of Sermons (Pt. 3, pp. 106-107)
(14) Science of Soul (p. 159)

1

Individual Soul

India is a land of saints and seers and in every age its holy soil has produced Yogis and Sanyasis who have left an indelible mark on the pages of history. In the distant past Swami Śankaracharya restored the Vedic religion amongst majority of Indians, by driving Buddhism from the country almost lock, stock and barrel. His interpretation of Upanishads and Brahma Sutras is till this day, considered as most accurate and authentic. His philosophy of Advait *Vedānta* or pure monism is an honest rendering of the essence of *Vedas*. Later on Swami Dayanand Saraswati gave a call for return to *Vedas*. His famous work 'Light of Truth' or *Satyartha Prakasha* contains his original views about many traditional concepts which were being blindly followed in the past. He was bitterly criticised for his unconventional views but he adhered to his courage of conviction and gave to the world an absolutely new interpretation of *Veda Mantras*. He modified to a large extent the prevalent belief among masses about God, Soul and Matter. The names of Swami Vivekananda, Swami Yogananda, Swami Ramtirath and many more such Yogis and Sanyasis have also emerged from the same soil to give a new direction and enlightenment to the world. Each such saint has contributed his own original mite. Even at present many sects are flourishing side by side with one another following their own concept. Iskon, an organisation founded by A.C. Bhaktivedanta Swami Prabhupada which considers Krishna as the Supreme Personality of Godhood, has established itself in every nook and corner of the world and commands a large following.

Twentieth century witnessed the emergence of Swami Yogeshwaranand Saraswati, the greatest Yogi of his time. He perfected the philosophy of Yoga and mastered the art of *Samādhi*. He developed a deep intuitive vision which enabled him to verify through mystic experience everything pertaining to *Brahman, Jivātman* and *Prakriti*. He boldly discarded the old concepts and beliefs if those were found to be incompatible with his intuitive experience.

He was a devout follower of Yoga school of *Patāñjali* and yet he disagreed with him on quite a few vital points. To illustrate such disagreement, he differed with *Patāñjali* about control of *Citta Vrittis. Patāñjali* has said that yoga is the control of modifications in the *Citta*.[1] But Swami Yogeshwaranand found this aphorism as without basis because, according to him, complete elimination of *Samskāras* of our actions which cause modifications in the *Citta*, is impossible and, therefore, all *Vrittis* of *Citta* cannot be controlled.[2] Secondly *Patāñjali* has listed five kinds of *Vrittis* of the *Citta* but Swami Yogeshwaranand counts a few more *Vrittis*. He says that when soul which is the custodian of life, acquires association with *Citta* (sub-conscious mind-stuff), then *Citta* becomes a living organism giving rise to activity which is also a *Vritti* (tendency) which *Patâñjali* has not taken into consideration. In his opinion, this is a tendency because it gives rise to desire in the body and creates activity. Since knowledge which is an attribute of *Citta* (sub-conscious mind stuff) and abides in it, also gives rise to activity, both knowledge and activity are *Vrittis* (tendencies or modifications) which are akin to breathing and sound. He says that *Kapil* and *Patāñjali* the authors of *Sāmkhya* and Yoga *Sutras,* have not dealt with these tendencies.

According to Swami Yogeshwaranand, our *Citta* is a knowledge–oriented organ and knowledge creates activity. Knowledge and action are ever related. When the soul associates with body, action arises first of all and then knowledge follows. Therefore, the first *Vritti* (tendency) of the *Citta* is life which no one has spoken of. Life is sustained by breathing and beating of the heart which are *Vrittis* and which only Swami Yogeshwaranand has talked about. By his own concept of *Vrittis*, Swami Yogeshwaranand has, to some extent, expanded the scope of *Patâñjali Sutra* (1-2) which says *"योगश्चित्तवृति-निरोधः.* *Patâñjali* has classified all types of *Vrittis* under five heads namely, *Pramâna* (right knowledge), *Viparya* (wrong knowledge), *Vikalpa* (imagination), *Nidra* (sleep) and *Smriti* (memory). To these five *Vrittis*, Swami Yogeshwaranand has added two more namely *Prāna* (Vital Air) and *Śabda* (Sound) or knowledge and action which must also be controlled. As the movement of the heart continues, so also does the movement of the breath. Thus, the tendencies or *Vrittis* of the breath and of the sound (word) are never absent and must necessarily be included amongst the *Vrittis,* prescribed by *Patāñjali*. He says, "I have devoted considerable study to this subject. For 50 or 60 years I have conducted research into it. My opinion is that breathing comes before memory because without breathing there can be no memory. Sound goes with breathing because beating of the heart which produces sound, is not possible without breathing. So, I maintain that there are seven attributes of the mind (*Citta*) including these two".[3] He says that the *Vrittis* (tendencies) of breathing and of the sound of the heart are never absent whether one is in the waking state, dream state, deep sleep state or in the Turiya state of consciousness. He regrets that *Patāñjali* did not take cognizance of these *Vrittis*.[4] Further, Yoga recommends complete control of *Vrittis* to attain *Samādhi* for realisation of self and *Brahman*. He does not agree with Yoga school on the subject and says that *Vrittis* cannot be totally controlled because *Samskāras* (impressions) of our past actions, cannot be totally remitted. Till the very end of life a total and complete cessation of *Samskāras* never takes place, whether in waking state or dream state or deep sleep or even in meditation.[5] Natural vibration as a functional process of *Citta* continues to exist even in the state of *Samādhi*. Memory is a functional modification of *Citta* which helps in realising different objects in *Samâdhi*. As long as any activity takes place in the *Citta, Vrittis* will continue to arise. Any cognition whether of an object or *of Âtman* or even of the Absolute *Brahman* Himself, is the cause of *Vrittis*. Hence, so long as the *Citta* remains in association with the soul, there is no possibility of its control. *Samskāras* are countless in numbers and a large measure of these *Samskāras* pertain to timeless previous births. All these *Samskāras* cannot be worked out and remitted in a single birth. And more and more *Samskāras* are added with every subsequent birth. These *Samskāras* can never be exhausted in totality and, therefore, *Vrittis* cannot be entirely controlled.

About the definition and attributes of soul, he has views which, sometimes, do not conform to the established concepts. Similar are his views with regard to the qualities of *Brahman* and the concept of *Mokṣa*. He does not consider the individual soul as the doer and reaper of fruits of actions nor does he accept soul as immutable or eternal. For him, soul is a created thing which comes into being when the all pervasive divinity establishes contact with cosmic *Citta*.[6] He also affirms that the eternity of the soul lasts only till the Doomsday when *Citta* merges in its material cause and the captive Divinity is released from its grip. Similarly, he considers *Brahman* (Supreme Self) as actionless and assigns the role of creation to *Prakriti* (matter) which materialises due to *Brahman's* proximity or presence in it.[7] All these variations are discussed in the body of this book at appropriate places. Presently, the question is how should an inquisitive reader accept the veracity of truth of various discoveries made by Swami Yogeshwaranand. He held some views initially which he modified later on after intense concentration of mind in which that truth was intuitively revealed to him. He admits that his earlier views were based on his understanding of the matter at that time but those views were revised by him on attainment of refined knowledge in deep *Samādhi*. We must discuss whether such knowledge as he claims to have acquired in deep *Samādhi*, has any acceptable validity even though it is not verifiable by senses. He verified the truth in his state of super consciousness (*Samādhi*). He followed a regular practice of recording in a register, kept for that purpose, all that he experienced in *Samādhi* and went on modifying the truth by deeper and still deeper analysis with inner light. We may call it an intuition or a mystic experience; but is intuition dependable proof of knowledge?

There are different kinds of proofs which are accepted as valid sources of knowledge by different schools of philosophy. These proofs are as under:

> "The *Cārvakas* admit only one means of right knowledge, viz., perception (*Pratyakṣa*); the *Vaiśeṣikas* and Buddhas admit two viz., perception and inference (*Anumāna*); the *Sāmkhyas* admit three, viz., perception, inference and verbal testimony (*Agama* or *Śabda*); while the *Niayāyikas*, whose fundamental work is the *Nyāya Sutra*, admit four, viz., perception, inference, verbal testimony and comparison (*Upamān*). The Prabhakaras admit a fifth means of right knowledge called presumption (*Arthāpatti*), the *Bhāttas* and *Vedāntins* admit a sixth, viz., non-existence (*Abhāva*), and the

> *Paurānikas* recognise a seventh and eighth means of right knowledge, named probability (*Sambhava*) and rumour (*Aitihya*)".[8]

As mentioned above *Sāmkhya* admits of only three independent sources of valid knowledge which are perception, inference and *Śabda* and considers the rest as included in these three. Of the proof mentioned above *Pratyakṣa* being direct cognition is believed as more authentic than the others. However, even direct cognition can be misleading or unacceptable unless it satisfies the following conditions:[9]

(1) It is not of the relation of words with the thing signified such as 'water' with the fluid called water;

(2) It should not be of a temporary or transient character and should not be observed under unfavourable circumstance such as the thing seen in the darkness; and

(3) It should be free from all elements of doubt and be certain in character, such as things seen from a distance like a mirage in the desert which is taken for oasis.

In the light of the above definition of *Pratyakṣa*, a question may be asked whether intuition can be accepted as direct perception. In the East, these days tremendous reliance is placed on intuition or mystic experiences. Some seers consider a mystic experience not only as valid but as the only true source of knowledge. However, in the West the tendency has been to regard mystic experiences as hallucinatory or psychotic. But a perceptible change is taking place even in the west, where, in the recent times, some humanistic scholars, are considering the mystic state to be an integral part of the process of self–realisation.

In a recent publication *Consciousness: East and West*,

the authors M/s. Kenreth R. Pelletier and Charles Garfield have made extensive deliberation on the subject of meditation and the mystic experience gained in meditation and have finally come to the conclusion that meditation can indeed be a potent tool in the development of human potential.[10] In India, there has been in existence for centuries, the culture of deliberately inducing altered state of consciousness through meditation. A disciplined methodology has been propounded by every religion to experience higher order of reality. Meditation has been prescribed from ancient times, as a technique to bring about an altered perception of the world, the self and the Ultimate Reality. In fact, meditation is universally accepted as a state of passivity involving introspection which enables one to attain "*Swarúpa Sthiti*" or one's own original nature.

While western researchers proceeded according to the knowledge based on psychology, Dr. R.D. Ranade adopted the methods prescribed by Indian sages and seers based on their personal experiences in meditation. Ranade has been one of the greatest mystics of his times and has been highly revered for his views on the mystic experience. According to him, hallucination is an *adhoc* experience which could be different each time. There are neither stages nor continuity in hallucination. It is far inferior in content and meaning, from intuitive experience. In the case of mystic experiences there is not only continuity but also more and more certainty in each successive experience. He, therefore, not only accepted intuition as a valid source of knowledge but insisted that it was the only valid source of true knowledge because one directly cognizes the self through intuition.[11] Such knowledge does not have any relation with the words signifying the object nor is it temporary or transient and is absolutely free from any doubt. The criteria of validity of intuitive experiences, is that these are clear, vivid and objective like sense experiences and are not isolated but continuous. Universality of mystical experiences is another criterion of validity which means that there is a striking similarity in the experiences of most of the mystics.

If according to Ranade and hosts of other realised *Ṛṣiś, Seers, Yogis, Scriptures* and also according to the western psychologists as mentioned above, intuition is a valid source of knowledge, then the knowledge acquired by Swami Yogeshwaranand in deep contemplation can be considered as having the force of validity and can be regarded on par with the intuition of saints. He abandoned his home at the tender age of fourteen years in search of knowledge of soul and God and till the age of fifty lived either in the huts made of wood or in the caves in deep forests in the midst of wild animals. Even though this fact, by itself, is not sufficient proof of the veracity of his intuitive knowledge, it can weigh in his favour. Our scriptures accept even testimony as a source of knowledge but Swami Yogeshwaranand does not rely merely on testimony but also on direct cognition of the reality, in super-conscious state.

Patāñjali has added one full chapter on *Vibhutis* or super–normal powers acquired by a Yogi when he passes from various stages of *Samādhi. Dhārana, Dhyāna* and *Samādhi* taken together are called *Samyama*. By mastering the art of *Samyama*, the light of knowledge, emanating from concentration, shines forth and as *Samyama* gets firmly established so does knowledge attained in *Samādhi* get purer and purer.[12] Explaining the object of *Samyama*, *Patāñjali* has stated that knowledge of the past and future would be revealed to the Yogi through *Samyama*. Similarly by fixing *Samyama* on latent impressions or *Samskāras* of Karmas, knowledge of previous birth can be acquired and by practising it on notions, the knowledge of other's minds is obtained. Later on, in the same chapter, *Patāñjali* has said that *Prātibha* (intuition) is the state of knowledge before attainment of discriminative knowledge between *Puruṣa* and *Prakriti* and when *Prātibha* is attained the Yogi comes to know every thing. Thus, intuition has been widely accepted as revealing knowledge of all objects including knowledge of God and soul. Trance can be acquired by drugs and other external aids but intuition arises within from concentration of mind with pin pointed fixation. The two types of experiences are not on par with each other.

Intuition is, thus, a thoroughly reliable source of knowledge and the version of Swami Yogeshwaranand that all his knowledge was certified as true by his inner intuitive vision, seems to be compatible with what is stated by other mystics.

In his earlier works namely *Science of soul* and *Science of Divinity*, he accepted soul as the doer and reaper of fruits of actions but in his later work *Essential Colourlessness of the Absolute*, he retracted from his earlier stand. Being conscious that the said change is conspicuous in his later works, he has himself offered explanation which reads as under :

> "In several places or contexts, in the course of the books, the *Science of soul* and the *Science of Divinity*, the embodied soul and the Supreme Being have both been described as responsible agents of all their doings. That was done out of deference to, and in acceptance of, the traditional attitude with a view to making pertinent things easily understandable for the eager aspirants. As a matter of fact, it should be taken as a superimposition of the attribute of freedom and responsibility in action on the pure nature of both of them. I would candidly affirm that I do not regard God as well as the individual soul to be responsible agents and, consequently, the logical reapers of fruits of actions attributed to them. In

> my opinion, merely by dint of their close proximity, they become the Inspirers or Efficient Cause of motion, action and perception in the 'Citta' within the body and the non–conscious Material Entity in the larger context of the Cosmos".[13]

That Swami Yogeshwaranand revised his earlier views should not cause any surprise if we realise that the subject of subtle conscious entities is so abstract and elusive that even the best of thinkers, sages and philosophers have often drawn erroneous and one–sided conclusions. Such errors will occur even in future. All contemplation in the most intuitive state of *Samādhi* can reveal only a fringe of the Infinite *Brahman* and of finite individual soul. Swami Chinmaya Nanda has said that 'God defined is God defiled'.[14] If God reveals himself fully and completely, He will cease to be God. Therefore, updating of Knowledge about Him, even by intuition, is a never ending process. All the later discoveries of Swami Yogeshwaranand have come about through sharp vision in superconscious state. Indeed such discoveries cannot be proved by the laws of physics and mathematics or by any other empirical law. Going by Dr. R.D. Ranade the Divine Vision which arises in contemplation, alone can impart true knowledge of soul and God. In *Nyāya* philosophy also there is mention of three kinds of extraordinary perceptions. These are :

(1) *Sāmānyalakśana*;

(2) *Jñānalakśana*; and

(3) Yogaja.

The third kind of extra–ordinary (*Alaukika*) perception namely Yogaja, is the intuitive perception which arises from supernatural powers generated in the mind by meditation.[15] It further says that those who have acquired spiritual perfection, for them intuitive knowledge of every object is constant and spontaneous. Although the *Vedāntins* do not accept the first two extra-ordinary perceptions, they have desisted from repudiating *Yogaja.*[16] In fact every school of thought in Indian philosophy generally accepts *Yogipratyakśa* as extraordinary perception which is also supported by *Ṣruti* and *Smruti*. Even according to Jains, when all *Karmas* that obstruct knowledge, are removed from the soul, there arises in it absolute knowledge or omniscience which they call *Kevala-Jñāna*. In the same way distant objects which are minute and have form, can be known by *Avadhijñāna* while by *Mana-Pryāya*, one can have direct access to the present and past thoughts of others.

With regard to intuitive and subtle experiences, Swami Yogeshwaranand has clarified that all such experiences belong to the subtle body and it is not possible to see them without *Samādhi*. However, he says that to reach the stage where one can have such intuitive experiences, necessitates a disciplined and sustained practice which is embodied in the eight-fold Yoga of *Patāñjali Sutras.*

As stated earlier knowledge of God, soul and matter can be acquired only by Yogic perception or intuitive experience. Swami Yogeshwaranand also acquired such knowledge in the same way. In this book *Science of Diviniy* he clearly states:

> "The idea rests not on books but on our Yogic perception. Though it is not supported by other scriptures, we are expounding it here because we believe it to be right. We are not indulging in refutations, but explaining what we have perceived as facts, and the world also believes only in experiences. We consider it our duty to present to the world what we have actually realised in Samprajnjāta Samādhi. We were for many years in the state of Samprajnjāta Samādhi in the snow-clad regions of the Himalayas and

> perceived these phenomena and now describe them because we think they are useful for humanity".[17]

The method by which one can realise *Brahman* in five cosmic elements (*Panchatanmātras*) is claimed as his exclusive discovery because no other teacher has described the knowledge of *Brahman* in this manner. He says that it is his original research and the method is described on the basis of his personal experience. According to this method, Brahman can be realised at every stage from primordial matter to five elements.[18] In the same way knowledge of soul can also be acquired at every stage of evolution of matter. But he says, that such knowledge can materialise only by concentration in accordance with what is stated by *Patāñjali* in Yoga *Sutra* 3-33.[19] According to this *Sutra*, when *Prātibha* arises, the Yogi comes to know everything. In *Vyāsa Bhāshya, Prâtibha* is defined as knowledge which is obtained without being taught but which arises out of one's own *Prātibha* (intuition).[20] Swami Yogeshwaranand claims to have acquired *Prātibha* due to which his *Brahmarandhra* remained well-lit all the time even when he was not absorbed in *Samādhi*. Having suitably discussed intuition, we now proceed to analyse attributes of soul.

ATTRIBUTES OF SOUL

All orthodox schools of Indian Philosophy have differences amongst themselves about the nature and attributes of soul although the existence of the soul is accepted by all of them. According to *Nyāya* *इच्छा द्वेष प्रयत्न सुख दुःख ज्ञानानि "आत्मनो लिङ्गम" इति.*[21] It means that desire, aversion, pleasure, pain and intelligence are the marks of the soul. They claim that these are the qualities which abide in soul. Their argument is that these qualities could not belong to the body or the senses and that there must be some other entity to which they belong and that entity is soul. How do we know that such an entity as soul exists? According to *Mimāmsa*, self-consciousness is enough proof of its existence. Unlike *Mimāmsa*, *Nyāya* does not accept the notion of our self-consciousness as a proof for the existence of soul. The creation of *Ātman* is never experienced by us nor its destruction like the destruction of the body. So, they say that, the soul must be eternal. It is not located in any particular part of the body. It is *Vibhu* because it exists every where simultaneously. However, it is unconscious in itself but acquires consciousness with the collocation of bodily limbs whereafter activity arises in it. These are the views of the *Nyāya* School about soul.

Sāmkhya philosophy admits two eternal principles namely that of *Puruṣa* (soul) and of *Prakriti (matter)*. *Prakriti* is the root principle of matter from which every created thing has arisen. According to *Sāmkhya*, souls are many but these are neither partible nor do these possess any qualities. If the souls had not been many then with the birth of one all would have been born and with the death of one all would have died.[22] The Jains believe that the soul possesses *Anantajñāna, Anantadarśana, Anantasukha and Anantavirya*. However, *Sāmkhya* defines soul as being devoid of any qualities or attributes but it is of the nature of pure consciousness. *Sāmkhya* view of soul also differs from *Vedānta* inasmuch as it does not consider soul to be of the nature of *Ananda* or bliss. *Sāmkhya* believes that *Ananda* (bliss) is an attribute of *Prakriti* to which all pleasures and pains belong and, that, it does not belong to the nature of soul. Secondly, *Vedānta* believes that individual souls (*Jivas*) are an illusory manifestation of *Brahman*, the Supreme soul. But *Sāmkhya* considers these souls as apart from *Brahman*. It also says that the self cannot be realised as an image of knowledge because it is a distinct, transcendent principle whose real nature is beyond knowledge. The self is like light without which no knowledge can be revealed. *Puruṣa* is the principle of intelligence and unless touch is established with this principle, no knowledge or action can arise. Here, *Sāmkhya* differs even from *Buddhism* which analyses knowledge into diverse constituent parts which, when held together, bring about conscious states. Intelligising means interpreting the events of knowledge happening to a person so as to make them a system of experience. For *Sāmkhya*, therefore, there is a separate *Puruṣa* for every individual and such a *Puruṣa* is of the nature of intelligence. *Vedānta* differs from *Sāmkhya* on this point also and says that *Ātman* is one, is a pure being and pure bliss – Sat, *Citta*, *Ānanda*. That single reality is the only truth but by the illusion of Maya, it appears many. *Mimāmsa* cannot do without accepting the existence of the soul or else who would perform the rituals prescribed in the *Karmakānda* of the *Vedas* and who would enjoy the pleasures of heaven gained through such sacrifices? While accepting the reality of the soul, *Mimāmsa* regards it as different from the mind–body apparatus. It is eternal and omnipresent and one soul resides only in one body and, so, there are innumerous souls. *Mimāmsa* does not accept the soul as atomic because when we have a sensation in the head, we also feel it in the leg.[23] The Jaina theory that the self is of the size of the body which expands and contracts as per the body is also not acceptable to *Mimāmsa.* They say that since experiences of one man are different from the experiences of the other, the self must be different in different persons. So, according to them, it is better to regard the soul as all–pervading as described in vedic scriptures.

The word *Ātman* originally used in *Rigveda* has a dual meaning. It denotes on the one hand the essence of the universe and it also denotes on the other the vital breath (*Prāna*) in beings. In later Upanishads the word *Brahman* is used for the essence of the world and the word *Ātman* is used to denote the essence in man and yet the Upanishads treat both as one and the same. We may concede that *Brahman* is the innermost essence of the universe but what is the innermost essence of man? In *Chāndogya* Upanishad Prajapati addresses Indra and Virocana on this subject as under:

> "The self which is free from sin, free from old age, from death and grief, from hunger and thirst, which desires nothing but what it ought to desire and imagines nothing but what it ought to imagine, that it is which we must try to understand."[24]

There is an anecdote relating to the above discourse. On hearing the above version about the self, the gods and the demons represented by Indra and Virocana respectively, approached Prajapati to enquire in detail about the self as depicted above. Prajapati asked them to look into a vessel of water and they could find the self in it. Their answer was, " we see this our whole self even to the hair and to the nail." Prajapati said, "well that is the self, that is the deathless and the fearless, that is the Brahman." Virocana was satisfied with the answer but Indra entertained doubts. He came back again and again to Prajapati with a fresh doubt each time and Prajapati gave him a course of successively higher instructions about self as body, as the self in dreams and the self in the dreamless sleep. Finally he told Indra, this body is the support of the self. The self as embodied is affected by pleasure and pain but pleasure and pain do not touch the bodiless soul".[25] This anecdote only shows that the gods sought a constant and unchanging essence in man. The description of such an innermost essence of man is that "he is the seer of all seeing, hearer of all hearing, and the knower of all knowledge. He sees but is not seen, hears but is not heard, knows but is not known. He is the light of all lights. He is like a lump of salt, with no inner or outer, which consists through and through entirely of knowledge." Bliss is not an attribute of it but it is bliss itself. However when such an innermost essence is embodied, then it is called self which is effected by pleasure and pain, When the same self is not embodied, it is not effected by pleasure and pain. This is the view of the Upanishads about Self.

The above are the versions of different schools of philosophy which have been briefly discussed because they have a bearing on the *Sāmkhya* Yoga school with regard to the nature and attributes of the soul on which the philosophy of Swami Yogeshwaranand is based. Closely related to the nature of soul is the knowledge of objects which enable the soul to cognize the objects or gain inner and outer experiences. How does this knowledge arise to the self? In his commentary on *Patāñjali* Sutra 4 of *Samādhi Pada, Vyāsa* says that whenever modifications of the *Citta* take place, the *Puruṣa* has similar modifications. Quoting *Pancasikhacārya*, he says that "there is one appearance, that appearance is knowledge".[26] The *Sāmkhya* philosophy states that by mere proximity of the *Puruṣa, Citta* attains a pseudo consciousness and because of the afflictions (*Vrittis*), there is false identification of 'consciousness' with the activities. Thus, the reason for *Puruṣa's* knowledge of modifications is its relationship with *Citta*; and this relationship is beginningless because *Citta* is permanent according to *Sāmkhya*. *Sāmkhya* maintains the permanency of the *Citta* on the ground of its capacity for recognition of objects. It says that recognition is the knowledge which was known earlier and is recalled now and this is possible only if the knowledge which existed earlier continues even now, meaning thereby that the knowledge is permanent because otherwise recognition would have been impossible if the knowledge had been transitory. On this basis *Sāmkhya* concludes that *Citta* or intellect, as *Sāmkhya* calls it, which recognises the objects, is permanent. In the same commentary *Vyāsa* poses a question as to in what form does consciousness, though changeless, exist at the time of activity or modification of the *Citta*. The question arises because in Sutra 3 of *Samādhi Pada, Patāñjali* says that "at that time, the seer abides in itself." He himself answers the question by saying that during activity the seer has similarity with *Citta* in its modification. He says that the modification of the *Citta* is like the image and its reflection. Elaborating the point he says that in activity those modifications of the mind are like the flame of the lamp – impermanent and changing; or like liquid copper placed in a crucible. They take the shape of the objects which are in contact with the *Citta*. Therefore, though the *Puruṣa* is pure consciousness which is unchanging, even so these reflections in the *Puruṣa* of the modifications of the *Citta*, are considered the modifications of the *Puruṣa* himself. Yet by these modifications, no change is caused in the *Puruṣa* because, as already stated, just as the appearance of crystal as red is false, the modifications in the *Puruṣa* are also false. On this ground *Sāmkhya* proves that (*i*) modification in *Puruṣa* are similar to the modifications of *Citta* and (*ii*) that the modifications in *Puruṣa* are false and the *Puruṣa* remains unchanging.

Nyāya does not accept the reason mentioned by *Sāmkhya* to prove that Citta is permanent and hence, knowledge is also permanent. The reason given by *Sìmkhya* is that *Citta* can recognise the objects by *Smriti Vritti. Nyāya* refutes not only the conclusion drawn by *Sāmkhya* but also the reasons leading to that conclusion. *Nyāya* says that recognition of the objects is not done by the *Citta* but by the soul. The reason is that knowledge cannot be attributed to an unconscious object like *Citta*. *Nyāya* argues that if knowledge as a mode of the permanent *Citta* is not different from it, then we have to admit various sorts of knowledge to be permanent. But as a matter of our daily experience, we do not receive various sorts of knowledge simultaneously. Hence, knowledge is not identical with *Citta* according to Nyāya.

Sutra 22 of *Kaivalyapada* of Yoga Sutras says that consciousness without any activity, knows its own intellect when it obtains by a reflection, oneness with mind. In the next *Sutra* it says that the *Citta* coloured by the seer and the seen grasps all objects. Here in these two Sutra *Patāñjali* says that when the *Puruṣa* is reflected in the *Citta*, it becomes one with the modification caused by the object in the *Citta* and then the *Puruṣa* is known as knower, experiencer etc. although in reality it is unchanging. It all means that knowledge arises by two–way reflection namely the reflection of *Puruṣa* in the *Citta* and also the reflection of *Citta* in the *Puruṣa*.

Unlike *Vacaspati Miśra, Vijñāna Bhikṣu* believes in the theory of double reflection which says that just as there is reflection of the *Citta* in the consciousness, so also it should be accepted that there is reflection of consciousness in the *Citta;* otherwise the knowledge of *Puruṣa* cannot be explained because of the contradiction of the subject and object in oneself knowing directly. It is only by superimposing *Ātman* on the *Citta* that knowledge like a pot etc. can be obtained.

In the above mentioned *Sutra, Patāñjali* has tried to explain as to what is implied by consciousness (*Puruṣa*) illuminating the *Citta.* Since *Puruṣa* is unchanging, its assuming the form of the modification of the object in reality means that it is the modification of the *Citta* alone. Therefore, *Citta* is affected by *Puruṣa* in the same way as it is affected by the object. *Citta* is all comprehensive as it is able to take in both, the seer and the seen. The modification that "I am the knower as also the modification that I am the body" arise in the *Citta*. Apart from explaining how knowledge of an object arises by its reflection in *Citta, Patāñjali* has also explained in the said Sutra, the cognition of *Puruṣa.*[27] *Puruṣa* is not the prop of intellect which means that it is not an object of contemplation as pot is. The word *Puruṣa Pratyaya* used by *Vyāsa* only means the realisation that intellect has been illumined by self-luminous *Puruṣa*. One retains in *Samādhi* the memory relating to *Puruṣa* which is the object of knowledge, and by analogy it is spoken of as the reflection of consciousness.

The Philosophy of self-realisation of Swami Yogeshwaranand has been studied and discussed in the light of above observations with regard to soul, and with regard to the process of acquiring knowledge about the objects and the *Puruṣa*. Wherever Swami Yogeshwaranand departs from the established doctrines on these matters, has been discussed in detail in the ensuing chapters. He had personal experience in his superconscious state which gave rise to certain independent concepts which may make valuable addition to the philosophy of self. While broadly adhering to *Sāmkhya* Yoga philosophy, he has deviated from it in some crucial aspects which have been suitably analysed and concluded. However, it is necessary to understand the process of evolution of *Prakriti* (matter) and the concept of *Antahkarana Catuṣtaya* (four-fold inner organ) in order to fully appreciate the Philosophy of Swami Yogeshwaranand. Therefore, the next two chapters have been devoted to these two factors namely evolution of *Prakriti* and *Antahkarana*.

EVOLUTION OF THE UNIVERSE

According to the Philosophy of Swami Yogeshwaranand, *Brahman* (Supreme Self) is Omnipotent, Omnipresent and the sub–stratum of all things whether created or uncreated. *Prakriti* with all its aspects of time, space and causality abides in *Brahman*. In its most original form, *Prakriti* is the balanced state of three *Gunas* (qualities) namely *Sattva* (purity), *Rajas* (passion) and *Tamas* (inertia). In its balanced state which is also its most stable state, *Prakriti* is invisible because *Prakriti* is also subtle like *Brahman*, but *Brahman* is more subtle. *Brahman* and *Prakriti* are eternally associated with each other and it is due to this association that *Prakriti* evolves into various stages of creation and also appears to be conscious. After each *Pralaya* (the great deluge), an agitation is caused by the Divine will, in the balanced state of *Prakriti* which disturbs its equilibrium. Then *Prakriti* commences its process of creation of the universe by the force of fructifying Karmas of the *Jivas* (individual souls). Since *Prakriti* is constituted of three *Gunas* namely *Sattva, Rajas* and *Tamas*, every effect or resultant product of *Prakriti* is also constituted of these three *Gunas*. Therefore, the universe in which *Prakriti* finally evolves itself, is also made of the said three *Gunas*.

On its equilibrium being disturbed, when *Prakriti* starts evolving, the first evolutes are *Mahā Ākāsha* (ether in its subtlest form), directions, time and *Mahat* which is an intelligent principle. Being constituted of three *Gunas*, *Mahat* also becomes three fold viz. *Mahat Sattva, Mahat Rajas* and *Mahat Tamas*. *Mahat Sattva* is also called the cosmic mind–stuff or *Samasti Citta* or *Citta Sattva* because it is the *Sattvic* portion of *Mahat* from which cosmic *Citta* is produced. This *Samasti Citta* is the material cause of all individual *Cittas*. Individual *Citta* is formed of the subtle and infinitesimal portion of cosmic *Citta* and exists as its effect. Individual souls derive *Bhoga* or enjoyment from the active portion of the cosmic *Citta*. The relationship of the individual soul and the *Citta* is like the relationship of the owner and the owned (*Swa–Swāmibhāva Sambandha*). This relationship is also known as *Bimba–Bimbi–Bhāva* or the relation of the object reflected and the reflector. In this relationship, the soul is the object reflected and *Citta* is the mirror which reflects the soul.[28]

Mahat Rajas gives rise to a *Rajas* predominating

evolute which is called *Samasti Buddhi* or cosmic intellect. An active and infinitesimal portion of this *Samasti Buddhi*, forms the individual *Buddhi*. Hence, *Samasti Buddhi* is the material cause of all individual intellects. Here, Swami Yogeshwaranand, has made a very clearly marked distinction between *Samasti Citta* and *Samasti Buddhi* which are material causes of individual *Citta* and individual *Buddhi*. Teachers of Yoga and *Sāmkhya* do not make such a distinction because they treat *Citta* and *Buddhi* as one and the same principle. On this account *Sāmkhya* Yoga schools accept *Antahkarana* as consisting of three limbs and call it *Antahkarana Traiya*. In this view of the matter, Swami Yogeshwaranand considers *Antahkarana* as consisting of four limbs instead of three as accepted by *Vedānta* and Upanishads. By making this segregation between *Citta* and *Buddhi*, he has made it easier to understand the difference between *Samskāras* and *Vrittis* and their respective functions. He says that he has ascertained the qualities, functions and characteristics of these four organs on the basis of his own direct experience in *Samādhi*.

So far, we have mentioned about two evolutes of *Prakriti* viz. *Mahat Sattva* and *Mahat Rajas*. The third evolute of *Prakriti* is *Mahat Tamas* from which arises *Samasti Ahamkāra* (Cosmic Ego) which again is of three kinds namely *Sattva Ahamkāra, Rajas Ahamkāra* and *Tamas Ahamkāra*. The *Sattva Ahamkāra* gives rise to five senses of knowledge (*Jñānendriyas*) and *Rajas Ahamkāra* gives rise to five senses of action (*Karmendriyas*). *Tamas Ahamkāra* produces five *Tanmatras* or subtle *Mahabhutas*. An equal portion of *Sattva Ahamkāra* and *Rajas Ahamkāra* produces cosmic mind (manas). All the *Samasti Ahamkāras* mentioned above are the material causes of individual *Ahamkāras*. Mind is capable of taking work or commanding both types of the senses because it has *Sattva* as well as *Rajas Ahamkāra* in it. Again it is because of equal proportion of *Sattva* and *Rajas* in it that the mind is extremely powerful, active and fast. Its speed is remarkable and although it can perform only one action at a time it appears to be doing so many things simultaneously due to its extremely fast speed.

It has already been mentioned that *Tamas Ahamkāra* gives rise to five subtle *Tanmātras.* Like any other object of *Prakriti,* these *Tanmātras* also consist of three *Gunas* viz. *Sattva, Rajas* and *Tamas*. These subtle *Tanmātras* are the material cause of subtle bodies and subtle objects enjoyed by such subtle bodies. *Sattvic Tanmātras* become the material cause of the subtle bodies of Devas, human beings, animals, insects, trees and plants. Differences that are visible in these subtle bodies are due to variation in the degree of *Sattva, Rajas and Tamas* present in them. Similar is the case in respect of differences in physical bodies. From *Rajas Tanmātra* are created subtle objects which offer enjoyment to subtle bodies. From *Tamas* predominating *Tanmātras* arise *Pancha Mahabhutas* or gross five great elements. These *Mahabhutas* also comprise of the three *Gunas* aforesaid. With the predominance of *Sattva* in them, the five great elements give rise to physical bodies of the *Devas*, men, *Gandharvas,* and other supernatural beings. With the predominance of *Rajas* and *Tamas,* the elements create the physical bodies of animals, birds, insects, flies and similar beings.

Swami Yogeshwaranand says that *Rajas* predominating gross elements abide in the ether and in the spaces between the different worlds and bring forth the objects of enjoyment for beings. Elaborating this, he says that the air-pervading ether and water particles found therein as also water in clouds, fire in the form of lightning and in the particles of earth, are all instances of *Rajas* predominating forms of *Mahabhutas.*[29] *Sāmkhya* does not talk about such forms of *Rajas* predominating *Mahabhutas.* Proceeding further with the evolution of

Prakriti, Swami Yogeshwaranand says that from *Tamas* predominating *Mahabhutas* are formed all solid masses such as earth, planets heavenly bodies etc. It is interesting to note that according to Swami Yogeshwaranand, men and *Devas* were created only after the creation of the world of birds, animals and insects along with necessary food for them. Initially the creation of men etc. was asexual but later on it was with sex.

This is the process of creation as envisaged by Swami Yogeshwaranand. He says that the association between *Brahman* and *Prakriti* has been in existence from times immemorial and will continue to exist till eternity. There will never be any time when God and matter will act independently. Creation takes place only with their contact or joining together but in this association *Brahman* remains actionless. All changes and modifications take place only in *Prakriti*. Even coming into being of *Jīvātman* (individual soul) also occurs in the same chain of the process of creation of *Prakriti*. According to Swami Yogeshwaranand, in the creational chain of cosmic modifications when *Prakriti* reaches the stage of *Citta* formation, the Divinity being already present therein, assumes the character of *Jīvātman* and begins to be called the soul. He says:

> "In that manner, undergoing its successive stages of subsidiary creation when 'Prakriti' reaches the formation state of the Cittas (the subconscious fundamental layer of mind), that particular presence of the Universal Consciousness limited to the bounds of every finite Citta comes to be entitled 'the living soul'. Henceforth, the submerged impression of Samskāras, latently carried over from the earlier round of creation, when at the time of Doom, along with them the Citta had merged in its immediate cause, now getting revised, as it were clutch fast and stick to the Universal Spirit in the narrow strip of the Citta

> to which they belong. The conscious factor held and encompassed within the material precincts of the Citta thus comes to be known as the 'living spirit' in man, bird, or beast." [30]

The above sequence of evolution differs slightly from what is stated by *Sāmkhya*. *Sāmkhya* says that the first evolute of matter is *Mahat*. Then *Ahamkāra* was created and all the latter creations have come out of *Ahamkāra*. *Sāmkhya* mentions the following enumerations relating to the principles (*Tattvas*):

(1) pure consciousness (*Puruṣa*)
(2) primordial materiality (*Múlaprakriti*)
(3) intellect (*Buddhi or Mahat*)
(4) egoity (*Ahamkāra*)
(5) mind (*Manas*) – both as sense capacity and an action capacity
(6) hearing (*Śrotra*)
(7) touching (*Tvac*)
(8) seeing (*Cakṣus*)
(9) tasting (*Rasana*) (*Buddhindriyas*)
(10) smelling (*Ghrāna*)

(6)–(10): the five sense capacities

(11) speaking (*Vāc*)
(12) grasping / prehending (*Pāni*)
(13) walking / motion (*Pāda*)
(14) excreting (*Pāyu*), and (*Karmendriyas*)
(15) Procreating (*Upastha*)

(11)–(15): the five action capacities

(16) sound (*Śabda*) (17) contact (*Sparśa*) (18) form (*Rúpa*) (19) taste (*Rasa*) (20) smell (*Gandha*)	the five subtle elements (*Tanmātras*)
(21) space / ether (*Ākāśa*) (22) wind / air (*Vayu*) (23) fire (*Tejas*) (24) water (ap) (25) earth (*Prthvi*)	the five gross elements (*Mahābhútas*)

Among the twenty five principles of *Sāmkhya* mentioned above only the first two viz. *Puruṣa* and *Múlaprakriti* exist independently. These are ungenerated, are beyond time and space, stable without parts and independent. According to *Sāmkhya*, *Puruṣa* is inherently inactive but primordial materiality (*Múlaprakriti*) is inherently generative. Items (3) to (25) mentioned above are the various sub–divisions of primordial *Prakriti* and are generated in the same order. Swami Yogeshwaranand differs from *Sāmkhya* in the order of generation of the evolutes of *Prakriti*. According to him, the exact order of evolution of *Prakriti* from its original (Alinga) or primordial form, is as given further.

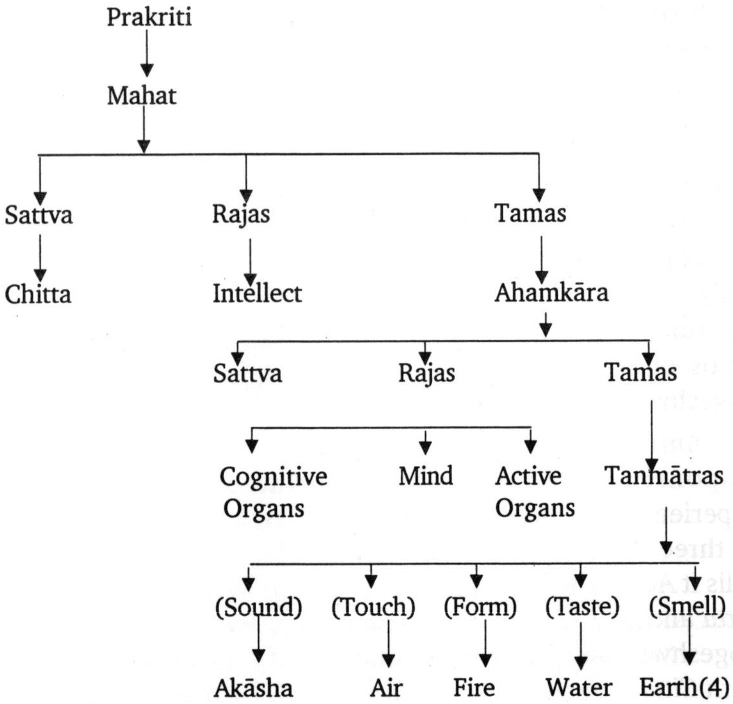

The difference is very significant. He does not accept the *Sāmkhya* concept that after *Mahat, Ahamkāra* was produced and all the rest of the products have come out of *Ahamkāra*. He divides *Mahat* into *Mahat Sattva, Mahat Rajas* and *Mahat Tamas* and says that *Ahamkāra* has been generated only by *Mahat Tamas* and not by the other two. From this, he has evolved his philosophy which accepts *Citta* as having been produced from the *Mahat Sattva* and has independent existence apart from *Buddhi*.

Thus, Swami Yogeshwaranand considers *Citta* and *Buddhi* as created by *Mahat* and not by *Ahamkāra*. Because *Citta* is made of *Mahat Sattva*, and is knowledge oriented object, it is able to reveal the knowledge of self. Similarly *Buddhi* which is produced from *Mahat Rajas* is also knowledge predominating and possesses the faculty of analysis and judgement. If these were products of *Ahamkāra* which has the quality of ignorance, these would not be able to perform their respective functions. By treating *Citta* and *Buddhi* as products of *Mahat* and not of *Ahamkāra*, he has considerably improved upon the *Sāmkhya* philosophy of creation. It enables one to clearly understand the functions of *Citta* which works with *Samskāras* and of *Buddhi* which works with *Vrittis*. The *Nyāya-Vaiśeṣika* concept that mind alone performs all the functions of *Manas, Buddhi, Ahamkāra* and *Citta*—the four limbs of *Antahkarana,* creates confusion which Swami Yogeshwaranand has effectively removed.

Antahkarana is the internal instrument which is responsible for all our internal as well as external experiences. *Sāmkhya* believes that *Antahkarana* consists of three limbs namely *Manas, Buddhi* and *Ahamkāra* and calls it *Antahkarana Traiya* (three-fold). *Sāmkhya* considers *Citta* and *Buddhi* as one and the same. According to Swami Yogeshwaranand, *Antahkarana* is four fold (*Chatuṣtaya*) with *Citta* being an entity apart from *Buddhi*. The soul uses *Anathkarana* as an instrument to gain experiences, both gross and subtle. *Anathkarana* operates in the *Súkṣama Śarira* (subtle body) as also in the *Kārna Śarira* (causal body). Compared with causal body, the subtle body is somewhat gross and comprises of two parts. One part is known as *Manomaya Kosha* (mind sheath) which is action predominating and other is *Vijñānamaya Kosha* (intellect sheath) which is knowledge predominating. Both of these *Koshas* are inert by themselves because their powers of action and knowledge do not belong to their respective *Koshas*. These energies emanate from the *Kārna Śarira* (causal body) or *Ānandmaya Kosha* (Bliss sheath).

To make the subject more intelligible, it may be well understood that the castle of *Jīvātman* namely the human body consists of three bodies and five sheaths. The three bodies are gross body (*Sthula Śarira*), the subtle or astral body (*Súkṣama Śarira*) and the causal body (*Kārna Śarira*). The *Pancha Koshas* or the five sheaths are *Annamaya Kosha* (food sheath), *Prānamaya Kosha* (vital air sheath), *Manomaya Kosha* (mind sheath), *Vijñānamaya Kosha* (intellect sheath) and *Ānandmaya Kosha* (bliss sheath). *Annamaya Kosha* and *Prānamaya Kosha* operate in the physical body while *Manomaya* and *Vijñānamaya Koshas* operate in the subtle or astral body. The fifth sheath namely *Ānandmaya Kosha* operates in the causal body. It can, thus, be seen that among the four limbs of *Antahkarana, Citta* and *Ahāmkara* are directly related to *Ānandmaya Kosha* (bliss sheath) and *Kārna Śarira* (causal body) while *Manas* and *Buddhi* are related to *Súkṣama Śarira* (subtle body). *Manomaya Kosha* comprises of (1) ten *Indriyas* (senses), (2) five *Tanmatras* and (3) Mind. When *Manomaya Kosha* is joined to *Buddhi,* it comes to be known as *Vijñānamaya Kosha* (intellect sheath). *Ānandmaya Kosha* (bliss sheath) consists of *Citta* and *Ahāmkara*. It has thus been made clear by Swami Yogeshwaranand that *Antahkarana* is possessed of four limbs and these limbs are *Manas, Buddhi, Ahāmkara* and *Citta*.

As stated earlier, according to Swami Yogeshwaranand the creation of the universe takes place by evolution of *Prakriti* with its three *Gunas* which is also the material cause of the universe. That *Prakriti* is the material cause of the universe, is also affirmed by *Vedas*. *Yajur Veda* says, "All pervading Being alone is the lord of the imperishable *Prakriti*—the material cause of the world—and of the soul and is yet distinct from both".[32] *Rig Veda* also makes a similar mention. It says:

> "The *Prakriti*, which is likened to the trunk of a tree whose branches are the multiform universe which is resolved into its elementary condition at the time of dissolution is also eternal. The natures, attributes and characters of these three are also

> eternal. Of the two — God and the soul — the latter alone reaps the fruits of this tree of the universe — good or evil — whilst the former does not. He is the All-Glorious being who shines within, without and all around. God, the soul and the *Prakriti*, all these are distinct from one another being different in their natures, but they are all eternal".[33]

The scripture clearly says that God, the soul and the matter are eternal. Similar mention is also made in *Śvetāsvatara Upanishad* where it is said that the *Prakriti*, the soul and God, all of them are uncreated and they are the cause of the universe. They have no cause and have been existing eternally. The eternal soul enjoys eternal matter and is wrapped up in it while God neither enjoys it nor is He wrapped up in it.[34] Thus, it is stated in Vedas that God, the soul and the *Prakriti* are three eternal entities and while God is the efficient cause, *Prakriti* is the material cause of the world. *Prakriti* being devoid of intelligence can neither make or unmake itself, but is always made or unmade by a conscious intelligent Being. Therefore, all orderly changes in material things depend for their occurrence on the pervasion of God in matter.

Some confusion is created by Mundaka Upanishad when it says that just as a spider does not take anything from outside but draws out filaments from its body with which it spins its web, so does God evolve the world out of His own self, becomes metamorphosed into it and enjoys Himself.[35] Taittriya Upanishad also says that by the mere act of willing He became transformed into the universe.[36] This confusion is, however, removed by *Vaiśeṣika* Sutras in which it is said that the effect only reveals whatsoever pre-existed in the cause. *Brahman* and the world being so dissimilar in nature, *Brahman* cannot be the cause of the universe. He evolved this gross universe out of subtle *Prakriti*. Moreover, if we say that *Brahman* is the material cause, He has to be regarded as transformable, conditioned and changeable because matter transforms. Besides, the nature, attributes and characteristics of the cause are transferred to the effect. On that ground we have to accept as does Swami Yogeshwaranand that God is the efficient cause and *Prakriti* is the material cause of the universe which is created for the enjoyment and release of individual soul.

Since *Prakriti* is an aggregate of *Sattva, Rajas* and *Tamas*, every object that has evolved out of *Prakriti* must contain these three *Gunas*. The ratio in which these *Gunas* are present in different objects will be different but no object is formed only by one *Guna* in exclusion of the other *Gunas*. In every object one *Guna* predominates but other *Gunas* are also present in an auxiliary form. For instance *Tamas* is predominant in earth and *Sattva* is predominant in ether, but other *Gunas* also have their subsidiary presence. Similar is the case with all other objects created by *Prakriti*.

Swami Yogeshwaranand considers *Prāna* (subtle breath) as the first modification of *Prakriti* (matter) when it comes into contact with *Brahman*. He says that the first motion that results from the said contact is called *Prāna* which is extremely subtle in the beginning but it tends to become more and more gross with the growth of knowledge, strength and activity. According to him, the *Prāna* produced by the contact of *Prakriti* and *Brahman* is the primal energy or power of *Prakriti* and because one of the *Guna* (quality) of *Prakriti* is *Rajas* (passion), activity is the ever enduring quality of *Prakriti* and, therefore, there is never a complete absence of activity in it. Thus, the knowledge that arises in *Prakriti* due to its contact with *Brahman* is represented by *Sattva* (purity), the motion called *Prāna* is represented by Rajas (passion) and the absence of any particular activity leading to evolution, is represented by *Tamas* (inertia). It is, therefore, proper to regard *Prāna* as the energy by which *Prakriti* proceeds to evolve by changing its state to knowledge, power and activity. Even in the individual *Citta*, the energy of *Prāna* appears first, then knowledge arises in the form of memory and still later arise the strength and activity. This sequence of evolution shows that *Prāna* is the first evolute of *Prakriti* and not *Mahat* as stated by *Sāmkhya*. Here Swami Yogeswaranand differs from the sequence of creation accepted by *Sāmkhya* which considers *Mahat* as the first evolute when *Prakriti* moves from its non–manifest or invisible state. He says that treating *Prāna* as the first evolute is his personal contribution to the *Sāmkhya* system as no other teacher has viewed the evolution of matter in this manner. He is of the view that change, motion, activity and *Prāna* can arise only in *Prakriti* but *Brahman* who is Omnipotent, Omniscient and intelligent cannot have any qualities and attributes. It is *Prāna* which originates first as an evolute of *Prakriti* from the state of reabsorption of *Prakriti* and, thereafter, the entire creation proceeds from it. According to him, *Sāmkhya* has overlooked this important point, while talking about the process of evolution of matter and says:

> "It is possible that Kapil Muni, the founder of the *Sāmkhya* School might have overlooked this point and assumed the existence of only *Prakriti* and *Puruṣa* during the condition of reabsorption. His philosophical treatise does not indicate or suggest the existence of *Prāna* in this state. Our experience, however, indicates that *Prāna* is the first evolute as a result of the contact of *Puruṣa* (the intelligent principal) and the non–intelligent *Prakriti*. Even if we suggest that this evolution is change of state, it poses no problem. *Prakriti* evolves from a unitary state to become dual–and later triple–aspected etc. with the coming into existence of *Sattva*, *Rajas* and *Tamas*. *Prāna* is

> instrumental in bringing about this transformation. Substance and attributes are different as well as identical.
>
> Thus, according to Kapil Muni and some *Sāmkhya* teachers, the three *Gunas* of *Sattva, Rajas,* and *Tamas* are the first evolutes of *Prakriti* and the combination of the three *Gunas,* in equal proportion, is the balanced state of *Prakriti* and that during this state there is no activity or movement of any sort. In our opinion, however, the first evolute is *Prāna* which keeps *Prakriti* dynamic even in the state of reabosrption; this *Prāna* goes on to enable *Prakriti* to evolve the three *Gunas* of *Sattva, Rajas* and *Tamas.* So long as *Prakriti,* in any state, is in proximity to the intelligent *Brahman* there will always be some motion or activity in *Prakriti*".[37]

Swami Yogeshwaranand has designated as *Prāna,* the motion generated by the contact of *Brahman* in the quiescent state of *Prakriti.* In the case of the individual, the motion generated by *Prāna* in the *Citta* occurs due to its contact with *Brahaman* and becomes the cause of further evolution of *Prakriti* and, therefore, it is *Prāna* which manifests change or activity. This view is supported by *Vaiṣeśika Darśana* in *Adh.* 1 *Sutra.7*. *Praṣnopanishad* also supports this view when it says, "Just as the wheel is supported by spokes within it, even so, all the activities of the cosmos are supported by *Prāna.*[38]

ANTAHKARANA CHATUṢTAYA
(Four-fold Internal Organ)

The concept of the *Antahkarana Chatuṣtaya* assumes tremendous significance in Yoga philosophy which deals with discrimination between *Puruṣa* and *Prakriti.* Because it is through this instrument that we gain experiences of the outer world and also have vision of lights of subtle and casual bodies, it becomes necessary to fully understand the form, colour and functions of each of the four limbs of *Antahkarana*. We have briefly discussed *Antahkarana* in the previous chapter but it is necessary to have a thorough knowledge of this organ. The four limbs of *Antahkarana* are (1) mind or *Manas*, (2) Intellect or *Buddhi*, (3) Ego or *Ahamkāra* and (4) Sub–conscious Mind–stuff or *Citta*. *Nyāya* and *Vaiśiṣeka* schools believe that Mind alone performs the functions of all the four limbs and, therefore, Mind corresponds to *Antahkarana*. *Sāmkhya* and Yoga systems accept *Antahkarana Trayi,* a three–fold internal organ comprising of *Manas*, *Ahamkāra* and *Citta*, considering *Buddhi* as included in *Citta*. Upanishads, however, treat *Antahkarana* as comprising of all the above mentioned four limbs, each limb performing specific functions peculiar to it. *Vedāntins* follow the concept of Upanishads and, therefore accept that *Antahkarana* is formed of the aggregate of the four parts mentioned above. Swami Yogeshwaranand also accepts *Antahkarana* as consisting of the said four parts but qualifies that he ascertained the qualities, characteristics and functions of the four limbs on the basis of his direct experience in *Samādhi* which he has described in detail so that an aspirant may be able to realise it directly. This will give an opportunity to the practitioner to compare or contrast his own experience with that of Swami Yogeshwaranand. He, however, affirms that *Citta* has, necessarily, to be taken as apart from *Buddhi* because only on this basis one can understand the formation of *Vijñānamaya Kosha* (Intellect Sheath) and *Anandamaya Kosha* (Bliss Sheath). Even subtle and casual bodies cannot be realised separately if *Citta* and *Buddhi* are not considered as two separate limbs of *Antahkarana*.[39]

Because the knowledge of the limbs of *Antahkarana* can be obtained only in *Samādhi*, the experience is likely to be different with different aspirants depending on which of the three *Gunas* of *Prakriti* was dominant at the relevant time. For this reason, there is a difference of opinion with various *Achāryas*. Since one can have access to self–realisation only through *Antahkarana,* it is imperative to have mastery over this instrument. Swami Yogeshwaranand says that since the functions of various parts of *Antahkarana* are closest to the soul, he felt the necessity of ceaseless meditation and analysis of the subject so that he could properly realise it. He, however, candidly admits that in spite of careful study of the scriptures and with deep reflection in meditation, he could not ascertain a clear description of the principles of *Antahkarana.*[40] Yet, his description of the four limbs is the result of long years of study and examination in meditation as well as the study of scriptures and of the schools of philosophy. We cannot verify his meditative experiences through gross senses. According to him, *Citta* and *Ahamkāra* are directly related to *Anandamaya Kosha* which abides in casual body (*Kārna Śarira*) while *Manas* and *Buddhi* are related to *Manomaya Kosha* which abides in subtle body (*Súkṣam Śarira*). It may be clarified that *Manomaya Kosha* comprises of ten *Indriyas* conjoined with Mind and encased by *Pancha Tanmātras* whereas *Vijñānamaya Kosha* comprises of *Manomaya Kosha* joined with *Buddhi.* We now take up each limb of *Antahkarana* separately and discuss its formation, functions and characteristics.

(1) Manas (Mind) – the First Limb

Earlier, it has been stated that according to *Sāmkhya,* in the process of evolution of *Prakriti,* the first evolute that was formed, is *Mahat* with the three *Gunas* of *Sattva, Rajas* and *Tamas.* From *Mahat–Tamas* was created Cosmic *Ahamkāra.* From the *Sattvic* portion of Cosmic *Ahāmkara* were created the senses of perception (*Jnānemdriyas)* and from *Rajasic Ahamkāra* were created senses of action

(*Karmendriyas*) while with equal portions of *Sattvic Ahamkāra* and *Rajasic Ahamkāra* was created Mind (*Manas*). Thus, Mind has a mixture of *Sattva* and *Rajas* and it is for this reason that Mind can command and take work from both types of *Indriyas*. Because of the presence of *Sattva,* it engages the *Indriyas* of perception to perceive and because of the presence of *Rajas*, it engages the *Indriyas* of action to perform actions. Whatever perceptions or impressions are brought to it by senses, Mind immediately conveys these perceptions to the intellect for analysis and judgment. It cannot hold a perception for longer than a moment and also cannot hold more than one perceptions simultaneously. It has to be noted that *Tamas* is not predominant in Mind and, therefore, Mind is ever active. However, in the dream state, the Mind stops functioning because dream state cannot supervene so long as the conscious Mind is active. Of the conscious and unconscious, the former does not allow the latter to manifest itself or make conscious its contents during its activity.

Nyāya Sutras say that Mind is atomic and eternal.[41] The same Sutras further says that it does not gain knowledge of two objects simultaneously.[42]

This description is very scanty and does not bring out the whole truth about Mind. According to what is experienced by Swami Yogeshwaranand, the Mind is a small luminous mass of unemanated light which has the sensation neither of burn nor of touch. It shines in its own orb and, affected by the three *Gunas,* its form, colour and activity are constantly changing. The colour of its light is generally like that of Venus or like the dust particles in sunlight passing through a hole. But when under the influence of *Sattva*, the Mind assumes the colour of peaceful moon. When engaged in terrible actions, it emits rays of red or smoky blood colour which appear like the sparks of firewood. When *Tamas* prevails and it is under fear or uneasiness, Mind becomes contracted, polluted and shriveled and remains fixed in a particular situation. Thus the Mind receives vibrations from senses and transmits to *Buddhi* and prompts the senses to perform, by spreading its light. Although it is impossible to depict in any visual form or orate the subtle experiences of Mind under the influence of *Gunas,* Swami Yogeshwaranand has attempted to depict his experience as nearly as possible. *Illustration No.1* appended herewith depicts, to some extent, his experience. In the said illustration, *Manomaya Kosha* is shown under the influence of lust, anger, fear and grief. Intellect which is influenced by *Rajo Guna* is shown as yellow coloured and the ripples arising in it are due to lust, anger, fear etc. Mind which is also under the same emotions, is tinged with blue in its whiteness and is seen accepting the object of the senses. The senses of perception and action are shown as agitated by the said emotions which arise due to *Rajas*. It will also be seen in the said illustration that the Mind is active and by reflecting the objects, it is causing ripples in the orb of intellect. *Illustration No. 2* will give a reasonably fair idea of the abode of Mind. The yellow orb shown in the said illustration, is the orb of intellect. On top of it is the orb of Mind that shines like Venus. The subtle centres of the senses of knowledge are shown as white circles and those of senses of action as orange circles. In the transverse section of the heart, orb of *Brahman* is of white colour which is pervading the heart. It sustains the yellow orb of subtle *Prakriti*, the rosy orb of subtle *Prāna*, the blue orb of ego and the shining white orb of *Citta*. *Jīvātman* is shown inside *Citta* in white colour. By itself *Jīvātman* is colourless but it is only symbolically that it is shown as white in the Illustration because white colour approximates to colourlessness. These illustrations afford a rare opportunity for us to augment our knowledge on the

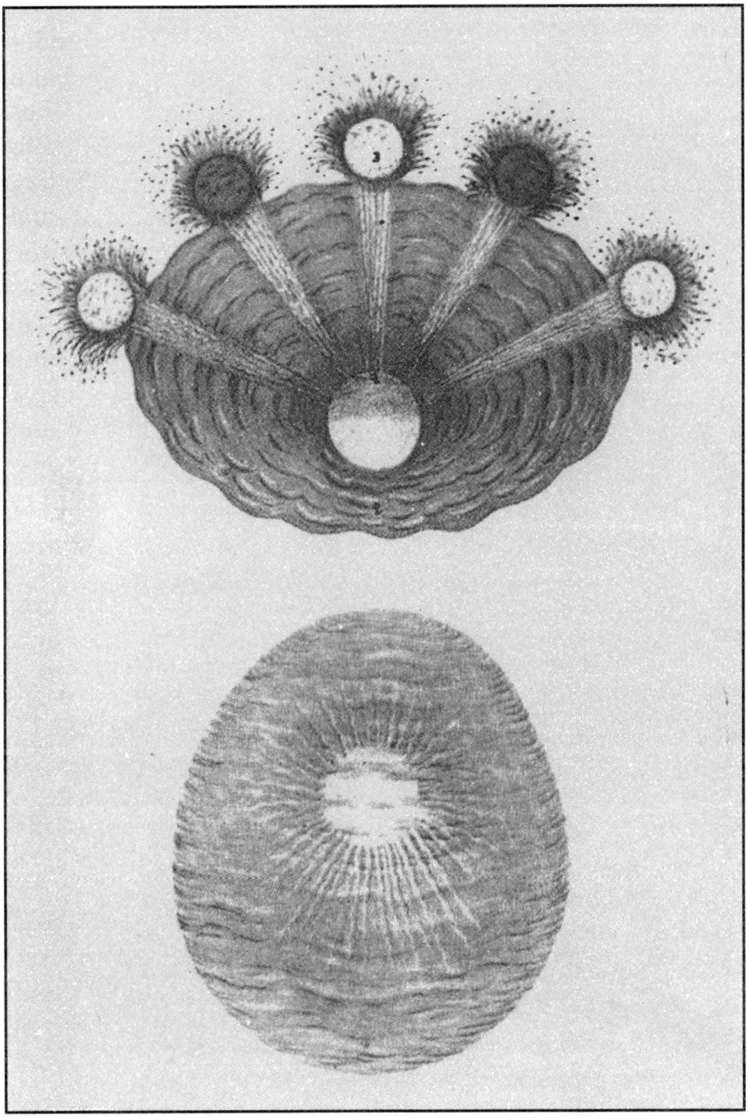

Illustration No.1: *Manomaya Kosha under the influence of lust anger, fear and grief [Science of soul p. 203]*

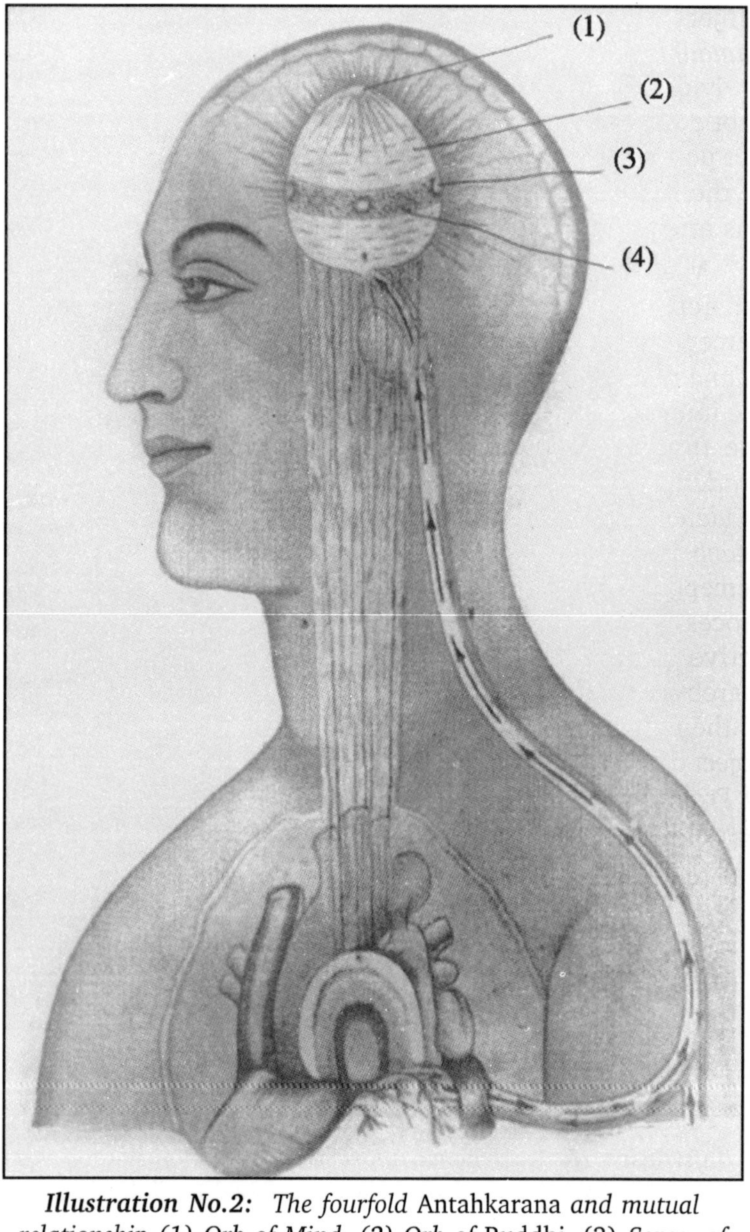

Illustration No.2: *The fourfold* Antahkarana *and mutual relationship (1) Orb of Mind, (2) Orb of* Buddhi, (3) *Senses of perception. (4) Organs of action [Science of soul p. 116]*

subject after verifying its truth in a particular state of *Samādhi*. So far as we know, no other Yogi has left such a vivid record of his mystic experiences with regard to subtle organs like the limbs of *Antahkarana*. Though it is not possible to ascertain the truth of his mystic experience of the limbs of Antahkarana, yet Swami Yogeshwaranand has attempted to widen the knowledge on the subject.

Mind constantly reflects the perception of an object, an action, a conversation etc. as also the internal perception of the senses. This function of the Mind is called *Ādāna* or taking and when these reflections are offered to the intellect, the function is called *Pradāna* or giving. Thus, the fundamental characteristic of Mind is *Ādāna* and *Pradāna*. In the reverse order, in its process of *Ādana Prādāna* Mind receives judgment from *Buddhi* (Intellect) which it passes on to the senses. When Mind offers any perception or reflection to the intellect for judgment, the process appears as if a fish is moving in a well. It is always active in carrying out the orders of the intellect and, thereby, engaging the senses of both types in performance of their respective functions. Like any other organ or any object of the world, Mind is also affected by the three *Gunas* of *Prakriti* and its three states under the three *Gunas* are described as under:[43]

(a) *Under the influence of Sattva:* Mind, under the influence of *Sattva*, appears like peaceful, tranquil and steady moon as if inactive. Its colour is of the luster of moon and although it appears as stationary, it is ever changing.

(b) *Under the influence of Rajas:* In this state, it shines like Venus, tinged with blue colour. It is fickle but endowed with tremendous speed so that it covers long distances with its luminous rays. It keeps the intellect and senses unsteady and causes the senses to move to distant places with speed to

obtain knowledge of divine objects. It has special brilliance when it is engaged in receiving knowledge.

(c) *Under the influence of Tamas:* Under *Tamas,* the colour of Mind is slaty, smoky and dull like mist and it suffers from the defect of procrastination of action which means that it postpones action endlessly and also makes body and senses as inert and inactive. It not only makes the senses inactive in the performance of their functions, it also becomes inactive itself.

Just as heat is the quality of fire, so also fickleness is the quality of Mind and for that reason Mind is endowed with unsteadiness. Since speed is also its function, it brings knowledge and experience of any object in different degrees but when its rapidity is disorderly, it becomes an obstruction rather than help in attaining proper knowledge.

As mentioned earlier, the main functions of Mind are *Ādāna* and *Pradāna.* In performing these functions Mind works as a messenger. It performs the function of *Ādāna* by receiving from the senses, the sensation of objects, knowledge and action and it performs the function of *Pradāna* by receiving from the intellect the decision and judgement and conveying to the senses. The Mind is not concerned with argument, analysis or decision which falls in the domain of intellect. *Ahamkāra* which is action predominating performs unmanifest subtle functions of the *Citta* and since Mind has also evolved from *Ahamkāra,* it is also action predominating. Mind does not interfere with the activities of the *Citta* nor does *Ahamkāra* interfere with the functions of subtle body in the *Bramarandhra* or the *Manomaya* and *Vijñānamaya Koshas.*

The Mind being action predominating, it engages, by its very nature, the senses of knowledge in bringing knowledge, senses of action in performing actions, the

Buddhi in analysing and giving directions, the *Prānas* in spreading knowledge, life and action and the gross body in procuring gross enjoyments for the soul. Mind renders the senses transparent by lending its light to them which enables them to see, hear, smell etc. the distant objects which are hidden and unknown to gross senses. While Mind becomes concentrated and absorbed in *Samādhi* and brings the knowledge of the object concentrated upon, in *Pratyāhāra* (withdrawal of senses) it withdraws its rays and becomes of very small size. It is also a function of the Mind to draw *Samskāras* from the *Citta* abiding in the heart and deposit these *Samsakāras* in the orb of intellect for fructification. Of the four limbs of *Antahkarana*, Mind is the most active. It has tremendous speed and can do actions instantaneously. Even in the *Vedas* it is said that of all the lights, the light of Mind reaches the farthest.[44]

(2) Buddhi (Intellect) – the Second Limb

Intellect is the knowledge predominating limb of *Antahkarana* and, therefore, it performs the function of ascertaining and determining. Cosmic *Buddhi* is formed from the *Rajasic* portion of *Mahat* and from an infinitesimally small portion of Cosmic *Buddhi*, is formed the individual *Buddhi*. So material cause of *Buddhi* is *Mahat Rajas*. When viewed in deep contemplation, intellect will appear like an oval mass of unemanated light like the light of sun which is free from any sensation of heat and touch. Like Mind, intellect also expands and contracts keeping itself to the size of the body. Again like Mind it is also influenced by the three *Gunas*. Its seat is in the *Bramarandhra* but it is permanently related to the casual body in the heart, through the medium of Mind. Every moment, the *Samskāras* which are rearing to fructify, arise from *Citta* and attracted by the rays of the Mind, are conveyed to the orb of intellect where these are converted into gross form for enjoyment by the senses.

Correspondingly, the Mind receives impressions from senses, conveys them to the intellect which analyses and converts them to subtle impressions which the Mind delivers to the *Citta*. It is also through Mind that the intellect conveys all gross enjoyments to the soul. Therefore, all the fructifying *Samskāras,* the senses and the Mind, are under the control of intellect and obey its command. It is, therefore, said in spiritual parlance that when intellect turns towards enjoyments, it causes bondage of the soul but when dispassion is acquired, the soul turns to liberation. As already stated, *Buddhi* is influenced by *Sattva*, *Rajas* and *Tamas*, the three *Gunas* of *Prakriti*. The state of intellect under these *Gunas* is, respectively, as under:

(a) *Under the influence of Sattva:* the intellect is inclined towards Dharma. Swami Yogeshwaranand details the following characteristics of Dharma which arise when intellect is influenced by *Sattva*:

"wisdom, dispassion, prosperity, mercy, absence of cruelty, non–violence, truthfulness, non–stealing, *Brahmacharya* (continence), non–convetousness, purity, contentment, austerity, study of scriptures, surrender to God, theism, inclination towards virtuous conduct, interest in arriving at the truth by analytical reasoning, justice, endurance, serenity, self-control, humility, patience, faith, affection, devotion, happiness, cheerfulness, delight, bliss, selflessness, freedom from attachment, parental affection (*Vātsalya Bhāva*) retentive memory, reflection, contemplation, meditation, discriminative power, peace, one–pointedness of mind, fixity in pure feelings to bring forth objective and analytic superconsciousness (*Samprajñāta* and

Asamprajñāta Samādhis), firm belief in God etc."[45]

In *Sattvic* state, the light of *Buddhi* is pleasing and effulgent like sunrise, peaceful and free from waves. The light has golden luminosity and possesses the power to discriminate between vice and virtue etc. Even in pure *Sattvic* state, the purity of *Buddhi* varies in degrees and in the state of *Samâdhi*, the light of *Buddhi* is called *Ritambharâ Prajñâ* (truth-bearing consciousness) which is brightest and which appears like mercury light.

(b) *Under the influence of Rajas:* It tends to acquire certain defects which arise from fickleness caused by the presence of *Rajas*. The inclination of such intellect is towards unrighteousness (*Adharma*), ignorance (*Ajñāna*) and lack of dispassion (*Anaishwarya*). The *Rajasic* intellect has more of self–assertion, self–justification and also gives rise to negative emotions. It leads to wrong judgement, imagination and doubts. Since the tendencies in this state are demonic, the light of the intellect is orange in colour, red mixed with yellow and, at times, it is rosy red but fickle.

(c) *Under the influence of Tamas:* The intellect becomes prone to the following defects:

"ignorance, violence, cruelty, ejection, atheism, inertia, indiscrimination, laziness, sloth, carlessness, fear, lamentation, dullness, deceit, fraud, false pride, theft, folly, debauchery, bad conduct, meat eating, eating and drinking other impure food, cheating, forgetfulness, pride infatuation, delight in sinful deeds and so on."[46]

While visualising *Tamas* predominating intellect, it will be observed that some of the inclinations will appear similar to those as in the intellect under the influence of

Rajas but by close examination one can ascertain the difference inasmuch as *Rajas* is coloured by passionate action and *Tamas* by darkness and inertia. The light of the intellect under the influence of *Tamas* is opaque and of smoky yellow colour. Such an intellect is full of impurities and, therefore, it is unable to reveal clearly the knowledge of any object.

In general, the functions of *Buddhi* are to deliberate upon the sensations of sound, touch, taste, sight and smell of the sense objects brought to it by senses through the medium of Mind and pronounce well–reasoned judgement. Intellect discriminates between *Dharma* and *Adharma*, between virtue and vice, between truth and untruth and the like. It offers sound counsel and acts like a powerful light–house to guide man on the righteous path. Thus, it is the function of *Buddhi* to reveal knowledge of objects in *Samprajñāta Samādhi* by ensuring one pointed concentration in *Samādhi*. When intellect attains to the form of *Ritambhara*, it enables one to realise the discrimination between *Puruṣa* and *Prakriti*. In substance what is mentioned above is that in the *Sattvic* state, when *Buddhi* is pure it removes the defects of ignorance (*Avidya*), destroys *Asmita* (gross egoism) and releases the aspirant from bondage and enables him to attain *Mokṣa*. On the other hand, when it is over–powered by *Rajas* and *Tamas*, it causes all sorts of afflictions for the soul and enmeshes it in the painful cycle of birth, death and rebirth. *Patāñjali* mentions five *Vrittis* of the *Citta* which need to be controlled so that the Mind can be fixed in *Samādhi*. Swami Yogeshwaranand says that all the functions of the intellect are also technically called *Vrittis*. In a larger sense, all *Vrittis* are thought waves, modifications and transformations. In view of this all transformations whether of *Citta* or intellect (*Buddhi*) can be termed as *Vrittis*. Intellect has numerous *Vrittis* which will be discussed at the appropriate place.

(3) Ahamkāra (Ego) – the Third Limb

Ahamkāra or ego is the principle which creates in us the feeling of 'I–ness' and 'mine–ness' – the feeling of exclusive individuality. In addition, it performs the following functions:

(a) It draws from the orb of intellect subtle *Samskāras* (impressions) of every decision or command and deposits them in the *Citta*;

(b) it sends towards intellect all *Samskāras* that arise from *Citta*, for conversion into gross form;

(c) it enables the soul to experience the feeling of '*Ahamasmi*' or 'I am' and also of '*Ayamasti*' or 'This is'; and

(d) after receiving knowledge of every action, direction, command, experience etc. from intellect, it marks 'mine–ness' on its impression, shows that impression to the soul and deposits it in the *Citta*. In fact, it conveys entire information of *Buddhi* to *Citta*. Like Mind and intellect, *Ahamkāra* is also capable of expansion and contraction but keeps to the size of the body.

In the process of evolution of *Prakriti, Samasti* (universal) *Ahamkāra* was created from *Tamasic* portion of *Mahat*. From active portion of *Samasti Ahamkāra* is created the *Vyasti* or individual *Ahamkāra* which is present in every being. Because of the presence of *Tamas* in it the colour of *Ahamkāra* is like that of a light blue jewel, lustrous as moon. It is oval shaped mass of unemanated light. Its circle envelops the orb of *Citta* in which abides the soul. Its own abode is in *Ānandamaya Kosha* (bliss sheath) in the casual body. Swami Yogeshwaranand says that it envelops the *Citta* in the same way as a shell envelops the almond or a cover envelops the pillow.[47] He further says that if seen by Divine Eye (*Divya Chakṣu*), it is very beautiful and looks like the neck of a peacock. *Ahamkāra* itself is enveloped by the orb of subtle *Prāna* like a luminous veil which infuses life force every moment and spreads this life force to the three bodies and five sheaths. The individuality or I–ness exists with *Ahamkāra* in the form of *Asmita* (egoism) and represents *Tamas* (inertia) and *Avidyā* (ignorance). We have already mentioned that the function of *Ahamkāra* is to stir up *Samskāras* in the *Citta* and send fructifying *Samskāras* to the orb of intellect and also to receive new *Samskāras* from the intellect and deposit them in the *Citta*. It will be noticed that we have assigned the same function to Mind as well. As this is likely to cause some confusion, it is necessary to clarify this point.

The abode of Mind is the subtle body and that of *Ahamkāra* is the casual body. Mind regularly shuttles between the senses and the intellect. In the same way, *Ahamkāra* moves between *Citta* and the intellect. Thus *Ahamkāra* alone gathers the *Samskāras* from *Citta* and brings these to the orb of intellect but these *Samskāras* are conveyed to the *Buddhi* through the medium of Mind. Therefore, both perform their respective functions as already mentioned which should not cause any confusion as the functions of the two are clearly different.

Ahamkāra is also affected by the *Gunas* of *Prakriti* and its colours and forms under the three *Gunas* are as mentioned below:

(a) Under influence of Sattva: When *Ahamkāra* is under the influence of *Sattva*, it assumes the colour of a pure blue saphire which is beautifully transparent. In this state it awakens awareness of the feeling of '*Asmi*' or '*Ahamasmi*'and also reveals to the soul, its essential nature. When *Ahamkāra* is in peaceful state, it stops the functions of *Citta* and subtle *Prāna* which helps in the attainment of self–realisation. *Sattvic*

Ahamkāra also acts as a very useful source for understanding the causal *Prakriti* and the realisation of *Brahman* in its orb enveloping all other orbs in the *Anandmaya Kosha*.

(b) *Under the influence of Rajas* : *Rajas* is the quality of power, possession and passion. Under the influence of *Rajas* the *Ahamkāra* brings a special luminosity to the *Sattvic* glow which appears like the glowing neck of a peacock. When *Rajas* predominates, the *Ahamkāra* becomes fickle and restless and engages *Citta* and subtle *Prāna* in constant activity and infuses life in all the *Koshas*. It is *Rajasic Ahamkāra* which puts the stamp of 'mineness' on each and every knowledge of sense experience. It also awakens the impressions of lust, anger, greed, infatuation as well as attachment and aversion. Because of the above feelings, it does not allow *Citta* to rest in peace and, therefore, control of *Vrittis* becomes very difficult.

(c) *Under the influence of Tamas* : In *Tamasik* state, *Ahamkāra* has sky blue colour which is slightly smoky. Under the influence of *Tamasik Ahamkāra*, the *Citta* becomes dull and conceited. It tends to self–praise and directs the *Citta* to unrighteousness. Such *Ahamkāra* excites and intensifies the painful *Samskāras* which arouse sinful feelings. *Tamasik Ahamkāra* obstructs the Divine Vision, takes away the faculty of right knowledge and nullifies the detached witness attitude of the *Puruṣa*, thereby creating intense attachment to the body, senses and sense objects.

Just as Mind is the help–mate of *Buddhi*, *Ahamkāra* is the help–mate of *Citta* but both are unaware of their functions. The Mind is not aware of its function of *Ādāna*–

Pradāna. Similarly, *Ahamkāra* which stirs up *Samskāras* in the *Citta*, has no knowledge either of the nature of these *Samskāras*, or of the fruit of Karma to be borne by them or even of the manner in which such *Samskāras* would bear fruit. Under *Rajas*, the *Ahamkāra* engages the soul in *Adharma*, *Ajñāna*, *Anaishwarya* and *Bhoga* and veils the orb of *Citta* with egoism, thereby making the *Jīvātman* conceive that the body, family, possessions and the world belongs to him. It kindles all types of possessive ideas by propping ego. Since it gets influenced by the three *Gunas* it is ever changing. Under *Sattva*, the feelings that arise are 'My heart is pleased', 'My intellect is clear', 'I am happy' or 'I have understood'. Under *Rajas*, the feelings are My *Citta* is depressed, 'My Mind is distracted', and all such similar depressing feelings. Under *Tamas* the feelings that arise are "This does not become clear to me", I cannot think of any thing", "My intellect does not agree to this" and all such similar perceptions. While *Ahamkāra* generally arouses the negative and misleading tendencies which cause unrighteousness, ignorance and attachment, it also performs a very unique and valuable function. It may be mentioned here that realisation of self takes place when *Jivâṭman* is reflected in the mirror of *Citta*. When this happens, there should be some agency to certify that the image so reflected is that of *Jīvâtman*. *Ahamkāra* is such an agency. When *Jīvātman* realises its true nature in the medium of *Citta*, the knowledge is qualified by *Ahamkāra* which creates the feeling of *Ahamasmi* or 'I am'. Normally ego veils the vision of *Jīvātman* but in the above situation it makes it possible for the soul to see its reflection and be sure about it. Without the assistance of *Ahamkāra*, *Jīvātman* would never attain self–realisation since *Ahamkāra* alone can show the relation of *Jīvātman* and *Citta* in the form of reflection and the object reflected.

The reason why ignorance holds a sway over *Citta*, is that *Ahamkāra* and *Citta* always work together but

Ahamkāra assumes supremacy over the functions of *Citta*. It is this *Avidya* which takes the gross body for the soul and all that is unreal as real with the result that one gets engrossed in painful afflictions such as *Asmita*, *Raga* *Dveṣha* and *Abhiniveṣa* (clinging to life). These *Kleshas* abide in the *Citta* in four forms namely *Prasupta* (dormant), *Tanu* (thinned out) *Vichhinna* (overpowered) and *Udāra* (expanded). Swami Yogeshwaranand says that *Avidya* which is an offspring of *Ahamkāra,* is that which veils the light of knowledge and binds the activity of *Rajas* so that instead of true perception, one sees the absence of it. He further says that if *Ahamkāra* overpowers *Sattva* in *Citta*, *Tamas* takes over to create ignorance, attachment, hatred, impurity and pain.[48] It is for this reason that *Jīvātman* assumes the role of actor and enjoyer which it is not. While *Sattva* dominated *Citta* acts as an aid for liberation, *Ahamkāra* causes bondage.

(4) Citta (Sub – Conscious Mind Stuff) – the Fourth Limb

When *Prakriti* commenced its process of creation and reached the stage of *Mahat*, then from *Mahat Sattva*, it created the cosmic *Citta* which became the material cause of individual *Cittas*. *Mahat* is deemed as the first evolute of *Prakriti* which is of the nature of an intelligent principle and *Sattva* is of the nature of purity. *Citta* being the product of *Mahat Sattva* is also pure as crystal, beautiful as a diamond and white as butter or the feathers of a duck. It is transparent and shines like mercury or polished silver but it is ever changing. To Divine Eye, it appears as pure, clear and as a small oval mass of unemanated light like all other limbs of *Antahkarana*. Every object created by *Prakriti* has three *Gunas* namely *Sattva*, *Rajas* and *Tamas*. Since *Citta* is also of the nature of these three *Gunas*, it has luminosity, activity and inertia. Mahrishi Vyasa has said the same thing while commenting on second *Sutra* of first chapter of *Patāñjali Sutras*.[49] Swami Yogeshwaranand describes the abode of *Citta* as under:

> "In the middle of the heart is a small ethnic cavity called the cave of heart, the size of the thumb of a baby or a white grape; it is not part of the physical organ. In this inner cave of the heart is the abode of *Citta* in the form of an oval mass of unemergent light; this *Citta* is the abode of *Jīvātman*. The modern experts of surgery have also seen a small hole–like part close to the blood repository in the heart which is a bit raised and which has a constant vibration on it. They have named it Auriculo–ventricular Bundle of Hiss. These surgeons have not yet been able to know the reality of *Citta* and *Ātman*. Our visualization of them at this place will be amply supported by medical science also. The effect of *Citta* and the *Ātman* is observed at this point first of all and causes the working of the heart whereby the activity is sent forward to the entire physical body through the veins".[50]

The relationship of *Citta* and *Jīvātman* commences from the beginning of each creation and is of the nature of reflector and the object reflected (Bimba–Bimbi Bhava). *Jīvātman* subsists in the womb of *Citta* and *Citta* itself abides in the cavity of the heart. *Illustration No. 3* shows the location of *Citta* and *Jīvātman* as envisioned by Swami Yogeshwaranand in *Samādhi*. It will appear from the illustration that there are six luminous orbs in the region of the heart. The orb of white colour is the orb of *Brahman* which pervades the other orbs. Orb of *Prakriti* is of yellow colour and that of subtle *Prāna* is of rose colour. The colour of the orb of *Ahamkāra* is blue–green and that of *Citta* is of white colour which is emitting rays. It can be seen that in the white orb of *Citta*, there is a very luminous orb which is *Jīvātman*.

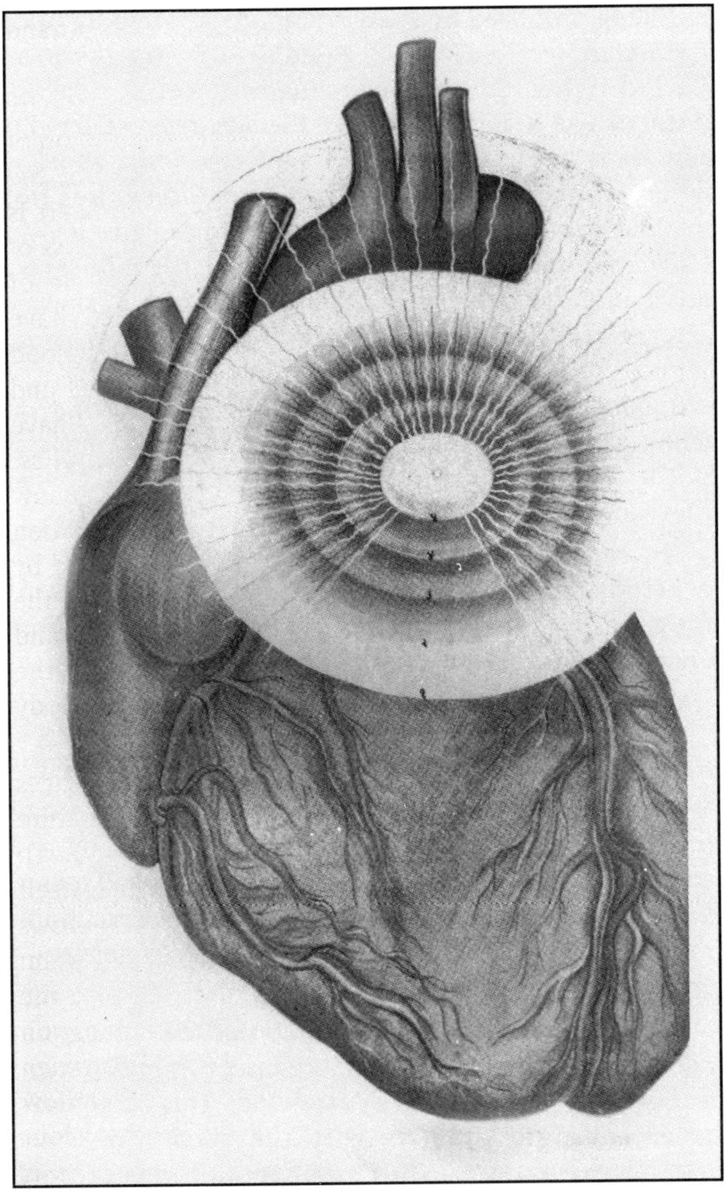

Illustration No.3: *In the Heart Region there are six luminous orbs [Science of soul p. 262]*

Being produced by *Prakriti*, *Citta* is affected by *Gunas* of *Prakriti* just as Manas, *Buddhi* and *Ahamkāra* are affected. When *Sattva* predominates, *Citta* is clear like crystal or like a diamond or like the sun–rays reflected on snow. It is bright like mercury light and white as butter and is transparent. In such *Sattvic* state, *Citta* is free from any doubts, is peaceful, bestows bliss and can give a vision of *Jīvātman* and *Paramātma*. *Citta* under the influence of *Sattva* imparts feelings of *Dharma* (Virtue), *Aishwarya* (Prosperity) *Jñāna* (wisdom) and *Vairāgya* (dispassion). Swami Yogeshwaranand says that as long as *Sattva* predominates, the *Citta* is filled with the placidity of divine feeling and is endowed with soft luminosity. In this state *Citta* assumes a minute form by contracting and thereby self–realisation becomes possible.[51]

In the *Rajasik* state, *Citta* becomes turbulent and boisterous and is ever changing. *Rajasik Samskāras* arise in it which give rise to attachment, hatred, jealousy, pride, conceit, pleasure and pain. It is full of *Sankalpa* and *Vikalpa*, thoughts and imaginations. In this state *Citta* holds both types of *Samskāras viz.* of virtue and vice, knowledge and ignorance, passion and dispassion etc.

Tamasik Citta is possessed of dull light, is related to ignorance, indiscrimination, vice and is tainted by cruel actions. Action of the intellect is subdued and bad feelings of evil inclinations crop up. Since good *Samskāras* do not arise in *Tamas* predominating *Citta*, man does not tend to perform good actions.

Above is the detailed description of the colour, form and the functions of the four organs of *Antahkarana* as visualized by Swami Yogeshwaranand. This shall enable the aspirants to compare with the version of Swami Yogeshwaranand, their own experience of such organs in meditation. In this way one can have direct perception of *Antahkarana*, *Jīvātman* and *Brahman*.

Puruṣa (soul) is unattached, actionless, unchanging, pure and enlightened and also free from pleasure and pain but *Citta* superimposes these qualities on the soul (Jīvātman). Then the soul identifies itself with *Citta* and seems to enjoy or suffer pleasure and pain. From the time of its creation and till it merges in its cause, *Citta* remains active. It is ever changing by its very nature and brings experience of *Bhoga* to *Puruṣa*. But in the state of *Samādhi* when the aspirant reaches the stage of *Asamprajñāta Samādhi*, *Citta* is controlled by *Samskāras* of extreme dispassion (*Para–Vairagya*) and leads to realisation of self and *Brahman* under certification by ego. Subtle *Prānas* are generated by *Citta* which energise first the ego and then all the five *Koshas* and three bodies. Even *Jīvātman* realises its own essential nature (*Swarúpa Sthiti*) by way of reflection in the mirror of *Citta*. Functions of *Citta* do not cease even in deep sleep and *Turiya* state because when one rises from sleep or *Samādhi*, one is able to recall the experience gained in that state. Remaining in the *Ānandmaya Kosha*, *Citta* conducts the whole body with its functions which are subtle, unmanifest and hence, profound and mysterious. Here a question may be asked as to how do we verify these functions of *Citta* and also of the other limbs of *Antahkarana*. Swami Yogeshwaranand says that these can be visualised only by the Divine Eye and can be understood by sharp and one pointed intellect.[52] Another question that naturally arises is that the *Antahkarana*, with its four limbs, is made of *Prakriti* and is inert and lifeless because *Prakriti* itself is inert and unconscious. Then how and where from do these limbs receive energy to perform their functions. Swami Yogeshwaranand answers these questions as under:

> "The entire *Antahkarana* is the centre of energy for the *Jīvātman*. Essentially, this *Citta* generates the energy of knowledge and action, rather like positive and negative electrical energy. The

> energy is generated to such an extent that it is difficult to measure it; because of its subtlety it is very difficult to visualize it with the general light of meditation. Rising from the lake of *Citta* and coming out of the orb of ego, this process appears in the form of subtle *Prāna*. Out of these currents, the positive current of knowledge nourishes *Citta* and *Buddhi Tattwa,* and the negative current of activity goes on offering energy of action to ego and Mind (*Ahamkāra* and *Manas*). In yogic language, the essence of the life-principle is *Súkshma Prāna* which shines like luminous vapour outside the orb of ego. It mixes with the astral body which is seated in the brain wrapped in five *Tanmātras.* It sustains, nourishes, irrigates and conducts the physical body that is constituted of five gross elements. Just as in the astral body, organs of action and senses of perception perform their particular functions of knowledge and action, even so *Citta* and *Buddhi* predominate in knowledge and ego and Mind predominate in action; they are the limbs of *Antahkarana*.[53]

The mention of positive and negative currents by Swami Yogeshwaranand, is only symbolic. Because *Citta* and *Buddhi* are knowledge predominating, he has related positive current to these organs and because ego and mind (*Ahamkāra and Manas*) and are action predominating, he has related negative current to them. There is no other reason for their distinction.

At the time of death our physical body perishes but the subtle and the casual bodies survive and form an aggregate with five *Tanmātras;* assume the form of a luminous *Śiva–Pinda* and leave the physical body. Swami Yogeshwaranand makes an interesting mention about the forms of various bodies when these bodies move to the other world after death of the physical body. He says that the forms of astral or subtle bodies of Yogis who have conquered the elements are similar to their physical bodies. However, *Sattva* predominating bodies have special luminosity and shine like the moon. Such bodies are well–developed like their physical bodies and their faces are also beaming with happiness. *Rajas* predominating bodies are tall, of golden colour and beautiful but somewhat thin. *Tamas* predominating bodies are brown or of smoke colour and smaller in size. Their appearance is not very pleasant and their movements are also dull. Swami Rama of Himalayan Institute has given a somewhat similar description of the various types of bodies departing from the gross bodies at the time of death, but the description is neither as lucid nor as elaborate.

Citta is otherwise dull and unconscious but due to its contact with conscious soul, it also appears conscious. Just as an iron bar which is kept close to fire, acquires all the qualities of fire such as heat and light, in the same way when *Citta* comes into contact with soul, it also acquires the qualities of soul and appears to be conscious. The process by which this consciousness pervades the *Citta* and then the whole of *Antahkarana* is called *Kriyā*. It is because of *Kriyā* that the *Antahkarana* appears conscious and the various limbs thereof perform their respective functions. Swami Yogeshwaranand says that the said process of *Kriyā* can be seen only in *Samādhi* when it can also be seen how *Citta* offers various enjoyments to *Puruṣa*. Like *Kriyā*, *Jñāna* (knowledge) is also the energy that arises from soul. When *Jīvātman* takes its abode in *Citta*, it gives rise to two types of energies namely *Jñāna* and *Kriyā* or knowledge and action. These energies pervade the *Antahkarana* and the five sheaths and throughout life we perform our activities with these two energies. *Jñāna* enables *Citta* to perform the action of knowing while *Kriyā* enables it to perform its action of doing.

Commenting on *Citta Vritti Nirodhad*, the second *Sutra* of Part-I of Yoga *Sutras*, *Vyāsa* has said that when *Citta* is full of *Sattva*, then *Rajas* and *Tamas* appear to be absent. At that stage there is inward flow of *Citta* which is called *Antarmukhi Vritti*. Then *Citta* gets absorbed in *Viveka–khyati* or discriminative knowledge of *Puruṣa* and *Prakriti* and the resultant realization of *Puruṣa* is known as *Ātma Sākshātkāra* or realisation of self. According to Swami Yogeshwaranand, this leads to *Dharma Megha* (the cloud of virtue) which helps the soul to rest in its essential nature.

The other flow of *Citta* is *Bahirmukhi* or outward flow. This flow has dual inclination of *Rajas* and *Tamas* and, therefore, *Citta* is never calm. In the outward flow of *Citta*, good *Samskāras* do not arise. Evil desires taint the intellect and make the *Mind* fickle and senses turbulent. Senses turn to the objects for enjoyment and cause agitation in Mind. The basic nature of the senses is to move outwards to the sense objects and not inward to the soul. On the nature of such *Vrittis Vyāsa* has stated that tendencies which increase impure *Samskāras* in the *Citta* and which strengthen ignorance by generating the *Vāsnas* of virtue and vice are *Kliṣta* or painful.[54] The reason for giving rise to this pain is karma. Thus, all those *Vrittis* which are the support of all the good or bad subliminal impressions (*Samskāras*) are *Kliṣta* or painful.

Swami Yogeshwaranand has clearly indicated the difference between *Vrittis* and *Samskāras*. Defining *Samskāras*, he says that all the subtle functions and subtle feelings of pleasure and pain and all gross actions, gross objects and gross knowledge, as well as gross functions, cast their impressions on the subtlest and most sensitive part of the *Citta* and are termed as *Samskāras*. Enjoyment in the form of pleasure and pain are presented to the *Puruṣa* through all such subtle and non–manifest functions. Thus all these *Samskāras* which are inclined to

Bhoga, rise from the *Citta* and on entering the intellect sheath assume gross forms which cause gross enjoyments for the *Puruṣa.* These gross forms are used by the intellect and are named as *Vritis*. According to Swami Yogeshwaranand, all functions of *Buddhi* which are numerous and infinite, are called *Vrittis* and when *Vrittis* cast their shadow on the most sensitive part of *Citta*, then the shadow is called *Samskāra*. *Citta* and *Ahamkāra* and, in fact, the casual body as a whole, carries out its functions by *Samskāras*. In the nutshell, all functions of *Buddhi* are known as *Vrittis* and the subtle forms of these *Vrittis* are called *Samskāras*. And *Samskāras* exist in the *Citta* but *Vrittis* exist in the intellect. The distinction is further clarified by the fact that intellect is coloured or reflected by knowledge of objects brought by *Indriyas* but *Citta* is coloured by *Samskāras* of such aknowledge. Therefore, *Citta* has only two *Vrittis* of *Jñana* and *Kriya* which have been divided by *Patāñjali* into five *Vrittis*.

It has to be noted that unless the *Buddhi* and *Citta* are coloured by some object, they cannot convey any knowledge to us. We get knowledge of only such objects as are coloured or are reflected in the *Citta* and in the intellect. Therefore, *Buddhi* and *Citta* are always full of *Vrittis* and *Samskāras*. However, being inert and lifeless both *Citta* and *Buddhi* are unaware of their own functions. It is *Puruṣa* alone who goes on watching these functions every moment. Since *Jīvātman* abides in *Citta*, it is ever aware of every movement of *Citta*. Because *Citta* and intellect are confined to only one place, they can know only one object at a time. However, because their actions are very rapid, it appears as if they were doing so many actions at a time.

We have stated in some earlier context that *Citta* is the repository of our *Samskāras*, the seed impressions of our subtle and gross actions. We have carried with us such impressions of innumerous births in the past. We have accumulated and added to that stock, the *Samskāras* of this birth as well making it a huge collection. Our *Citta* is an infinitesimally small portion of Samasti *Citta*. A question arises whether that huge pile of accumulated *Samskāras* can be accommodated in our small *Citta*. The answer is that so many *Samskāras* cannot be confined to individual *Citta*. To solve this problem, every *Citta* is directly related to the cosmic *Citta* through the current of Divine Rays. This relationship persists at all times. All the *Samskāras* which are not likely to bear fruit immediately are carried from individual *Citta* to cosmic *Citta* through the said current of Divine Rays and the *Samskāras* which are ripe for fruits, return from cosmic *Citta* to the individual *Citta* through the same route. When a powerful *Samskāra* of the individual *Citta* is ready to bear fruit, it draws similar *Samskāras* from the cosmic *Citta*. That is the reason why good or bad *Samskāras* bear fruit for a long time once the fructification starts. Those who are adept in the practice of *Samādhi* can envision this process. Swami Yogeshwarnand says that when external operations of *Antahkarana* cease and *Manas, Buddhi Ahamkāra* and *Citta* perform only inner functions, then in the sate of *Samādhi*, the contact of *Vyasti Citta* with cosmic or *Samasti Citta* can be seen by the practitioner. One can see in *Samādhi* a stream of a sparkling light joining this *Citta*, passing through the heart and merging in the etheric sphere. The stream of *Samskāras* which flows from individual *Citta* to the cosmic *Citta* and *vice versa* can be seen by practicing *Samyama* on it. This is the experience of Swami Yogeshwaranand which appears to be in accord with the *Vibhuti Pada* of Yoga *Sutras*. Elaborating this experience, he says:

> "If you follow this stream you can see that these are being carried along with the stream and deposited in the womb of the mother Prakriti (cosmic *Citta*). Then, rising from there, these

> *Samskāras* join with the stream of rays, in the form of luminous vapour raining down on every *Citta*. Among these *Samskāras*, the ripe ones remain in the *Citta* and fructify through the force of memory; the remaining ones flow through the stream, joining with the other accumulated *Samskāras* in the cosmic *Citta*. The fructifying *Samskāras* stick to every *Citta* and, being awakened by memory, they successfully engage the intellect in enjoyments. These fructifying *Samskāras* are seen sometimes as rays and sometimes as sparks, rising from *Citta* and entering into *Buddhi* (intellect); they also have differences of colour. In the state of meditation, by the power of *Samayama*, this is seen clearly. By the divine law and by providential prompting, every *Citta* accepts the fructifying *Samskāras* only and rejects the remaining ones, and they, flowing through the stream, join their other companions in the cosmic womb and are thus accumulated there. This is the manner in which *Samskāras* abide in the human *Cittas* and, according to this process, maintain their coming and going from the deep storehouse of *Prakriti*".[55]

Visualisation of the flow of *Samskāras* from individual *Citta* to cosmic *Citta* and vice versa are shown in *Illustration No. 4*.

There is a space in the skull which is three inches inside from the eye–brows and two inches from the tamples. This space is called by the scriptures as *Brahmrandhra* or the thousand petalled lotus or the tenth door. It contains five lights of *Jñānendriyas*, five lights of *Karmendriyas*, five lights of *Panchatanmātras* and one light each of the Mind and intellect, totalling in all to seventeen lights. Astral body or subtle body abides in *Brahmrandhra* and illumines the *Brahmrandhra*. These lights can be visualised only with the

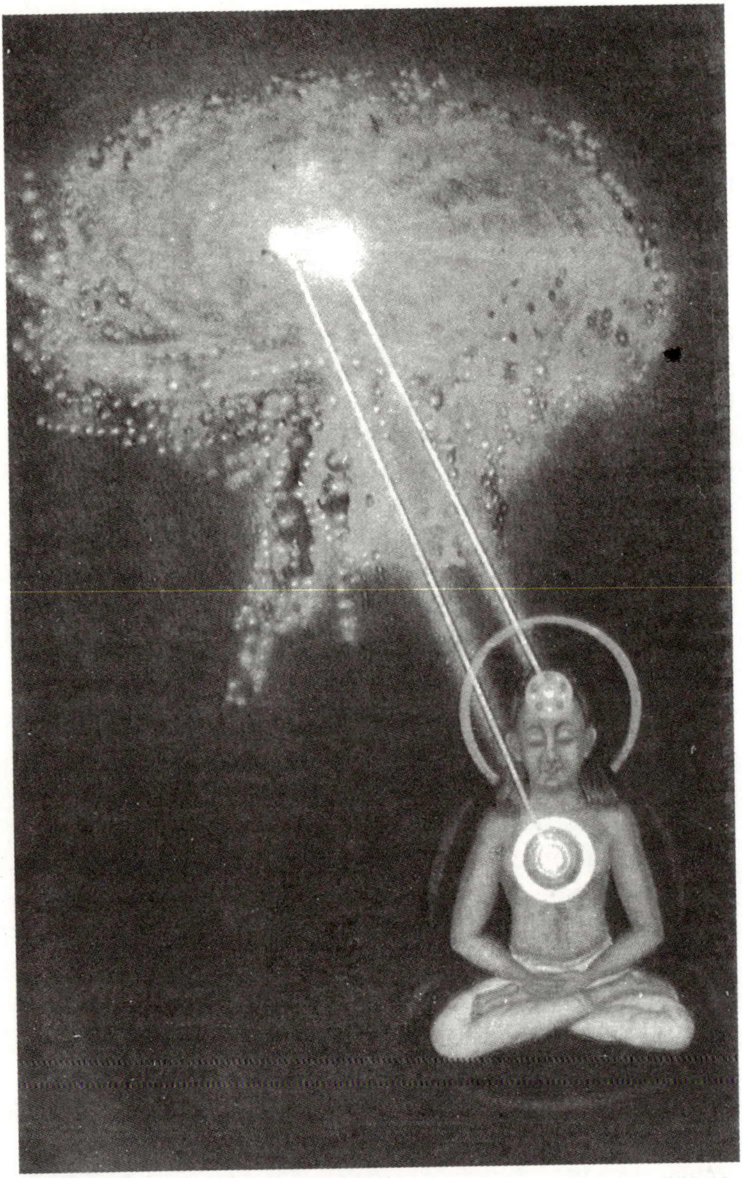

Illustration No. 4: *Relationship of Individual and cosmos during the state of meditation. [Science of soul p. 286]*

divine eye and by entering this region. The knowledge and vision of these lights as well as of the lights abiding in the region of heart where exist the *Citta*, the *Jīvātman* and the *Ahamkāra*, is not brought about by a mystic experience alone. There is a definite method by which one can reach these regions and have a vision of all the subtle organs that abide in those regions and finally to have a vision of the soul.

Swami Yogeshwaranand gives a detailed explanation about these lights and also offers guidance about how to segregate these lights and realise them separately. He says that those who enter the *Brahmrandhra* through meditative vision, see these lights in the preliminary state like the flame of a lamp or of many lamps, as many shining stars or like glow worms. Often one sees it like a leafless tree with luminous branches with shining clouds hovering over it or one sees a dense dark shadow. At this stage the Divine vision of the practitioner is not so perfect and, therefore, he sees a conglomeration of lights which are all mixed up. These lights are different from outer lights which are endowed with heat and touch and can be perceived by the senses. But the inner divine lights are different as these are constituted by subtle principles of *Prakriti*. These are luminous Divine energies which sustain human activities. All subtle functions whether of *Brahmrandhra* or of the orbs of heart are visualised by the Divine eye alone.

The activity of the inner lights is very fast and is difficult to describe in words. Swami Yogeshwaranand says that the said vision cannot be experienced unless complete perfection is attained in *Sādhana* (practice). Once this *Sādhana* is perfected, it is wonderful to see how mind and intellect engage themselves in their subtle activities through the medium of lights being reflected by the objects of senses. He says that it is beyond the capacity of a human being to describe in words the lights of the orbs and their movement. It is a unique and very beautiful view which cannot be expressed adequately in words. The knowledge of these lights cannot be acquired only by initial effort but the hidden principles reveal themselves when the aspirant becomes steady in his meditation. He says that even the subtlest objects relating to astral and casual bodies can be seen directly by meditative vision. Therefore, he insists that since all true objects of vision can be seen by Divine eye alone, these have to be understood by heart.[56] It is to understand the form, colour and functions and also to gain exhaustive knowledge of the subtle entities of which he has given various illustrations by way of explanation. He says:

> "Just as geographical and geological knowledge is made easier through maps, so illustrations can enable one to understand these matters. A teacher who is perfect in *Samyama* controls the Mind of his disciple by his will and enables the vision of the disciple to fix itself in *Brahmarandhra* or in the *Citta*. He contines to point out the subtle objects by the force of his own will; he explains their functions also just as teachers explain geography through maps"[57]

The manner in which Swami Yogeshwaranand has explained the knowledge of the five sheaths and three bodies is altogether different from what has been said by other seers and sages. He says that defects enter into the experience due to imperfection in individual realisation. We cannot know an object merely by its name and form but by cognising the object itself. He, therefore, considers it against testimony as well as against direct perception, the claim of those who say that the individual soul abides in the brain and not in the heart. He re–affirms that as long as one does not acquire the power of Divine vision through practice of meditation, one cannot arrive at the conclusion by study alone. Till then, the vision may be impure and may lead to wrong knowledge. It is, therefore, necessary to know and experience that the source of consciousness is in the *Citta* which is the abode of the soul and which is located in the heart.

Swami Yogeshwaranand was not only a great Yogi but was also bold and fearless in his approach to many vital and important aspects of reality, He, therefore, rejected many concepts and doctrines which have prevailed from endless past and which are believed by a vast majority of people as beyond question. Some such doctrines are discussed in the ensuing chapters.

REFERENCES

(1) Yoga Sutra 1-2 : योगश्चित्तवृत्तिनिरोधः
(2) Beads of Sermons – (Pt. II, p. 80)
(3) Beads of Sermons (Pt.5, p. 175)
(4) Beads of Sermons (Pt. 6, pp. 98-99)
(5) Essential Colourlessness of the Absolute (p. 130)
(6) Essential Colourlessness of the Absolute (p. XIII)
(7) Science of Divinity (p. 2)
(8) Nyāya Sutras of Gotama (p. 3)
(9) Light of Truth (p. 52).
(10) Consciousness : East and West (p. 140)
(11) Mysticism by R.D. Ranade (p. 7)
(12) Yoga Sutra (3-5) तज्जयात्प्रज्ञालोकः
(13) Essential Colourlessness of the Absolute (p. XIV-XV)
(14) Mandukya Upanishad (p. 8)
(15) An Introduction to Indian Philosophy (p. 204)
(16) Advaitasidhi (pp. 137-139) quoted in ibid
(17) Science of Divinity (p. 332)
(18) Science of Divinity (p. 11)
(19) Yoga Sutra (3-33) प्रतिभादा सर्वम्!
(20) Yoga Varttika of Vjñāna Bhikṣu Vol. III (p. 128)
(21) The *Nyāya Sutras* of Gotama (p. 6)
(22) A History of Indian Philosophy (Vol. I p. 238)
(23) A History of Indian Philosophy (Vol. I p. 401)

(24) Indian philosophy (Vol. I p. 152)
(25) Chindogya Upanishad (VIII - 7-12)
(26) *Yogavarttika* (Vol-I, p. 43)
(27) Yogavarttika (Vol-4, p. 49)
(28) Science of Soul (pp. 119-120)
(29) Science of Soul (p. 124)
(30) Essential Colourlessness of the Absolute (p. 194)
(31) Science of Vital Force (p. 138)
(32) Light of Truth (p. 243)
(33) Light of Truth (pp. 243-244)

द्वा सुपर्णा सयुजा सखाया समानं वृक्षं परिषस्वजाते!
तयोरन्य: पिप्पलंस्वादुत्यनश्नन्नन्यो अभि चाकशीति!!

(Rig Veda 1- 164-20)

(34) Light of Truth (p. 244)
(35) Light of Truth (p. 247)
(36) Light of Truth (p. 248)
(37) Science of Vital Force (pp. 10-11)
(38) Praṣnopanishad: 2-6 *अरा इव रथनाभौ प्राणे सर्वं प्रतिष्ठितम्*
(39) Science of Soul (p. 122)
(40) Science of Soul (p. 125)
(41) Nyāya Sutras (3-2-59)
(42) Nyāya Sutras (3-2-56)
(43) Science of Soul (p. 128)
(44) Science of Soul (p. 131) *दूरंगमम् ज्योतिषां ज्योतिरेकम्!*
(45) Science of Soul (pp. 134-135)
(46) Science of Soul (p. 135)
(47) Science of Soul (p. 138)
(48) Science of Soul (p. 144)
(49) Yogavarttika Vol.I (p. 31)

चित्तम् हि प्रख्या-प्रवृति-स्थिति-शीलत्वात् त्रिगुणाम्

(50) Science of Soul (p. 146-147)
(51) Science of Soul (p. 148)

(52) Science of Soul (p. 150)
(53) Science of Soul (pp. 151-152)
(54) Yoga Varttika (Part-1 p. 55)
(55) Science of Soul (pp. 165-166)
(56) Science of Soul (p. 190) स्वयं तदन्तः करणेन गृह्यते-
(57) Science of Soul (p. 191)

2

Reinterpretation of Certain Doctrines

DEFICIENCY OF KNOWLEDGE IN SOUL

There is an acknowledged doctrine among scholars that the soul (*Jīvātman*) is finite and, therefore, limited in knowledge, but it is capable of attaining full enlightenment from God or from realised preceptors and, on receipt of such enlightenment, the soul obtains final release from bodily bondage. This concept, of the limitation of knowledge of the soul, has been critically analysed by Swami Yogeshwaranand. According to him, if limitation of knowledge in soul is inherent in it, then it will last as long as the soul lasts because inherent traits are inalienable from the substances. Just as motion of air and heat of fire, are their respective inherent traits, and must co-exist with the respective substances, the deficiency of knowledge in soul must also co-exist with it. It means that on removal of deficiency of knowledge in soul, the soul will also cease to exist because, as already mentioned above, the substance and its traits are inalienable.

Now if we presume that the deficiency is not the original trait of the soul but was inducted into it later on or is caused by some outside agency, then it assumes the relationship of cause and effect. Every cause lends its intrinsic qualities to its effect. Hence, if the deficiency is the effect of some cause, then it is necessarily transient and will disappear, at sometime or the other, when the cause is extinguished. But the concept pre–supposes that the deficiency is primordial and existed from inception of the soul. Because the soul is finite, it is believed that its knowledge is also limited. If this be so, then its capacity for further knowledge will also be limited which means that its knowledge will neither be increased nor decreased and it will be beyond both development as well as deterioration. In these circumstance, how will the soul acquire knowledge either from *Brahman* or from a realised teacher ? Indeed, it will not be possible at all for the soul to acquire any additional knowledge. The soul, being an atomic conscious entity, can never have knowledge of this vast, unfathomable, universe nor can it have mastery over the shoreless ocean of Infinite Conscious Spirit. Hence, Omniscience for the soul is out of question because the soul will always be possessed of limited knowledge.

Although later on Swami Yogeshwaranand believed that the *Jīvātman* cannot acquire knowledge from God, earlier he held different views. In his first work viz. *Science of soul*, he has said that the divine subtle objects remind us of *Brahman* who is the creator of these objects. He says that it is through the aid of *Brahman* that the individual soul is protected from *Prakriti* and it is through His grace alone that it acquires knowledge of the infinite Treasure of *Prakriti*. Elaborating it further he says that, just as by the aid of sun, the eye is able to see, even so, by the grace of *Brahman*, the *Jiva* is enabled to attain the knowledge of the vast universe.[1] These two statements are self contradictory, but Swami Yogeshwaranand has frequently upgraded his knowledge of subtle realities through deeper and deeper vision in *Samādhi*. Therefore, such modification in his views is perfectly valid and quite natural. Discussing deficiency of knowledge in soul, he further says that if the deficiency of knowledge is eternal as the soul is eternal, it cannot be dispensed with because a thing which has no beginning can also have no end. Hence, this deficiency must continue forever. God and soul are both conscious entities. Since God is perfect and His knowledge is also supreme, soul should also be similarly conceived, except that the soul, being infinitely small, its knowledge is also small in comparison with that of God and it has no capacity for either increase or decrease of knowledge. It is, therefore, clear according the Swami Yogeshwaranand that the soul is not deficient but limited in knowledge which can neither be increased nor decreased by any means, whether by God or man.

Vijñāna Bhikṣu is known for his efforts to reconcile *Advaita* and *Sāmkhya*–yoga systems and, for that reason, he calls *Puruṣa* as witness. He says that the *Puruṣa* which is the power of consciousness, stays as consciousness alone in itself at the time of *Asamprājnata Samādhi*. According to him, the underlying idea of the *Sutra* of *Patāñjali* (1–3) is that just as the crystal is not red in the absence of China–rose and remains as itself, so also, when the modifications of the *Citta* are absent, the *Puruṣa* stays in its own nature. The proximity of China–rose and crystal, which makes the crystal appear read, is one of the standard examples of error and *Vijñāna Bhikṣu* has quoted this example to facilitate easy understanding of the point that knowledge of the objects is acquired when the object is reflected in the *Citta* and *Citta* is reflected in the *Puruṣa*. Thus, whatever modifications are present in the *Citta* at the time of activity, the *Puruṣa* also has similar modifications. He says that the reason, for *Púruṣa's* knowledge of the modification of the *Citta,* is its beginningless relationship with *Citta*. Since the *Citta* is predominantly *Sattva* because it is a product of *Mahat Sattva*, it has the capacity to reflect the *Puruṣa* as the mirror reflects the objects and the modification of the *Puruṣa* refers to its reflection in the mirror. According to Yoga Philosophy also it is the reflection of the *Puruṣa* in intellect which brings knowledge of objects in the intellect.[2]

Let us first understand the real nature of the soul. If it were initially inert or unconscious, then it would not be different from *Citta*. *Sāmkhya Darśana* makes it clear that, owing to its conscious character, soul is not possessed of *Sattva*, *Rajas* and *Tamas*, which are attributes of *Prakriti*.[3] Therefore, the soul was a conscious entity from the very beginning and, on this account, it is like *Brahman* who is also conscious and who is Prefect and complete in knowledge. Soul will also have to be viewed similarly. Hence, there is no question of deficiency of knowledge in the soul.

If God cannot impart knowledge to soul then how does soul get emancipated by Him? Swami Yogeshwaranand says that God does not impart any knowledge about essential realities to man even though He is All-Pervasive Conscious Entity, a Subtle, Partless, Eternal Conscious Being. To prove his point he gives a concrete example. He says that of the two newly born babies, one may be left in a cave in the deep forest, entirely to the care and compassion of God, while the other may be entrusted to a living teacher. At the end of a specified period of fifty or seventy years, you will find that the baby which was left with God in the deep forest, far from the civilised world, turned out to be a total barbarian, absolutely ignorant of the reality even of God. If God could impart knowledge, He would have surely bestowed the best knowledge on the one who was confined only to the presence of God and had no contact at all with any man or woman from the outside world. In this way Swami Yogeshwaranand proves that the idea of God's revelation of knowledge is unfounded. However, he says, that the knowledge of God, soul and the creation can possibly be obtained from a man who has "deep insight into reality, is intuitively and fully aware of the nature of soul as well as of God, can critically discriminate between dead matter and its conscious controller, and stands firmly self realised".[4] God is not associated with such matters, but, because of his close proximity, He makes matter motion ridden so as to evolve and create the universe. Matter appears to be conscious only because of pervasion of God in it. Otherwise it is inert, lifeless and incapable of creation. Since, He can help in achieving the objective of creation of universe by His mere presence, it is not necessary for Him to perform any action Himself. Action is necessary only for a finite being but Infinite Super Conscious Spirit is in no need of being doer of things. For the same reason, Yogeshwaranand asserts that God can neither remove deficiency of knowledge nor can He impart knowledge and grant emancipation to the soul.

As regards Sanskrit language, there was a time when there was only the language of the *Vedas*. In the period of Upanishads another similar language was evolved. The same language was further evolved during the period of *Darśanas*. Later on the same language was split into many languages. While scholars adopted the *Vedic* language, common people evolved their own language. The *Brahmanas* were written in a language which was a mixture of *Vedic* and Upanishadic language. Thus three languages came into being namely *Vedic,* Upanishadic and *Dārśanic*, the last language being rich in grammar and vocabulary. Languages develop with time, as required by the particular period, and this process goes on for ever. Languages of other countries were also similarly developed by their own people and not by any Divine Being. Based on the above arguments, Swami Yogeshwaranand makes an emphatic declaration that:

> "There is no language given by God as such. *Ved Mantras* were not written and structured by God. If God had written them, then why does not He write now .... Our intelligence keeps developing in our brain .... My books

> have been authored by me by developing my own intellect .... I received no lesson from God. In fact, I consider that God plays no part in our intellectual development".[5]

The above are the most revolutionary views about God and Swami Yogeshwaranand must be aware that his views could tend towards apparent atheism. Therefore, to ward off such an impression, he has clarified as under:

> "I am not an atheist. My belief in Him is stronger than yours. But I do take note of the fact that His major acts are performed by Him alone and not by any one else. For example He causes the movement of the earth. This is beyond us. The sun rises in the east in the morning and sets in the west in the evening. Such stupendous works should be assigned to God. But when you bring God to do your domestic work and regard Him as your private servant, I have to part company from you".[6]

Even elsewhere, he has mentioned that:

> "This does not mean that I am denying the existence of God. Only I donot accept the commonly held belief about the functions of God. It is generally stated that it is God who brings about everything and that there is nothing we do ourselves. Does it mean that it is God who cooks my food and not my servant? The sum and substance of my view is that we should make use of our reason before we accept any belief. People say that Prophet Mohammad was conveyed messages by God which were incorporated in the Holy Quran. It is believed that the *Rshis* (Sages) received verses of the *Vedas* from heaven. I hold that these books were written when languages were being developed in the beginning".[7]

His concept of God (*Brahman*) is a very sensational departure from generally accepted facts about God. He says that there is no proof of God possessing any qualities, not even the qualities of knowledge, action and strength. The point raised by him is very significant and gives an unusual turn to the concept of God and His qualities. Let us examine the issue qualitatively and ask even if God had qualities, could He have created the universe? Creation can take place only if God and matter combine. None of the two can do it alone and, therefore, God is dependent on matter for creation. But His role ends after He pervades *Prakriti* just as the role of the male ends after impregnating the female. After that, every thing is governed by the law of *Karma* which does not permit any interference from any quarter including from God. But, in our shallow knowledge of Him, we attribute every event to the will of God. This is most certainly a new concept and an additional knowledge brought forth by Swami Yogeshwaranand.

Another very important contribution made by Swami Yogeshwaranand to the philosophy of yoga, is with regard to tendencies or the seed impressions of *karmas*. *Patāñjali* has grouped all tendencies of the world under five heads and has said that cessation of these tendencies leads to firm concentration in *Samādhi* and enables one to attain the final goal of emancipation. Swami Yogeshwaranand does not agree with *Patāñjali* and says, "I am strongly of the view that the yoga *Sutra* which states that tendencies can be reined in, is without basis".[8] He says that *Samskāras* can never be fully eliminated. Even dreams cannot be controlled, let alone the tendencies. Also during *Samādhi*, when we are in search of knowledge of self and God, memory continues to operate. He says that study and research of science, perception of soul and of God, are all tendencies. Our senses have the natural inclination towards sense objects and these always remain in pursuit thereof. The functions of our mind and intellect, which are ceaseless, also give rise to tendencies. There are, indeed, some methods by which we can control the effect of such tendencies but those methods are effective to a limited extent. Hence, complete elimination of tendencies is impossible. This concept is in total contrast with the Yoga *Sutra* which says Yoga is control of *Vrittis* of *Citta*.

Like *Nyāya–Vaiseṣika* and *Mimāmsa*, Yoga aslo accepts the existence of many souls in many bodies which are different from Brahman. Only *Vedānta* treats soul as non–different. Swami Yogeshwaranand agrees with the unity of *Brahman* and also does subscribe to the concept of multiplicity of souls for reasons which are mentioned in the next Chapter.

MULTIPLICITY OF SOULS

There are certain specific characteristics which are attributed to *Sāmkhya* such as dualism of consciousness and materiality (*Puruṣa* and *Prakriti*), the *Guna* theory, the plurality of *Puruṣas* etc. *Sāmkhya* accepts the notion of diverse souls in diverse bodies which is an important constituent of its philosophy. The plurality of consciousnesses has been discussed in great details by *Vijñāna Bhikṣu* in his work *Vijñānamrtbhāṣya*. That there are innumerous souls in innumerous bodies, is also a common experience of all of us. There is a conscious soul occupying each material body and, because men are born and die at different times, it is logical to conclude that each soul is different from the other. Individuals have different experiences and different pleasures and pains. All this goes to show the multiplicity of souls. Therefore, to say that there are diverse souls, will fully conform not only to the philosophy of *Sāmkhya* but also to practical experience. We, however, need to examine as to what is meant by 'diverse' souls. The term may connote either a separate spirit in every individual body or one common spirit reflected as individual soul. If we consider each separate spirit of the type of doer and reaper of fruits, then it will lead us astray because the soul is never the doer of actions. It is *Citta* which performs actions and is, accordingly, the doer of deeds. Some schools assign the role of a responsible agent to the soul. If we accept this role and concede the agency status to the soul, then we will be reducing the soul to an entity which is changeable, transformatory and transient. In such a case, there will be no difference between the soul and the *Citta*. However, if we do not assign the role of doer and reaper of fruits to soul, then there is no need to believe in innumerous spirits in innumerous bodies. One single universal spirit, inhabiting all the material bodies, will be good enough to enliven each single body for the duration of its life. Swami Yogeshwaranand says, "a diversity pertaining to these material creations, the body as well as the *Citta*, has been misconstrued as the diversity of the souls inhabiting them".[9] According to him, when the spirit is free from doer–reaper traits and is not subject to any attributive liability, there is no need to assign diversity to it.

In this connection, it is generally observed that the tendency to perform action and gather the results is always present in the body. The feeling of being happy or unhappy or any other similar feeling, is ever arising in the *Citta*, which out of sheer ignorance, transfers it to the soul. This is done because, the soul is a conscious entity and is quite capable of energizing material substances. *Vedānta* believes that consciousness in individual soul is the same as in the Supreme soul. This being so, it does not appeal to logic to have two conscious entities when one can do the job of both. Moreover, when the two entities are both conscious, how would we distinguish between the two? If we say that one single universal conscious principle is operating in all the bodies, an objection may be raised against it on the basis that experiences of different individuals are different. If the individual soul and the supreme soul have similar consciousness, then these experiences should also be similar. But it is never so. In this respect it can be said that it is the diversity of *Cittas* which is responsible for their differences and not the Universal Spirit. The real fact is that action and their fruits belong to the material organ known as *Citta* or *Antahkarana* and belong neither to individual soul nor to the Supreme soul.

In his book *Sāmkhysútravritti, Anirudha*, a great scholar of *Sāmkhya,* who lived in 15th century AD, has discussed in suitable details the problem of multiplicity of consciousness.[10] He argues that the plurality of consciousness follows from diversity. The limiting adjuncts or disguises, as it were, cannot by themselves account for diversity, as *Vedantins* might argue. If the adjuncts are real, then diversity is also real. On the other hand, if the adjuncts are unreal, then obviously they cannot account for diversity for the reasons that something real cannot arise out of something unreal. On the basis of the above argument, he suggests that the only solution is to accept the plurality of consciousness in addition to the adjuncts. This is not only the personal view of *Anirudha* but it is also the fundamental principle of *Sāmkhya*. Even *Vijñāna Bhikṣu* does not differ with Anirudha on this point. Swami Yogeshwaranand has reconciled the difference in the concepts of *Vedānta* and *Sāmkhya* and showed that the souls are not many. This enlarges the scope of *Sāmkhya* philosophy and bridges the gap between *Vedānta* and *Sāmkhya* on this point.

As we know, matter is inert and lifeless and is incapable of performing any action by itself. Unless some conscious force comes into contact with it, it remains lifeless. It is because of the proximity of soul that *Citta* appears to be conscious. Now what is that conscious force namely the soul, by whose proximity the material *Citta* has also become conscious? Is it atomic or of the size of body it occupies? If we accept it as atomic, we will be faced with many problems. We will also have to consider whether the said atomic size of the soul, is an impartible whole or whether it is constituted of parts. If it is made up of parts, then it has to be changeable like *Citta* and, in that case, there will be no difference between the two. If it is taken as impartible whole, then that single whole has to be only one entity and has also to be the greatest and the subtlest of all so that it is capable of penetrating every other thing. Such an entity can only be *Brahman*, the Supreme Lord. It, therefore, proves that the soul is composed of parts and is not a single whole. While on this point, a doubt arises as to how the one Supreme Being gets divided into so many souls filling so many bodies. The explanation that Swami Yogeshwaranand gives, is self evident. He says that of the five gross elements (*Pancha Mahabhutas*), *Akāsha* (ether) is the most subtle and pervades the other four which are different from one another and yet it does not get divided for that reason. It remains undivided but appears to occupy the space in all the relevant elements. In the same way, the Supreme Being may be viewed as contained in different bodies by remaining undivided in the manner of *Ghatākasa* and *Mahākasa.*[11] He pervades every existing thing from within and without but His differentiation into different bodies is a mere illusion or perverse understanding. The differentiation lies, in reality, in the bodies and not in the Universal Cosmic Consciousness. We fail to appreciate the real nature of God's pervasiveness and get deluded by unwarranted conclusions. The presence of the soul in body and the activity carried on therein, can very well be carried on by the Supreme Spirit. We believe that one is finite and the other is infinite though both have the same traits of consciousness. But it is the conscious force, present in both of them, which causes the motive force. The finiteness or the infiniteness of the spirit has no bearing, whatsoever, on the mobility or movement of the bodies. Hence, a single Universal Conscious Force, fills various bodies and, therefore, there is no need either to believe or to conjecture about the presence of diverse souls in diverse bodies. Swami Yogeshwaranand endorses the above view and says:

> "The work and utility which you would like to have out of a finite soul in association with a body we would rationally appreciate as issuing forth out of the Proximity of one Universal Spirit equally closely associated with all the bodies in existence. That Omnipresent Conscious Entity is without parts, an Actionless Motive Force, Perfectly Dispassionate, Changeless, Immutable, an Undivided whole, as well as the Subtlest of all subtle things in the world. Nothing else approaches it in its extreme subtleness; that is why it is able to penetrate the very core of all things everywhere. That is also the reason that other separate conscious Beings are not all apprehensible to reason".[12]

If we accept the existence of numberless souls and also accept that God pervades them all, then it will give rise to a corrolory relating to it. Only a subtle substance can pervade the gross one. In such a case individual soul will have to be believed to be gross or less subtle as compared with God. God is subtler than the subtlest and is, therefore, all pervasive. In *Samādhi Pada* of Yoga *Sutras*, *Patāñjali* has said:

> "The all pervading spirit which is free from all pain and from desire for all those deeds which are productive of results, good or bad, pleasant or unpleasant, or of mixed character and who is

> distinct from and superior to all souls, is called God".[13]

It is clear from the above that God being more subtle than the other souls, pervades them. But both God and individual soul are conscious entities. It means that one conscious entity is gross and the other is subtle. To enable God to pervade the soul, it is necessary that there should be an inner passage in it. For this purpose, the soul has to have parts and being composite, it must necessarily be changeable. But changeability is the quality of matter and not of any eternal being. Let us take, for example, the *Citta*. It is a created organ formed of *Prakriti*. It is infinitesimally small and is finite. It has parts and is liable to change and transformation, and, is the effect of a cause which is matter. God pervades it as much as God pervades the soul. Therefore, if we accept *Citta* as a created thing, then with the similarities between *Citta* and the soul, as mentioned above, we have no choice but to treat the two alike. Swami Yogeshwaranand says, "as an object possessed of parts, the *Citta* is admittedly the product of some other substance, which is its cause; hence why do you not, likewise admit the soul as composite object to be the effect of a more general cause?".[14] It is evident that in all our presumptions, we have been mistaking *Citta* for a soul and, since there are innumerous *Cittas*, we consider them as innumerous souls. Because *Citta* is liable to transformation, *Citta* manifests many attributes. Since the soul is akin to *Citta*, it will also give rise to a succession of changing states. If the soul displays one attribute after the other, it must possess the quality of mutation like the *Citta*. But soul is a conscious entity and, being composite like *Citta*, it must have been caused by some material. Its first cause can be none other than a conscious entity. The only other conscious entity that can create such a conscious entity as the soul, is the Supreme soul (*Brahman*) but *Brahman* has not created the *Jīvātmans* because these are believed to be eternal. Therefore, the conclusion that can be drawn from the above arguments is, that the proposition of the existence of numberless souls which can be pervaded by God, cannot be proved.

There is also another angle to this situation. If the number of souls is endless and *Prakriti* is also endless, then the two together should be able to create the universe and there will be no need for intervention of God. If the souls were limited in number and also had an end, then these would have been unable to create any activity in matter and, thereby, would be unable to create the world. But countless as they are, they should be able to form the universe dispensing with the need for God to do it. But this is a futile proposition *ab initio*. This leads to only one clear conclusion that there are only two eternal entities, one of which is conscious and the other is inert; one is *Brahman* and the other is *Prakriti*. The two are eternally related to each other in the form of Pervader and the pervaded. This relationship is possible only because the All Pervasive *Brahman* is one Indivisible whole without parts. Since innumerous souls, though conscious, are composite with parts, their category of consciousness will be different. *Prakriti,* being inert and lifeless, cannot be the inspiring force and no inspiration will be required even from *Brahman* because the souls are themselves conscious beings like *Brahman*. To resolve all these conflicting views, it is necessary to accept the All Pervading spirit alone being present in all the bodies. Thus, the common belief that there are innumerous souls occupying innumerous bodies, has been shown by Swami Yogeshwaranand as baseless. While upholding the *Sāmkhya* concept of duality he has reconciled the *Vedānta* concept of unity of spirit with multiplicity of *Puruṣas* of *Sāmkhya*.

It is interesting to note that *Vijñāna Bhikṣu,* also approached *Vedānta* from *Sāmkhya* Yoga point of view and tried to establish that there was no conflict between pure *Advaitā* and the duality preached by *Sāmkhya* Yoga. His approach was that the souls (*Jivās*) were parts of *Brahman* and their relationship to *Brahman* was like that of a son to the father or like that of sparks to the fire.[15] In a somewhat similar manner, Swami Yogeshwaranand also accepts soul as the portion of divinity which comes into contact with individual *Citta*, in the process of evolution of *Prakriti*. He says:

> "In the creational chain of Cosmic Conversion, when *Prakriti* reaches the stage of *Citta* formation, the All-pervasive Conscious Principle already present there, assumes the character of *Jīvātman*, or, better still, begins to be called or conceived of as such. In reality, a separate and independent existence of embodied soul, or for that matter, any such exclusively eternal and conscious entity, is hardly ever borne out by subtlest approaches of the wakeful human mind".[16]

Elsewhere also in his works, he has mentioned, more than once, that the name of soul has been given to God when God becomes present in the mindstuff (*Citta*) in the process of evolution of *Prakriti*. This concept of soul is original contribution of Swami Yogeshwaranand and represents a great improvement upon the Yoga *Sutras* of *Patāñjali*. He does not give permanence to soul and says that during the period of doom (*Pralaya*), the soul and the astral body become nonexistent and what remains is only *Brahman* and *Prakriti*. There are, thus, only two eternal entities according to him namely *Brahman* and *Prakriti* and not three as depicted by Yoga. Swami Yogeshwaranand removes a lot of confusion by his theory that the soul is none other than Divinity itself trapped in Cosmic *Citta*. At the time of *Pralaya*, when every effect merges in its cause, the Cosmic *Citta* also merges in *Mahat* and then *Mahat* merges in Primordial *Prakriti*. The trapped Divinity, at that time, becomes free automatically and, if at all, we accept *Mokṣa* as attainable for the soul, it is only at the time of *Pralaya* and not in any particular life.

According to *Vijñāna Bhikṣu*, though *Brahman* is changeless and is of the nature of pure consciousness, He is the material cause of creation because of being *Adhiṣthâna Kārna* (presiding cause) of the universe His being the material cause, thus, depends on the changing *Prakriti* which inheres in *Brahman*. He further says that *Brahman*, at the same time, is the efficient cause of the universe through His pure *Sattva* limitation.[17] This, indeed, is the Advait view which *Vijñāna Bhikṣu*, is trying to support. However, *Vedānta* of *Vijñāna Bhikṣu*, does not identify *Jiva* (soul) with *Brahman* and maintains that *Jivas* are many. It is this concept that Swami Yogeshwaranand refutes and attempts to prove that acceptance of one all–pervading consciousness, is free from all doubts whereas belief in numerous individual souls is fraught with many defects. Thus, the concept of multitude of individual souls is neither logically defensible nor unassailable. Now let us see if soul can be considered as a fragment of the Supreme soul.

SOUL NOT A FRAGMENT OF SUPREME SOUL

We have already discussed in the earlier chapter that the soul is a composite entity, being composed of parts. The reason for such a conclusion is that God (*Brahman*) pervades the soul and God could pervade it only if there is space in it. If the soul were an impartible unit, God could never have pervaded it. It is believed that the relationship of God and soul is that of the Pervader and the Pervaded. Soul is subtle but God is still more subtle. Only a subtle entity can pervade a gross or less subtle entity. Just as iron is gross and electricity is subtle, the latter pervades the former and resides in the same space with it. In the same way because *Jīvātman* is less subtle than God, it is, God who pervades the human soul. Just as the relationship of God and the soul is that of Pervader and the Pervaded, their relationship is also that of One who is served and the one who is the servitor or that of the Ruler and the ruled. In *Chāndogya* Upanishad also, the Ṛṣi says:

"O, my dear son Swetaketu, that Supreme Spirit may be sought after. He is the soul of the whole universe as well as of the human soul. The Self–same spirit is the Great Reality. That Supreme Spirit is within thee."[18]

Vyāsa, however, does not attribute the 'owner' and 'owned' relationship to *Brahman* and *Ātman*. He attributes this relationship to *Citta* and *Jiva*. He indicates while commenting on *Yoga Sutra* (1-4) that the limiting factor is the beginningless relationship of 'owned' and 'owner' between intellect (*Citta*) and *Ātman,* by the words beginning with *Cittamayaskānta* and ending with *Sambandho hetu* used in the said sutra. He says that just as the magnet, by attracting to itself the piece of iron, renders help in the form of removal of the piece of iron and becomes the treasured possession of the master, because of its being a means of experience, so also the *Citta,* as well, by attracting to itself the collection of objects, which are similar to iron and rendering help by being fit to be seen, becomes the possession of the *Puruṣa*, the master, because of its being means of experience. *Vijñāna Bhikṣu* endorses this interpretation of *Sutra*.[19]

Swami Yogeshwaranand treats extensively the relationship of *Pervader* and *Pervaded* between *Brahman* and *Ātman* and makes it a ground to prove that the soul is not a fragment of Supreme soul. He proceeds to argue that, if we accept the soul and God both as pervading the body as mentioned in *Chāndogya* and *Taittiriya* Upanishads, we will be able to understand the import of these Upanishadic statements easily if we consider soul as the first or prior Pervader and God as Post Pervader. God being the Post Pervader, enters the body only after the soul has entered. It is, therefore, that He caused the soul to enter the body first and, thereafter, entered the soul Himself. This clearly confirms the version of *Chāndogya* Upanishad in which God says, "having created the universe and different bodies, I enter the body as soul and manifest myself under different names and forms".[20] Similarly *Taittiriya* Upanishad also says, "Having created the universe and different bodies, God himself entered them".[21] Having accepted, on the authority of scriptures, that God Pervades the soul, we cannot but agree that the soul is composite substance made of parts and because it is made of parts, it is liable to change, mutation and activity which is also the quality of *Prakriti*. There is a notion, prevalent among certain sages, that the soul is a portion or fragment of the Supreme soul. A porton is indeed a part of the whole and, therefore, it acquires with God the relationship of the part and the whole. When we draw a bucketful of water from the well, the water in the bucket is a portion of the well water. Some such relationship has to be assumed between God and soul, if we consider soul as a fragment of God. In cause and effect relationship, the effect does not take the form of new or created thing but that the substance has acquired a new state of being, out of its former existence, through change and transformation. It is merely an apparent change of condition of the original substance. But being a portion or fragment of the substance is entirely different from cause and effect proposition. Here, no change takes place in the original substance except that small portion of it has parted away. The difference between the portion and its substance lies only in respect of the place and mode of transference where the portion lies after separation. In the light of this submission, if soul is treated as fragment of God, then we will have to accept God as capable of division or disintegration into parts. Only then we could say that multiple souls have issued forth out of Him as His fragments. But a question can arise as to why should all the souls be atomic in size and not smaller or larger. This sort of fragmentation of God will also expose Him to many demerits. First of all His quality of omnipresence will become questionable. Then His being subtler than the subtlest, will cease to be his trait. There will also be a possibility that some extraneous factor may cause such fragmentation in Him and bring about innumerous souls. But we have never heard of or experienced any such thing pertaining to God. Moreover, if God can be fragmented into souls, the souls themselves could be further fragmented into still smaller entities and so on till infinity. It will give rise to an infinite regression. It is only our faith that prompts us to believe that the soul is a fragment of God; the same faith will impel us to accept further fragmentation of the souls. Moreover, for every action there is always a cause for action. Here what is the causal factor involved in the division of Divinity? There is none whatsoever known to us so far. Those, who believe that the soul is a part of God, also believe that the soul performs actions and reaps fruits. This gives rise to many unanswered questions such as:

(1) Whether the quality of action and fruits is inherent in the soul or whether it was acquired at some later stage;

(2) If the deeds and their effects are temporary phenomenon, then how did it originate and, if permanent, how and when did these get associated with the soul;

(3) If there is a causal factor which linked the deeds and fruits with soul at some particular stage, then these cannot be called eternal and the soul will

have to be accepted as short-lived, being created by separation from God and yearning to re-unite;

(4) If the soul reunites with God, what will happen to its pending *Samkāras?* If the soul merges in God along with these *Samskāras*, will it not render God a heterogeneous jumble, devoid of His inviolable qualities?

(5) After being created as a fragment of God, which world the souls will inhabit outside God and matter?

(6) If the tiny bits called souls, pervade *Prakriti* after separation from God, it will mean that God is not present therein and that three clear divisions are made between God, *Prakriti* and *Jīvātman*, each ruling its own region. It will restrict God's presence to a particular region, thereby restricting His omnipresence.

It is evident that the concept of part and whole between the soul and God fails to answer the above and many more such questions. Even if we concede, on the basis of tradition, that the soul is a fragment of God, still it cannot be proved. On the other hand, it will lead to a very unusual situation inasmuch as one region will be ruled by *Prakriti*, another by the soul and a third by God. The world will be parcelled among three ruling monarchs but the souls will be confused as to who these should accept as their main prop, whether *Prakriti* or the Supreme Spirit. The souls, which have fragmented from God, are believed to be merging in Him at the time of doom, or *Pralaya*, which means that the process of souls issuing forth and merging in God will be endless and God will become a splitting substance like matter. This will take away any distinction between God and *Prakriti*. Hence, there is no logic in the doctrine that the soul is a portion or fragment of God.

Here a question may arise as to what was created first – the souls or *Prakriti*. If souls were created first and *Prakriti* later, then what was their substratum and where did these exist without body, limbs and organs? The evolution of *Prakriti* to reach the stage of the universe, has taken thousands of millions of years. During the period that lapsed between the coming into being of souls and the emergence of the universe, the souls must have remained idle; doing nothing except for waiting for the world to be created. On the other hand, if the soul was created first and *Prakriti* later, then how and, at what point of time, did the soul acquire the gross, subtle and causal bodies as well as the fourfold *Antahkarana*? A problematic situation will be created in which the souls will be increasing in numbers without energising *Prakriti*. In the process, God Himself will become liable to change and mutation and because of this change, He will become subservient to some other power. This sort of subordination will deprive God of the main qualities of all pervasiveness and impartibility. For the above reasons, Swami Yogeshwaranand rejects the concept of soul being a fragment of God and states, "The infinite souls, as such, cannot be looked upon as Divine fragments of an Indivisible and All-Pervading Supreme Consciousness that is, by its very nature, absolutely pure, wakeful to its surroundings as well as superbly free and unrestricted in all respects".[22]

If the soul is not a portion or fragment of God, can it be said that it is a creature of God? This concept will make God the material cause from which the souls could have been created. But all material things are changeable and take to diverse transformations. In that case the soul will become a product of God and while *Prakriti* will be creating its inert products, God will be creating conscious souls. The products of *Prakriti* are inert and unconscious but those of God will be conscious. Through a long process of evolution spanning hundreds of millions of years, *Prakriti* has created the immensely vast universe but God stopped at the first crop of conscious souls. He has not engaged himself in further creation of souls nor have first borne souls given birth to further series of souls. Souls are not seen to be creating souls. In the case of *Prakriti* the motivating factor is God because it is only due to the pervasion of God that matter starts evolving itself. Some similar factor will be necessary in the case of God as well, if we suppose the Supreme Being to be material cause of conscious *Jīvātmas*. This will place God in a very peculiar situation. If He is material cause of conscious souls, how can we consider Him as the efficient cause in respect of *Prakriti? Sāmkhya Darśana* clearly states that if the All-Pervading *Brahman* be the material cause of the universe, He would be transformed into various material objects, just as the primordial matter, and therefore, He is not material cause of universe but the efficient cause. Kapila the author of *Sāmkhya Sutras* states, in unambiguous terms, as under:

> "The Upanishad namely Śwetaṣwatara Upanishad (4-5) also describes the primordial matter alone as the material cause of the universe of the world. Matter, being subject to change, is transformable whereas God, being unchangeable, is not metamorphosed into any other form".[23]

Kapila says that God is unchangeable and resides in the interior of the heart. It is unfortunate that many scholars yet consider Kapila as an atheist even when he accepts God as Unchanging. Even otherwise he does not deny the existence of God but only denies necessity of God for creation. In the Commentary of *Vijñāna Bhikṣu*, an attempt is made to explain the notion of God (Iśvara). According to *Vijñāna Bhikṣu*, God is not a problem for *Sāmkhya* because the arguments about nontheism of *Sāmkhya,* only show that the notion of God is not, really, essential for establishing the rationality of *Sāmkhya*. This does not, however, mean that God need be denied. In support of this argument, he quotes extensively from pre–Karika epic and also from *Puranic* passages to conclude that god has a useful role to play in *Sāmkhya* tradition. Reverting to the creation of conscious souls by God, Swami Yogeshwaranand discards the idea of souls being created by God. He says:

> "The rise of conscious soul out of the universal consciousness makes it changeful and transitory like earth. Under such as notion, God's indivisibility, Aloofness from action, Eternal Identity and all Pervasiveness will cease to be his characteristic traits. The central distinction between Him and matter vanishes at one stroke of fancy. As the material cause of finite souls, He must become changeable by nature. Therefore, the notion of the rise of '*Jivās*' out of Universal Spirit does not seem to be intelligently convincing".[24]

The proposition under discussion brings us face to face with another problem. Just as *Prakriti* cannot create any thing unless it conjoins with *Brahman*, it will be necessary for God also to have another motivating force to bring forth souls. But other than God there is no such entity one can ever imagine. God Himself is an impartible whole, not liable to change, not confined to any particular area and not involved in any action. Such a God cannot be material cause of any thing and, hence, the souls cannot be thought of as springing from Him. We cannot think of any other source also from which souls can be produced. Hence, the souls have to be considered as uncreated conscious entities, except for the fact that the soul is Divinity entrapped in *Citta*.

Here it is pertinent to point out that all the traits of a cause are transferred to the effect. The effect is no different from cause and contains the characteristics of its cause. This is called *Satkāryavāda* which is an important concept of *Sāmkhya*. The soul has many shortcomings such as ignorance, minuteness, etc. If the soul is caused by God, then all the deficiencies of the soul must be belonging to God as well. But can we ever attribute any flaw to God? If soul was the progeny of God, then, like God, it should also be pure, unsullied, intelligent and flawless which is not the case. The soul is limited in knowledge, suffers from pleasures and pains and is effected by many other dualities while God is absolutely free from these infirmities. Thus, soul cannot be the offspring of God even on this ground. Swami Yogeshwaranand endorses this view and says that there are compulsive reasons which force us to admit the soul as self-evident, dispassionate conscious entity not susceptible to law of cause and effect, inherently pure, intelligent and free from all stains and blemishes. If the soul possesses these traits, then alone the soul's emancipation is possible. Hence we conclude on the basis of above discussions that the soul does not emerge either from God or from any other source, whatsoever, but man erroneously considers it as a creation of Divinity while in reality it is an eternal and everlasting entity till the Doom's day. By refuting the usual doctrine of the soul being a fragment of *Brahman* or a product of *Brahman*, Swami Yogeshwaranand has brought to naught such orthodox beliefs which have received wide circulation without any one applying his mind to ascertain whether such beliefs can be logically acceptable. Swami Yogeshwaranand seems to have cleared the cobwebs surrounding *Jivās* and *Brahman* on these issues while trying to prove by logic that the soul is neither a fragment nor a creature of God.

SOUL AS PRODUCT OF FIVE ELEMENTS

Swami Yogeshwaranand has taken up for critical

analysis, the well known concept of *Cārvaka* school that the soul has arisen as a result of coming together of the *Mahabhutas* (four elements) because the human body is made of these four elements and consciousness results from their combination in the same way as 'inebriation arises from the use of intoxicants'. Cārvakas do not accept the reality of Ākāsha because it cannot be perceived by senses. They say that the soul takes its birth simultaneously with the body and is destroyed when the body is destroyed. The *Cārvakas* argue that the existence of the soul, after the destruction of the body, cannot be proved by direct cognition of senses and that sense perception is the only valid knowledge, according to them. To this Swami Yogeshwaranand says that the notion of Cārvaks that the soul is produced by four gross elements (*Mahabhutas*), namely earth, water, fire and air, is not only unfounded but totally contrary to common logic. These elements are products of nature and are inert and unconscious, while soul is a conscious entity. Inert things can produce only inert substances and conscious things can produce conscious substances because the effect is inherent in a cause or, in other words, the properties of the cause get transferred to its effect. The material objects can be perceived by our senses but the conscious principle can be comprehended only by intellect or *Citta* which is the faculty of intellection. All things that are not susceptible to perception by senses, are cognized by intellect or *Citta*. Hence consciousness, which is different from matter, cannot be perceived by senses but only by *Citta* which is knowledge predominating intelligent faculty.

Matter is perpetually undergoing change or transformation and it is due to the constant change that *Prakriti* has evolved itself from *Alinga Prakriti* (primordial matter) to the massive universe. But matter is inert and, therefore, cannot create any thing by itself. For every creation there must be a creator, the efficient cause. Any thing that has been brought into being, has two main causes namely the material cause and the efficient cause. The material with which an object is made, is the material cause of that object, but the conscious factor which has conceived, designed and created the object, is its efficient cause. In the case of ornaments, gold is the material cause and the goldsmith is the efficient cause. Then, there are auxiliary or subsidiary causes such as fire, hammer and other instruments which are used to make the ornaments. Since the universe is a created thing, it must also have the material cause and the efficient cause. In the case of the universe, *Prakriti* (matter) is the material cause and *Brahman*, the All Pervading Supreme Consciousness, is the efficient cause. Like the driver imparts motion to a vehicle, it is *Brahman* (The Supreme Being) who imparts motion to *Prakriti*. In the case of our inert body, motion is provided by the *Jīvātman* (individual soul). Hence a conscious factor is absolutely necessary for any matter to create an object. All created things have, necessarily, a material cause and an efficient cause. Since *Prakriti* is Pervaded by *Brahman*, and this pervasion is eternal, there is presence of consciousness even in the five elements, which is responsible for motion in those elements. When a man dies, apparently, only breath seems to have gone out of his body. But even if we reintroduce breath into it by pumping air, still he will not come back to life because consciousness has withdrawn itself. By whatever way we may argue, we are compelled to admit the fact of perpetual association of the conscious and the inert. No object can ever be produced unless three factors come together and these factors are (1) The subject, (2) The object, and (3) The instrumental accessory. In the case of the soul, it can neither transform itself into the subject nor the object nor even the instrumentality, at one and the same time. A material cause can never turn into an efficient cause and without the intervention of an efficient cause, no material cause can become active by itself and transform into effects. The soul is a conscious factor relevant to the gross body but things, that are beyond the limited capacity of embodied souls, are governed by the presence of universal consciousness called *Brahman*. The conscious and the inert factors must both combine to create an object. Without the efficient cause, a material object can neither change nor mutate nor transform. By itself the material cause cannot produce an effect, as it will ever remain inert. In the ultimate analysis, it is the efficient cause alone which generates activity and motion in every thing.

It may be said that the source of activity in a human body is the air in the form of breath and when such a source is present in the body, there is no need of a conscious soul for creating motion in it. But it needs to be clearly understood that the motion, arising from breath, can take place only because the body is in contact with consciousness. Even if breathing is a natural property of the body, yet this quality cannot manifest itself without its association with the conscious soul. In the case of dead body, such an association is snapped, with the result that all activity, including natural propensity of the body, comes to a halt. It is possible that a material cause can, by accident, work as an efficient cause as well. As an example, we take up the case of a sudden gush of wind which jumbles up live electric wires to cause a sudden flame or short circuit. In such a case, the human being, who is the main efficient cause, is absent and yet the gush of wind could cause a short circuit. But the motion caused by subsidiary efficient cause is devoid of conscious controller and, therefore, it is sporadic and short-lived. Hence, in every field, including the process of breath as the source of life–force, we cannot do but admit the presence of consciousness. Can the natural traits of an inert substance be manifested without the contact of conscious principle? If this was so, then the soul could have been produced by the combination of five material elements, but this has never happened. The five great elements move in the great void known as ether or space. If no such space had existed, the five elements of earth, water, fire, air and ether, would never have acquired motion. Ether is the space to provide motion to elements. But the Supreme Consciousness (*Brahman*) also pervades in the same void because He is all–pervasive. Now the question is how is the space created? Like earth water, fire and air are created from *Prakriti*, the space is also created from it. But it is the presence of *Brahman* at the core *Prakriti* which is responsible for motion or evolution of matter. All activity is caused by the combination of *Brahman* and *Prakriti*. *Prakriti* alone can neither create anything nor give rise to motion, unless consciousness conjoins with it. Unless we accept the association of All–Pervading Supreme Consciousness with *Prakriti*, we cannot explain any other reason for the universal activity. This brings us to an unavoidable conclusion that there are only two eternal entities and these are *Prakriti* and *Brahman*, the former is absolutely inert and the latter is superbly conscious. In the process of evolution of *Prakriti* from its aboriginal state, the five elements came into being after the creation of *Pancha Tanmātras* (five subtle elements). Hence these five elements are products of matter. But motion in these elements is caused by the presence of the Supreme Consciousness (*Brahman*). These elements become active and create objects only due to their contact with conscious principle. The intrinsic qualities of touch, taste, smell, sight and sound get transferred to their effects but knowledge or conscious cognition can never manifest itself in these elements even if these elements are separately conjoined among themselves. Being inert, these elements can only produce inert objects. The traits of a cause alone can be transferred to an effect. Since consciousness is absent in them, their effects cannot have consciousness in them. We can say that the consciousness which is pervading these elements can appear in the effect or the object produced by them. But this is not tenable because the Supreme Consciousness pervading the elements is beyond any change, mutation or transformation. Only these elements are subject to change and produce the effects but the objects produced by these will remain inert and unconscious because the elements themselves are inert and unconscious. It, therefore, proves that the conscious and embodied soul is not the product of five elements (or four elements as per Cārvaks) of matter. Based on the above reasons, Swami Yogeshwaranand draws the obvious conclusion that "the soul is a self-evident factor, without having been produced out of any other thing. It is eternal, changeless, conscious, intransmutable without birth".[25]

If, however, we accept a view contrary to the view that no conscious entity can be borne out of unconscious elements, a doubt can arise as to how Supreme Consciousness was born. It holds in its All–Pervasiveness the vast universe. After all, some Supreme Conscious entity has to be there to support the universe and it must also have some material cause. As a proposition, we may accept the five elements as the material cause of the embodied soul. If God or Supreme Consciousness is also accepted as produced by the five elements, then what will be the difference between the embodied soul and the Supreme soul? If we accept that both exist as conscious entities created by elements, then we must explain how these will be related to each other. The creation obtains its support from God who will be brought to the same level as the individual soul which is restricted to the space of physical body. This does not appeal to common logic and, hence, the possibility of God and human soul coming out of the five elements, is impossible to conceive. The relationship of God and soul, with matter, is not based on cause and effect but on the Pervader and the Pervaded. The former two entities, namely God and embodied soul, have not come out of five elements but are self–existing conscious entities. Consciousness, however, arises only when the soul comes into contact with matter. The fact that once the life force departs from gross body, consciousness cannot be restored by the combination of five elements, is enough proof that soul is not a product of *Prakriti*. The qualities of matter namely *Sattva, Rajas* and *Tamas* (purity, passion and inertia) are absent in consciousness which shows that consciousness is different from matter and exists as the efficient cause alone.

Even knowledge and action are not the traits or characteristics of consciousness but of inert matter, although consciousness is the efficient cause for knowledge and action, arising from elements. Let us take example of human body which is made of matter. This body contains many limbs and organs like mind, intellect, senses etc. which are also made of matter and are, therefore, unconscious. But all these limbs perform their respective functions only because of the presence of a single conscious soul. The body and its constituents will cease to function, if soul was not present. For all that has been stated above, Swami Yogeshwaranand rejects the concept of soul being the product of five elements or four elements as the Cārvaks say and says that "the five elements, in combination, do not, and cannot tend to produce the conscious factor."[26]

The phenomenon of creation has been the subject matter of all the six *Darśanas* and each *Darśana* has treated it in its own peculiar way. Depending upon their own personal understanding, the sages have found some contradiction amongst the *Śatdarśanas* about how the universe is created, but, in reality, there is no such contradiction. In fact there is total harmony amongst these *Śastras* on this subject which is common to all. According to *Mimāmsa* "nothing can be produced without proper application." *Vaiśeṣika* system says "nothing can be created without expenditure of time." In the philosophy of *Nyāya Śastra,* "nothing can be produced without the material cause." Yoga philosophy advocates that nothing can be made without necessary skill and knowledge and according to *Sāmkhya*, "nothing can be made without definite combination of atoms." And *Vedānta* says that "nothing can be made without a maker.'"[27] All this leads to a single conclusion that the creation of the world needs six different causes and each of the six schools of philosophy has taken upon itself to deal with one cause each. If we take all six *Śastras* together, then alone we will be able to explain the world phenomenon of creation. Taking singly, we are bound to land ourselves in confusion. The net result of joint reading of the philosophies propagated by these schools is, that *Prakriti* is the material cause and God is the efficient cause of the world and that both the entities are self–existing, everlastingly eternal, but one does not create the other and, hence, the soul is not a product of *Prakriti.* It will be observed from the above that while the notion of the soul being a product of five elements has been refuted by almost every school of philosophy, the mode of refutation adopted by Swami Yogeshwaranand appears to be logically more sound. His argument proceeds from the basic phenomenon of conscious and non–conscious entities and comes to conclusion on the basis of the same two entities. He has provided a fillip to the existing thinking on the subject by proving his point through comparison of the traits of conscious and inert objects.

JĪVĀTMAN — WHETHER ATOMIC?

In the earlier chapter we have refuted the concept of soul being a product of five gross elements. We now take up the view, which is also widely accepted, that the soul is smaller than an atom although, in subtlety, it is like *Brahman*. In one of the verses of *Kathopanishad*, it is mentioned that *Jīvātman* which is like *Anu* (atom), minute and subtle, and *Iśvara* (Supreme Self) who is greater than the greatest, both dwell in the cave of the heart.[28] This declaration of the Upanishad makes it very clear that *Jīvātman* is minute like atom and *Brahman* is the greatest and both these conscious principles abide in the heart of every body. Swami Yogeshwaranand has also termed soul as atom–like,[29] and, has said that it is located in the heart where the *Linga–Sharira* or the Bliss Sheath also abides. It uses the fourfold *Antahkarana* to operate the body to fulfil the purpose of *Bhoga* (enjoyment) and *Apavarga* (release). Since the soul resides in the cavity of the heart, the moment the heart stops functioning, it flies away and the activities of life come to an end. According to Swami Yogeshwaranand, the soul is wrapped in its own orb and is further enveloped by five other orbs. He says that from the point of view of size the orb of the soul is smaller than an atom but from the point of view of subtlety, it is similar to *Brahman*. This was his view when he wrote the book "Science of soul," but he changed his views subsequently and discarded the concept that the living soul is atomic. The concept seems to him to be self–contradictory and gives rise to many questions which cannot be easily answered.

According to *Nyāya* and *Vaiśeṣika* schools, the smallest particle of matter is an atom (anu) which is formed by 60 sub-atoms or *Parmānus*.[30] But the atom of these systems is inert and unconscious while soul is a conscious entity. If we term soul as atomic, we imply that the atom, of which the soul is made, is a conscious substance unlike the atoms of *Nyāya* and *Vaiśeṣika* systems. Therefore, it is unlikely for the conscious soul to have been produced by unconscious atoms. Then how did the conscious soul come into being and what is the material cause thereof? There is a common view about the soul that it is conscious as well as eternal. But an eternal entity cannot be made of parts and if any thing is made of parts, it has to be changeable. In the case of soul, if it is atom like, and an atom is made of 60 sub–atoms, then the soul must also be subject to change and transformation. But we do not attribute these qualities to soul which is considered as eternal, unchanging and everlasting without having parts. We may argue that *Prakriti* also comprises of parts, is changeable and yet it is eternal and, in its process of evolution, it gives rise to many effects. This may be so with *Prakriti* but the soul does not display any such qualities. There are no transformatory effects caused by the soul. We may, however, point out certain qualities in the soul which arise when the soul comes into contact with the body and quote these as an example of changeability of the soul. For example, consciousness arises when the soul contacts the body but unlike *Prakriti*, consciousness does not create any object nor does it give rise to transformatory results of created objects. It only means that change takes place in *Prakriti* and not in conscious soul which remains eternal and unchanging and, therefore, it is unlikely to be constituted as an atom. This is the line of argument advanced by Swami Yogeshwaranand to refute the concept that the soul is made of atom. This statement is, however, only partially true. It is valid in so far as he says that the atoms which are inert and unconscious, cannot constitute the conscious soul. It is not valid when he says that an atom is constituted of 60 sub–atoms. *Nyāya Sutra* (4-12-16) clearly states that an atom is that which is not capable of being divisible into further parts.[31] Therefore, if the soul is made of atoms, it cannot be further divided and is stable in itself which is true. But this cannot remit the fault that atoms are unconscious and the soul is otherwise.

The tiny conscious soul is neither changeable nor eternal in its essence. If it is transitory, it must have some material which caused it. Even the existence and purpose of countless such souls can be very well served by one single All–Pervading consciousness which is partless and which is present in innumerous bodies. Thus, according to Swami Yogeshwaranand, there is no such thing like an atomic conscious soul which has been elaborately discussed in the previous paragraph. He says, "One and only one, Omnipresent Universal Conscious Presence, solely exists to the exclusion of all other such presence."[32] He says that the apparent differentiation of souls, is seemingly a delusive impression caused by the external plurality of bodies. Like the vast sky is indivisible and even millions of containers placed in it do not take away its continuous vastness, in the same way *Brahman* remains indivisible in spite of the countless bodies which contain him. In *Śvetaṣvatāra* Upanishad, the soul has been compared to a ten thousandth part of the width of a hair.[33] In the same Upanishad some other similes have also been given of the soul such as the thumb or the glorious sun. The soul has been denoted by similar terms even in *Mundakopanishad.*[34] It will appear that the Upanishads have depicted the soul sometime as the thumb, some other times as the one thousandth part of the hair, and yet at other times, as tiny and atomic in size but all these Upanishads have described it as finite, limited and extremely subtle. However, one needs to know as to how did it acquire the finiteness, limitation of form and its subtleness. The Upanishads do not satisfy this inquiry. It is, however, a common sense view that the countless atom–like souls, which are said to be of the size of a thumb or grape etc., cannot be eternal and everlasting. These souls also cannot be a portion of any other entity, whether inert or conscious, which has been adequately proved in the earlier chapters. All these controversies can be laid to rest if we accept that there is one Universal Spirit which is pervading the whole universe and is also occupying innumerous bodies, but is circumscribed by the limitation of *Citta*, the organ of intellection. The misunderstanding arises because all of us assume the Universal Consciousness, present in different bodies, as individual souls and because the seat of this consciousness, namely *Citta,* is extremely small, the soul abiding therein is also considered as very small like the thumb or atom or grape. The fact, however, is that God's presence in that small place only appears to be small in the same way as the reflection of the sun gets diminished when the aperture, letting the light in, is small. Swami Yogeshwaranand holds a similar view and says that the assertion that the soul is tiny like an atom, is unfounded and incapable of being proved.

The Upanishads treat of the soul as *Vibhu* or pervasive. In this connection, attention is invited to *Kathopanishad* which states that having realised that the soul is immensely pervasive, the Yogi overpowers both pleasure and pain and does not grieve.[35] Similarly *Vaiśeṣika Darśana* also says that as the vast ethereal space is supremely pervasive, so is the Spirit pervasive in the universe.[36] The intention, underlying the above statements, is to convey that when the Yogi sees the spirit as reflected in *Citta,* he considers it as atomic and tiny because *Citta* is small. But when he visualises the same spirit as pervading the whole body, it appears as measuring upto the size of the body. Finally, when he aims to realise the same spirit as pervading the infinite universe, the spirit appears to him as an endless force existing every where. This explanation does not leave any scope for the existence of the atomic soul in the body. Moreover, *Brahman* and *Jīvātman* are both considered as conscious entities and both are accepted as abiding in the *Citta*. If this is so, then how do we distinguish the two and assign a separate identity to each? Although both are conscious, we consider the soul as the doer and reaper of the fruits of actions but God is absolved of the actions as well as the fruits. In all fairness both should be treated similarly. But if we treat *Brahman* also as doer of deeds then, like living beings, He will also be liable to the law of *Karma* and shall be accountable for His deeds. Thus, *Brahman,* as He is, He has to be regarded actionless, all–pervasive and eternal. The soul being of the same class as *Brahman,* cannot be atomic for if it were accepted as an extremely diminutive atom of consciousness, it will become liable to parts, and, every thing that comprises of parts, is mutable. Then the soul will lose its distinct identity and will be like *Prakriti* which also comprises of parts and is changeable.

In the foregoing chapters, two everlasting entities have been proved to exist. These two entities are *Prakriti* and *Brahman*. While both are eternal, *Prakriti* is essentially gross and *Brahman* is essentially subtle. The job of creating the world is assigned to *Prakriti* but being inert and actionless it cannot do that job alone. Activity is generated in *Prakriti* by pervasion of *Brahman* who holds *Prakriti* perpetually in close proximity. In its primeval state, *Prakriti* is in its most stable form because the three *Gunas,* namely *Sattva, Rajas* and *Tamas,* are present in it in equal ratio. In that state *Prakriti* is invisible because that is the most subtle form from where it commences the process of creation. This process goes on for billions of years till *Prakriti* decides to venture into the reverse process of dissolution, as a result of which, each effect of the work of *Prakriti* merges in its cause. This is called *Pralaya* which occurs periodically to allow *Prakriti* to rejuvenate itself so as to commence the evolution once again. The next evolution starts after the lapse of countless years when by His divine will *Brahman* disturbs the equilibrium of the three *Gunas* of *Prakriti*. After the creation of time, space and direction for the movement of *Prakriti,* the first evolute which manifests thereafter, is an intelligent principle called *Mahat*. *Sāmkhya* accepts this order of evolution but Swami Yogeshwaranand marginally differs which has already been mentioned earlier. It should be clearly understood that the change or mutation takes place only in *Prakriti*. *Brahman* remains ever changeless. When *Prakriti* evolves beyond *Mahat* and reaches the stage of cosmic *Citta*, then the divinity which is already present in it, conjoins the cosmic *Citta*. The most sensitive and active portion of cosmic *Citta*, with divinity entrapped in it, becomes the material cause of individual *Citta* which is generally called *Jīvātman* or the individual living soul. This knowledge is a special contribution of Swami Yogeshwaranand as no other Yogi, in the past, has explained the soul in this manner. He says, "the presence of Universal Consciousness confined to specific bounds of an individual *Citta* has been, for the sake of facility, named as *Jīvātman*. The *Citta* itself being a minute creation of Nature, the Conscious Presence within its narrow walls, has also come to be known and recognised as an atomy."[37] This shows that Swami Yogeshwaranand does not accept the version that individual soul is of the size of an atom, because it cannot be proved. If we accept soul as an atom, then it must be fissureable because an atom comprises of sub–atoms. And any object that is fissureable is composite of parts and, for that reason, it has to be changeable. But change is an attribute of *Prakriti* and not of soul which is termed in the scriptures as eternal, unchanging and an indivisible whole. Hence, soul cannot be atomic in size. He says that since the atomicity of the soul cannot be proved and consciousness is present in every part of the body, then why not hold that the soul is of the size of the body. This statement of Swami Yogeshwaranand betrays his want of exact depiction of the size of the soul. He has, no doubt, proved by logic, that the soul is not made of atom nor is it atomic in size. However, He has deliberately left unanswered the question as to what exactly is the size of the soul. He has asked the aspirants to find out the answer to this question themselves by going into deep meditation while concentrating on soul. Nevertheless, an established concept of long standing, has been struck down by him by adducing logical reasons.

REFERENCES

(1) Science of Soul (p. 180)
(2) Yogavarttika (Vol.I p. 41)
(3) *Sāmkhya Darśana* (1-147)
(4) Essential Colourlessness of the Absolute (p. 127)
(5) Beads of Sermons (Pt. II p. 18)
(6) Beads of Sermons (Pt. II p. 138)
(7) Beads of Sermons (Pt. II p. 19)
(8) Beads of Sermons (Pt-II p. 79)
(9) Essential Colourlessness of the Absolute (p. 141)
(10) Samkhyasutravritti (VI, 45-51)
Quoted in Encylopedia of Indian Philosophies (Vol IV, p. 372)
(11) Essential Colourlessness of the Absolute (p. 142)
(12) Essential Colourlessness of the Absolute (p. 143)
(13) Light of Truth (p. 217)
(14) Essential Colourlessness of the Absolute (p. 144)
(15) Yogavarttika (Pt. I, p. 9)
(16) Essential Colourlessness of the Absolute (p. XIII)
(17) Yogavarttika (Pt. I, p. 10)
(18) Light of Truth (p. 226)
(19) Yogavarttika (Pt.I, p. 52)
(20) Chandogya Upanishad (VI-3-2)
(21) Taittriya Upanishad Brahmand Valli (11-6)
(22) Essential Colourlessness of the Absolute (p. 151)
(23) Light of Truth (p. 218)
(24) Essential Colourlessness the Absolute (p. 153)
(25) Essential Colourlessness of the Absolute (p. 178)
(26) Essential Colourlessness of the Absolute (p. 180)
(27) Light of Truth (p. 259)

(28) Kathopanishad 1-2-20

अणोरणीयान् महतो महीयान आत्मास्य जन्तोः निहितो गुहायाम्!

(29) Science of Soul (p. 264)

(30) Essential Colourlessness of the Absolute (p. 230)

(31) The Nyāya Sutras of Gotama (p. 162).

(32) Essential Colourlessness of the Absolute (p. 232)

(33) Śvetaśvatara Upanishad (5-9).

(34) Mundakopanishad (3-1-9).

(35) Kathopanishad, (Sec II Verse 22)

महन्तम विभुमात्मानम् मत्व धीरो नशोचति

(36) Vaiśeṣika Darśana (7-1-22)

(37) Essential Colourlessness of the Absolute (p. 242)

3

Brahman (The Absolute)

ATTRIBUTES OF GOD

The absolute *Brahman* has been accorded the pride of place in our scriptures which no one else is entitled to or capable of attaining. He is subtler than the subtlest, greater than the greatest, unchanging, eternal, all pervasive and Omniscient. Vedas are replete with references to him wherein he is described as supremely peerless and unequalled in self-effulgence. He is the cause of motion in *Prakriti* which He pervades. Creation takes place due to his close proximity with matter *(Prakriti)*. *Vedas* emphatically state that by knowing Him alone, one can cross the ocean of death and misery, which means that *Mokṣa* which is the highest of the four *Puruṣarthas*, can be attained only by realising *Brahman*. Swami Yogeshwaranand says that *Brahman* pervades *Prakriti* which is the material cause of the universe, and a Yogi commences his search for *Brahman* by realising *Prakriti* and its modifications, one after the other, simultaneously with realising the presence of *Brahman* in every object of matter. He (the yogi), then develops detachment from the objects of the world and his soul experiences the elating presence of *Brahman* everywhere. Swami Yogeshwaranand has spent many long years in trying to know the reality of *Brahman* through contemplating on Him and realising Him through intuitive experience, but he finds himself unable, like all other seekers, to realise his final objective. The reason is that *Brahman* is experienced by his reflection in the *Citta* which is ever in motion and undergoes ceaseless modifications of form and colour, which obstruct His clear image. If the Yogi himself fails to have an absolutely clear vision of *Brahman* in the turbulent *Citta*, he will be unable to impart to others any fairly clear knowledge of Him. For example, pleasure and pain, love and hatred and all similar feelings, are experienced by all of us in the *Citta* but an accurate depiction of this experience is seldom possible. In the same way, *Brahman*, even though experienced, cannot be delineated in words. Swami Yogeshwaranand says:

> "Similarly, though *Brahman* does become an object of experience in life, a delineation of His form or outline is seldom possible. From this it is not to be construed that He is entirely Formless; for if an object has its existence in the world, it must need to have some conclusive mark or marks of distinction of its identity. Now, in the absence of any practical guideline about His Identity, what form is He to be conceived of or supposed to have? This, indeed, is a very baffling question. The image, in which *Brahman* is seen during realisation, has no other parallel like it with which it may be compared in delineation or description, giving a likely verisimilitude of His appearance."[1]

The only entity with which *Brahman* can possibly be compared, is the finite soul encaged in our mortal frames, because both are conscious principles and both are eternal and unchanging. Before we are able to compare *Brahman* with soul by quoting analogy of the latter, it is necessary that we realise the soul first. We should know ourselves first and only then proceed to comprehend the image of God. Swami Yogeshwaranand has given a detailed account of the soul, and, how to realise it, in his book *Science of Soul*. He has also given a largely detailed account of the knowledge and realisation of *Brahman* in his book *Science of Divinity,* based mostly on his personal experiences gained in deep contemplation in the highest form of *Samādhi*. Yet wide confusion prevails about the true concept of *Brahman* with the result that many dogmas and beliefs have been passed from generation to generation, and accepted by large masses, as true and sacrosanct. Out of the many such doctrines, which have been built around the existence of the Supreme Soul (*Brahman*), Swami Yogeshwaranand has taken up a few of these for critical examination and logical conclusion and which have been discussed in this work.

It is believed by critics as well as by some scholars of *Sāmkhya* that *Sāmkhya* excludes *Brahman* from its purview, and that it is in conflict with *Vedānta* and Yoga, who accept the reality of an eternal God. *Vijñana Bhikṣu* says that there is no such conflict because exclusion of God in *Sāmkhya,* is for practical purpose only but there is no condemnation of theism as such. *Vedānta* and *Sāmkhya* have, altogether, different spheres and purposes. The main objective of *Vedānta* is *Brahman* and if this objective is contradicted, then *Vedānta* will be devoid of its principle objective. The principle of *Sāmkhya* is the discrimination between self and non–self (*Puruṣa* and *Prakriti*). He says that, since it is an admitted fact that there is no wisdom equal to or greater than *Sāmkhya,*[2] its focus rests on its discrimination and not on the rejection of God. For this reason, cultured scholars of *Sāmkhya,* like *Praṣara,* maintain that there is a God that is transcendental and real.

As against *Sāmkhya,* which approaches God indirectly, by its absence of mention about Him, Yoga gives a clear definition of *Iśvara*. It says, "the all-pervading spirit who is distinct from and superior to all souls, is called *Iśvara*

(God)." In yoga Sutra 23 of *Samādhipada, Patāñjali* says that another way, other than *चित्तवृत्तिनोरध:* to gain *Samādhi* is *ईश्वरप्रणिधान:* which means a special devotion to *Iśvara*. Commenting on this *Sutra, Vyāsa* clarifies as to who is this *Iśvara*. He says that *Iśvara* is a special *Puruṣa* who is unaffected by afflictions, actions, fruits of actions and the latent impressions thereof (*Samskāras*). *Iśvara,* overcome by '*Pranidhāna,*' favour the Yogi for his deep desire for *Samādhi.*[3] In the Vedas, the term used for *Iśvara,* is *Brahman* which depicts the absolute, the ultimate Principle. The sages, who wrote Upanishads, found *Brahman* as beyond description and, therefore, *Vedāntins* say that whatever is mentioned about Him should be rendered as *neti neti* (not this, not this).

Accordingly Upanishads have bestowed many titles on *Brahman,* most of which are negative. Some such titles are:

(1) *Achala* (Immobile)

(2) *Achintaya* (inconceivable)

(3) *Akshaya* (inconceivable)

(4) *Alinga* (Without marks or attributes)

(5) *Anādi* (Withour beginning)

(6) *Avachya* (indescribable)

(7) *Avyakta* (unmanifest)

(8) *Nirguna* (Without attributes)

(9) *Nirdosha* (without defects)

(10) *Nishkriya* (Without action)

(11) *Nitya* (eternal)

(12) *Sarvagata* (all pervasive)

(13) *Sanātana* (ancient)

(14) *Svatahparmāna* (self evident)

(15) *Vyāpaka* (Omnipresent)

The above titles, and many more, given to *Brahman,*

indicate the attributes which are assigned to *Brahman* and on which these titles are based. On the basis of the said attributes, He is also addressed as Super–Soul, the Supreme Soul, the Soul of the universe, *Param Brahman, Paramātaman* etc. It is said that, in His Absolute state, *Brahman* is *Nishkriya* and, as such, He cannot be considered as the creator of the world, being actionless and utterly transcendent to the material world. In the matter of creation of the universe, the Upanishads say, that by an act of willing, *Brahman* became plural merely by wishing "I may be many" (*Aham Bahuṣyam*) and, thereby, the world came into existence. The Upanishads also speak of *Brahman* as *Tajjalan* which means that (tat) from which the universe is born (ja), into which it returns (la) and by which it is sustained (an).[4] With the emergence of certain schools of philosophy, in the further process of evolution, such as *Sāmkhya*, two ultimate principles came to be accepted which have attributes of *Brahman* and are eternal and self–existing. These principles are *Puruṣa* and *Prakriti* which are respectively cosmic spirit and cosmic substance from which the universe is evolved. Thus, it is some of the many concepts of *Brahman* (God) which are generally based on the attributes assigned to Him, which are taken up for critical analysis by Swami Yogeshwaranand, the result whereof makes a positive contribution to the existing knowledge and philosophy on the subject. We have mentioned above some of the attributes of God which are found in the Upanishads. If we accept these attributes as belonging to God, then a question will arise as to how these came into being. If these were born from *Brahman*, then He must be considered as the material cause of the world. In that case, He will become changeable like every material cause and, also, we will have to search for some other principle who is the efficient cause; but there cannot be any efficient cause of *Brahman* because He is the final cause of every thing and is uncaused Himself. If these attributes came into being successively, one after the other, then these attributes will ever remain in a flux and will be caused perpetually without reaching finality. On the other hand, if all His attributes were caused at one time, then these attributes cannot be endless, which goes against the concept of *Brahman* being unbounded. His attributes should also be boundless. To say, that His attributes are temporary, will mean that He is changeable, in which case He will be governed by the eternal law of *Karma* and will have to enjoy the fruits of actions like any other living being. Hence, we cannot defend the notion of temporary or acquired attributes of *Brahman*. Even if we presume that His attributes are permanent and enduring, it is not easy to establish this truth. We will have to enquire, in that case, into the relationship between *Brahman* and His attributes, inasmuch as, it will be necessary to know whether the attributes are independent of *Brahman* or whether these are dependant on Him. If it is the relationship of equals, then, like *Brahman,* the attributes must also be eternal because a relationship based on equality can be meaningful only amongst eternals. But such a situation will cause many problems such as how to distinguish the attributes of *Brahman* from those of *Prakriti* and how to distinguish *Brahman* Himself from *Prakriti. Brahman* is known to be all pervasive and His attributes are innumerous which are not only so many but also of different kinds. This presumption will give rise to many questions. The first question that will come to mind, is whether these attributes will stick to some portion or to all parts of *Brahman.* Another question that will arise is whether the attributes will be gross or subtle. If the attributes are believed to be gross, then *Brahman* must be pervading these like He pervades *Prakriti* which is also gross. But if these are subtle, then what will be the *locus standi* of these attributes, vis-a-vis *Brahman,* who is the subtlest of all. In either case, *Brahman* will have to be denied His quality of all pervasiveness which is unthinkable. Morever, if the attributes are different from *Brahman*, these will have to be independent of *Brahman*; but if the attributes are considered as identical with Him, then we will have to admit a cause and effect relationship between *Brahman* and His attributes. In that case, *Brahman* will be no different from *Prakriti*. Just as *Prakriti* is the original cause of every thing, and, is also the support of all subsequent changes and effects, in the same way God will also become the support of all the attributes that are formed. It will create a relationship of likes and unlikes which will reduce *Brahman* to a changing entity like *Prakriti*. As we know, *Prakriti* is constituted of *Sattva*, *Rajas*, and *Tamas* which qualities get transferred to every object made of *Prakriti*. In the same way *Brahman* too will be regarded to bring into being, all His successive creations, in the manner of *Prakriti* and there will be no difference between *Brahman* and *Prakriti*. God is Omnipresent and an Omnipresent thing does not need any attributes, and, because He is partless and actionless, He is absolutely free from either holding or supporting any attribute.

We may say that all we mean by His attributes, is His innate characteristics. Even then the above questions call for a suitable answer viz whether the innate characteristics are identical or different from Him. If these are different, then relationship can be either of the substantive–and–adjunct or of two entities which are independent of each other. If these are identical, even then *Brahman* will not be able to avoid the law of change and mutability and *Brahman* will cease to be indivisible and actionless. The innate quality of a thing abides as long as the thing abides. If one is destroyed, the other is automatically destroyed. On this basis, if any of His innate characteristic is destroyed, *Brahman* Himself will get destroyed, which is entirely untenable. Attributes and changeability are inseparable because action is produced by the changing phases of attributes. Being indivisible, *Brahman* does not possess any space or void to accommodate such attributes, and, being actionless, He does not bring about such attributes. This goes to prove that the Absolute is colourless and without attributes and maintains eternal sameness, and also aloofness, from any change or direct action. Action and behaviour do not belong to the Omnipresent Supreme Consciousness but to an object which is composite, changeable and finite like *Prakriti*.

When we look at primordial *Prakriti*, we find that it is infinite and subtle but, in spite of that, there is perceptible motion in it and, therefore, action is ascribed to it. Then why should we not ascribe the same attributes to *Brahman* who is also infinite and subtle? Here we must closely mark the fundamental difference between *Brahman* and *Prakriti*. Although both are infinite, *Prakriti* is composite while *Brahman* is more subtle than *Prakriti* and, therefore, pervades it. This pervasion causes contact between *Brahman* and *Prakriti* and this eternal contact enables the latter to engage in creation. It is this contact which causes movement in *Prakriti* and is also responsible for knowledge in it as well as the system of creation and the duration of subsistence of creation. Thus, stability, knowledge and activity are inherent attributes of *Prakriti* and attributes tend to appear in an object which is subject to change. *Brahman* is free from these attributes because He is neither subject to change nor to motion. On the other hand, nature (*Prakriti*), because of its contact with *Brahman*, moves on from one aspect of creation to the other. God is free from any such change and is never engaged in the process of creation which falls in the domain of Nature (matter). If we accept such attributes as belonging to *Brahman* as well, then both *Brahman* and *Prakriti* will be on par with each other. Swami Yogeshwaranand says, "the concept that the infinite Omnipresence is compatible with various attributes, whether of transitory, eternal or inherent nature, is wholly, untenably and logically, beyond justification."[5]

Because *Prakriti* commences the process of creation only as a result of its close contact with *Brahman*, He is regarded as the efficient cause of the world and not its material cause. Swami Yogeshwaranand says that an efficient cause, as a rule either takes the form of an effective proximity or of imposing a subjective agency on the created effect. He further says that if we accept the proximity of the first cause in the creation of the world, then it can adequately explain the real nature of *Brahman* as stable and actionless; but if we assume that His subjective agency is responsible for creation, then we will have to admit "His subjection to the law of recompense for His various doings and then He will be just like any of us mortal beings." *Brahman* is all–pervasive and, if subjectiveness of an action is attributed to Him, He will become limited and finite and will, necessarily, become subject to bondage and release. He will be actively involved as a responsible agent to whom law of *Karma* is fully applicable. *Karma* has been defined in *Vaiśeṣika Darśan* as an activity comprising of ascent or decent, forward or backward movement and expansion or contraction.[6] These are the five characteristics of action but none of these belong to *Brahman*. Hence *Brahman* cannot be said to have attributes or any manifest action. Action and attributes are mostly confused to be synonymous but Kanada distinguishes between the two. Action has been defined above and attribute has been defined by him in Adh.–1, sutra–16 of *Vaiśeṣika Sutras.* According to the said sutra, an attribute informs an object independently and is supported by it without being governed by its association or lack of it.[7] For *Kanada*, an attribute retains its separate identity from the object and its relationship with the object is that of "the shelter–giving room and the sheltered."

However, Kapila, the author of *Sāmkhya Sutras,* states an entirely different view. He says that the object and its attributes are like cause and effect. The effect inheres in the cause and passes on during the transformatory phase of the object. Thus he speaks of complete identity of the object and its attribute or the cause and its effect. But from the point of view of their functional utility, he admits of the difference between the formal nature of the object and its attribute or the cause and its effect. The reason is that both serve different purposes and perform different functions. Swami Yogeshwaranand argues that both Kanada and Kapila admit that there is a formal difference between the cause and effect, which is also his own view. To explain his view, he cites the example of earth whose special attribute is odour (smell). When earth passes through the set processes of modification and turns from the substance to an effect, the attribute of odour follows earth in each effect. Thus, according to him, the relationship between the substantive and the adjunct is that of difference–cum–identity and on this basis, he comes to the conclusion that *Brahman* is, of necessity, free from attributes, nor does He ever do any deeds. Effects belong to objects which are liable to change and transformation and so do the actions. It is for this reason that all activity is generated in matter only by inner proximity of *Brahman* and not by direct action. Thus, activity takes place in matter alone and *Brahman* ever remains free from action. Upanishads have created a confusion by saying that *Brahman* is possessed of knowledge, power and initiative. A doubt is caused as to whether *Brahman* and these attributes are independent entities or these exist as cause and effect. If these are considered as adjuncts, then like *Brahman*, the attributes will also be accepted as eternal, which means that *Brahman, Prakriti* and attributes, all the three are eternal. The attributes of knowledge, power and initiative already exist in matter. It is, therefore, idle to assign such attributes even to *Brahman*. Moreover, *Brahman* is perpetually in contact with matter, prompting the latter to action, which contact continues in each subsequent stage of movement of matter. If *Brahman* were to possess all these attributes, then *Brahman*'s pervasion in *Prakriti* would be futile and unnecessary and there will be no need for *Prakriti* at all. What will *Brahman* do with these attributes? Whatever He is expected to do with these attributes, is already being done by his Omnipresence and all–pervasiveness. Hence, *Brahman* is in no need of any attributes nor is there any place in Him to accommodate such attributes. Nothing can enter an impartible whole, and, a partless whole can be only one, which *Brahman* is. Matter goes on producing effects unremittingly, without any intervention of God, and, shall ever continue to move from stage to stage in creation, preservation and final dissolution. Arguing against possession of any attributes by *Brahman*, Swami Yogeshwaranand says:

> "In the present argument, matter and God both are Eternal Entities. *Brahman* is Eternally the same, Unbound to transition in subordinate Forms; Matter, too, is Eternal, but subject to the laws of transformation and causation. In reality, these two are the only existing Entities that are Eternal and Timeless. Matter, between them, of course, is non–living and inert, while the Supreme Being is an Absolutely Super–Conscious Principle. Ultimately, summing up the argument, we may well conclude that *Brahman* is proved to be without all dispositional traces of Knowledge, Power and Initiative, or a totality of attributes, or even numberless adjuncts whatsoever. An attribution of qualities in Him nullifies the concept of His Omnipresence as well as Undivided Oneness. Therefore, the Supreme Entity called God always remains, in all respects, a Colourless

> Absolute Principle in Existence; and reason, logic and intelligent experience all amply bear out His Absolute Colourlessness."[8]

The view of Swami Yogeshwaranand, that *Brahman* is ever free from attributes, sounds logical for attributes can belong only to changeable entities but *Brahman* is eternal and unchanging. Attributes belong to *Prakriti,* and, if attributes are assigned to *Brahman* as well, then there will be no difference between *Prakriti* and *Brahman*. Yet we cannot deny the most subtle difference between the two viz. *Prakriti* is inert and unconscious whereas *Brahman* is supremely conscious. This marks *Brahman* apart from every other entity as being actionless. As He is actionless, He is not responsible for motion in *Prakriti* which has created the universe. In fact the activity in matter, results from the pervasion of *Brahman* in *Prakriti* which also generates knowledge and power in it.

Swami Yogeshwaranand reemphasises that, when a chain of transformations occurs in *Prakriti* through its contact with *Brahman* and when cosmic *Citta* produces individual *Cittas*, then the Omnipresent *Brahman,* abiding in the individual *Citta,* comes to be known as *Jīvātman.*[9] This is the half–mark of his personal philosophy of soul and is his special contribution of wide import. It is the evolution of *Prakriti* which has changed one single *Brahman* into manifold in the form of countless *Cittas* created by cosmic *Citta*. It is just like a man standing before many mirrors, appears to be manifold. In the same way, one *Brahman* apparently assumes innumerous forms. *Śvetāṣvatara* Upanishad attributes knowledge, strength and action as natural or inherent attributes of God.[10] In many Upanishads, *Brahman Vidya* has been described as inherent power of God in the form of knowledge, strength and activity. It has already been stated that the relationship between *Brahman* and *Prakriti* is that of the Pervader and the pervaded, and, because *Brahman* has very close proximity with *Prakriti*, it gives an impression, that the said power is that of *Brahman*, but, in reality, *Prakriti* is transformable and it is because of this quality that it can create knowledge, strength and activity which *Brahman* cannot do because He is devoid of all qualities, is actionless without organs and all pervasive. It is, therefore, idle to accord any attributes to Him or else His Omnipresence, indivisibility etc. will become meaningless.

DISPENSATION OF FRUITS OF ACTION BY BRAHMAN

That God is the fountainhead of justice and, therefore, He alone is competent to dispense rewards of actions of individual souls, is a universally accepted adage in almost every system of philosophy. But Swami Yogeshwaranand rejects this concept for the ensuing reasons.[11] If God's role as dispenser of fruits is recognised, then we will also have to recognise in Him an agency, either independent or as His natural trait. However, no such agency is believed to be existing in God. It is also to be noted that, if He was required to dispense fruits of actions of each soul which are countless in numbers, it will be a tremendous task. Then what will happen to such a record when *Pralaya* takes place and every creation is annihilated? The records pertaining to each soul will also cease to exist, like all effects created by *Prakriti,* and, therefore, all souls will be alike and it will be impossible for Him to distinguish between liberated souls and bonded souls. It will be a problem for each soul to select a material body according to the force of its *Vāsnas* under the law of *Karma*. Moreover, when creation takes place afresh and the compulsive factor such as the actions (*Karmas*), is gone, the souls might not be inclined to return to the world and, therefore, the very purpose of fresh creation will be defeated. Also, if God is the dispenser of the fruits of actions of various souls, this is certainly an action in itself which will be attributed to God and for which He will be accountable under the law of *Karma*. If that happens, there will be no difference between the various souls and God and He will have to undergo the same plight. There is a *Mantra* of *Yajur Veda* which is often quoted as proof to prove that God dispenses the fruits of actions.[12] This mantra says that God is all pervading, lustrous, bodiless, flawless, sinewless, pure, unpierced by evil. He is Omniscient, knower of the hearts of all, censurer of the sinful and self–existent. He reveals through the *Vedas* all things for His subjects from His innumerous attributes and is free from birth and death. It can be seen that the interpretation placed on this mantra, by the scholars, is erroneous because it nowhere says that God awards the fruits of actions. Swami Yogeshwaranand explains this *Mantra* quite differently and says that the verb "*Vyadadhat*" means holding in His grasp. Being the subtlest and all–pervading, the Supreme Being holds *Prakriti* and its subsequent creations, in His complete grasp. This interpretation of the *Mantra* seems to be more logical and establishes that the Supreme Being is absolutely colourless, actionless and entirely dispassionate. The record of every action is kept in the *Citta* of every body in the form of *Samskāras* which are the seed impressions of the actions and which mature and fructify into fully grown fruits in good time. Like all seeds, the *Samskāras* also bear fruit under certain favourable circumstances brought about by the required factors. There are four factors, namely place, time, instrumental agency and relevant accessories, which enable a seed to sprout. These factors are discussed in detail as under:

(1) **The place Factor:** We take the example of a spiritually imbued person who is keen to attain self–realisation in right earnest. There is no body

in his house to impart to him the knowledge of self and even the surroundings are not congenial for that purpose. He, therefore, abandons his house, leaves his kith and kin and moves out in search of a competent preceptor. In the process, he crosses deep forests, braves the fear of wild animals, scales lofty hills and meets many saints and seers. We call this as the **place factor** which implies the selection of suitable place.

(2) **The Time Factor:** After immense toil and numerous trials and tribulations, he finally succeeds in finding an enlightened person who agrees to take him under his guidance. He adores his preceptor and willingly undergoes great hardships due to rigorous austerity. He practices Yoga, purifies his *Antahakarana* by the prescribed practices and discards almost every comfort to which he was accustomed at home. We call this as the **time factor** which pertains to the appropriate time which is essential for the attainment of desired objective.

(3) **The Instrumental Agency:** The instrumental factor, in his case, is the quality of the Guru or the preceptor with whose grace, he is able to proceed with the practice to attain the desired knowledge. The guide must not only be fully conversant with the subject but must be a self–realised soul full of kindness and with a deep desire to truthfully impart knowledge to him in the spirit in which a father gives his assets to his son. Only a guide, with the said qualifications, can be instrumental in his attaining the desired goal. This is called the **Instrumental Agency.**

(4) **The Relevant Accessories:** Just as certain aids and accessories are absolutely necessary for a

student of academic studies to pass his examination, suitable accessories are, similarly, needed by an aspirant of knowledge and of realisation of the self. Some such accessories are mentioned below:

(a) There should be care–free provision for his food, lodging and other needs of daily life.

(b) His place should be away from the hustle and bustle of city life so that no disturbance is caused to him in his practice. It should be either in a forest or on a remote river–bank.

(c) He should be kept in good health and should be free from diseases like sloth, indolence, procrastination etc.

(d) He should have unstinted faith in his guru, to whom he should be fully devoted, and his practice should be firmly grounded on *Yamas, Niyamas* etc.; and

(e) A strong urge to realise the self must permeate his whole being and he should be very willing to make every sacrifice, as may be required, to achieve the destination.

Thus, if all the four factors mentioned above combine, the aspirant for self-realisation will be able to reap the fruit of his actions, through the aspirant's own labour. Here God has played no role at all and the objective is achieved by the aspirant through the medium of four factors which have been brought about by his own individual labour, without utilising any help from God.

Let us take a simpler illustration to make the subject more intelligible so that it could be easily understood. There are certain fruits such as mango, banana etc. which grow in hot climate and there are certain other fruits such as apple, plums etc. which are grown in cold climate. Now if a person from hot climate entertains a strong desire to earn money by growing apples, what he will do is to shift from a hot place to a cold place and buy a piece of land there to set up an apple garden. Thus far, he has taken care of the factor of place or the local factor. He planted the apple trees in the land purchased for this purpose, tended the saplings, guarded the plants from vagaries of weather, nourished them with water and manure and ensured full growth of the trees to reach the stage when these are in a position to bear fruit. In this way, the time factor has been taken care of. Now is the time to dispose of the crop to earn money. For this purpose, he establishes contact with right sources in different markets. If he has no access to the wholesalers, he will fail in selling the whole crop and, his desire to earn good money from apple garden, will remain unfulfilled. This is what is called the instrumental agency. What still remains is the last factor of relevant accessories which he is required to provide in the form of coordinating means. He will need the plant and machinery to select, assort and pack the apples scientifically so that they remain fresh. He will also need a variety of transport vehicles to deliver his produce to various destinations. For short distance, he will require trucks, for long distances railways and for export, he will need the services of Airlines. When all these accessories are properly placed, it takes care of the fourth factor of relevant accessories. It can be seen, even from this illustration, that the presence of all the four factors is absolutely necessary for the *Karma* to bear fruit. In this, no necessity is felt or experienced of God to bring about the result. Hence, there is no basis for the assumption that God dispenses to the *Jivās,* the fruits of their actions.

It is often argued that the actions, being inert and lifeless, cannot obtain their own deserts. Hence, some conscious and just agency is required to award such deserts judiciously, and only God is fit to be such an agency.

Presuming that a conscious power alone can do this job, then a conscious entity in the form of individual soul is already present in the body. Because of its close proximity, the *Samskāras* of *Karmas* are constantly stirred from bottom of the *Citta,* where these are stored ,and prompted into acquiring the gross form and proceed to yield the fruit. This sets into motion all the organs such as ego, intellect, mind and senses which discharge their prescribed functions in bringing the subtle seed impression into mature fruit and also in the reverse order of the fruit assuming the form of the seed. In the whole process, man's own industry, which is expressed through his personal efforts, has been instrumental in the achievement of the fruit of *Karmas*. In the final analysis, it is only the *Karma* or its fruit which is the cause of a man's bondage and his emancipation. It proves that man himself is responsible for his actions as well as its fruits. Swami Yogeshwaranand strongly affirms this view and says:

> "As such, man's own industry is the central and the chief factor in the performance of an act, as also, in the reaping of its fruits. Due to the close proximity of the conscious soul within, man's earned impressions get enlivened into a fertile cycle of action and its natural fruit, and become an indispensable cause of his sense–voluptuousness, at last. For this, God's intervening assistance, or responsible dispensation of fruits of deeds is not, at all, needed."[13]

Similar *Samskāras,* whether they abide in the individual *Citta* or cosmic *Citta,* exist together and remain as a group. The main *Samskāra* becomes the nucleus and other *Samskāras* stick on to it and all these *Samskāras* co–operate with one another to act towards the satisfaction of achieving the final goal and these *Samskāras* collectively manifest in a single action. In a garden there may be a variety of trees but each tree draws from the same field, the nourishment relevant to its own specie and goes on energising and vitalising it. In the same manner, all similar efforts lend co–operation to each other and produce similar fruits. This is proved by the fact that when we fall on good days we derive happiness for a long time and when we fall on bad days we derive only suffering which remains also for a long time.

The *Samskāras* too have a similar tendency and, accordingly, a *Samskāra* or an action in the seed form, is attracted and supported by other acts of the same nature. Swami Yogeshwaranand says that an action in seed form, likewise, tends to be attracted by other acts of the same character and thus continues to expand discriminately its own width of scope. "In this way actions of every distinct category, charged with their specific fruits, continue to widen their expanse of probability."[14] At the same time, man's own area of effort is also widened. In the whole process of fructification of *Karma,* which covers the span from subtle impression to gross action, man's own labour is indispensable and God's supervision to dispense the fruit, does not come in the picture at any stage. A conscious entity which is already present in the body, is quite capable of supervising the entire process and, therefore, a second conscious entity, such as the Supreme Consciousness, is not required at all. The *Samskāras,* the resulting actions and the fruits thereof, are all inert and lifeless but because of the close proximity of conscious soul, the fruits of *Samskāras* of every body are brought to bear and are experienced in the *Brahmarandhra*. This is an automatic process but, through his ignorance, man super-imposes the action as well as its fruit on the spotless soul. As a result, he ascribes to the soul the properties of actions belonging to the *Citta*. The true fact is that action takes place in the *Citta* when it comes into contact with conscious soul. By itself the soul is free from action, unattached and pure. In fact *Citta* is also inert because it is a bye–product of cosmic

Citta which is formed of *Sattvic Mahat* which again, is an evolute of unconscious *Prakriti*. Unless it comes into contact with soul, it cannot generate action in it. The *Samskāras* arising in the *Citta* are also inert and deeds, resulting from inert *Samskāras,* are equally inert because all are made of matter which, too, is inert. So, therefore, there is no room in the conscious soul to give rise to action, but, merely because of its contact with the inner organ in our body, we assign action to soul and hold it responsible for bondage and release. It is a great irony that we hold the soul as a responsible agent for its actions and treat it as reaper of fruits but we do not apply the same rule to the Supreme Soul and absolve Him of the responsibility of action as dispenser of fruits. If law of *Karma* is applied to both of them, then both will be alike and God will not be different from the soul. It, therefore, proves that action does not belong to God and since He is beyond action, He does not dispense the fruits of actions. God and the soul, both, are actionless and are not involved in action nor are they responsible for reaping the fruits. Swami Yogeshwaranand says that, when tested on the touchstone of reason and logic, the doctrine of Gods' dispensation of fruits of actions of beings, fails to survive.

Swami Yogeshwaranand strongly affirms that no action is ever remitted or destroyed and each action must, necessarily, bear its corresponding fruit. We perform countless actions during our life but all actions do not bear fruit in the span of our present life. We, therefore, take birth again to work out the *Samskāras* of remaining actions. Obviously the accumulated *Samskāras* are carried over to the next body after we discard our present body. The vehicle which carries these *Samskāras* is the subtle body which is made up of five *Tanmatras*, ten *Indriyas*, mind and intellect, all in subtle form. In fact, the *Samskāras*, the impressions of *Karmas*, are lodged in the *Citta* which abides in the causal body. However, on the destruction of the gross body the subtle body conjoins with causal body and both together depart along with the *Samskāras.*[15]

Our scriptures have termed the *Citta* as *Karmāsya* because all the seeds of actions are lodged in the ground of the *Citta* which is also the field where the seeds of *Karmas* are sown and the crop is reaped. *Samskāras*, the seeds of *Karmas* are, also called *Vāsanas* which exist in four forms namely *Prasupta* (dormant), *Tanu* (attenuated), *Vichchhinna* (overpowered) and *Udāra* (expanded). *Samskāras* may abide in any of the four forms and bear fruit. At the time of *Pralaya*, when every effect merges into its cause, the *Samskāras* also merge in the causal *Gunas* but they are never destroyed. The *Samskāras* of our past lives become dull and are suppressed and lodged in the cosmic *Citta* but they are never destroyed. These *Samskāras* become operative when a desire arises. Thus, our *Vāsanas* determine which particular *Samskāra* should come to the forefront and bear fruit. With regard to the parched up state of *Samskāras*, which is mentioned in Yoga *Sutras*, Swami Yogeshwaranand says that all *Samskāras* return to their respective places in *Prakriti* and this state is called parched up state but, since the *Samskāras* are never destroyed, these return to the *Citta* on completion of the duration of emancipation and associate with the soul to bear their respective fruits. Here it will be interesting to understand how Swami Yogeshwaranand related *Samskāras* to memory or *Smriti*. Recollection of something experienced in the past, is called memory. These experiences of the past objects cause *Samskāras*, present in the *Citta*, to be awakened or recalled in the presence of an awakener, whether inner or outer. Memory awakens again and again the knowledge of subtle *Samskāras* formed when an object is experienced by senses. Thus, the seed of every such experience is the *Samskāras* or *Vāsanas*. At the appropriate time, these seeds are awakened in the

Citta by memory when a suitable stimulus is found, and then, the said seed sprouts, enters the intellect sheath (*Vijnānamaya Kosha*) and is converted into gross form. It blossoms there and bears fruit. These *Samskāras* are formed by one or more of the five *Vrittis* mentioned in Yoga *Sutras*. Swami Yogeshwaranand says that the *Samskāras* are engraved on the plate of the *Citta*, in a manner of saying, and, that *Samskāras* are formed according to experience and *Smriti* is formed according to *Samskāras*. And all these *Samskāras* are neither destroyed nor lost through the media of time, space and class, and, are awakened when there is an awakener.

We have already mentioned that the *Samskāras* are of four types of which the expanded *Samskāras* cause activity, pleasures and sufferings in the gross body where these always remain present. Attenuated or subtle *Samskāras* cause enjoyment and suffering in the subtle and causal bodies in this world as well as in the other world. The *Samskāras* can be experienced by subtle senses in the state of *Samādhi*. The dormant *Samskāras* exist in the heart and are responsible for experiencing bliss of God realisation as also of self-realisation. In the state of *Pralaya* when everything is reabsorbed in *Prakriti*, the *Samskāras* are dissolved in *Alinga Prakriti* where no experience of pleasure or pain takes place. Like cotton is converted into lint, lint into yarn and yarn into cloth, in the same way *Prakriti* also exists in every product created by it. In the course of its evolution, *Prakriti* transforms itself into causal body first, then into subtle body and lastly into gross body. Expanded *Samskāras* provide enjoyment or suffering to gross body but, if these expanded *Samskaras* are made attenuated by a Yogi through his effort, knowledge and dispassion, they are rendered incapable of bearing fruit in the gross body. The attenuated *Samskāras* provide enjoyment and suffering only to subtle body as these *Samskāras* abide in subtle body. Swami Yogeshwaranand says that after accomplishing their work in the subtle body these *Samskāras* become worn out, weak and impotent to bear any results and move to the causal body, where they become dormant. Since the senses, mind and intellect are not present in the causal body, these *Samskāras* are unable to bear fruit. However, since *Ahamkāra* and *Citta* are present in the causal body, it enables fructification of only those *Samskāras* which are associated with God and the soul because *Ahamkāra* and *Citta* are capable of enjoying the bliss arising therefrom.

Swami Yogeshwaranand denies that the *Samskāras* which are absorbed in invisible *Prakriti,* return to the gross body to cause enjoyment and suffering for, if they did so, the purpose of liberation will be of no avail. If they remain dissolved in the causal *Prakriti,* then alone liberation will be possible. However, when the duration of liberation gets over and the soul returns to the world to perform actions, it must pick up all those *Samskāras* which were lying buried in *Prakriti* and proceed to bear their fruits.

The gross body contains the other two bodies, namely subtle and causal, within it and because the various types of *Samskāras* abide in one or the other such body, these *Samskāras* are properly graded as subtle, subtler and subtlest. Although the *Samskāras* remain in their respective bodies, the expanded *Samskāras* of each action and other such relevant *Samskāras* of the same category, move together and remain dissolved in the relevant state of *Prakriti* and are stored therein. According to Swami Yogeshwaranand, the main *Samskāras* of the chief *Karmas* carry with them, the minor ones of their own type and on the commencement of fructification, forcibly return, bringing with them the minor ones.[16] As stated earlier, there are layers of gross, subtle, causal and extremely causal *Samskāras* which hold our *Samskāras* and which go and return along with all *Samskāras* of their own category. *Samskāras* of the same category bear fruit together. The main *Samskāra* is stored in the *Citta* while similar minor *Samskāras* are stored in *Prakriti*. When it is time to bear fruit, even minor *Samskāras* become like main ones and tend to bear fruit in the same way. If a Yogi stops forming new *Karmas,* but has not yet acquired *Param Vairāgya* (supreme dispassion), the *Samskāras* of earlier births do bear fruit. *Karmas* and *Samskāras* of the present life are generally more inclined to fructify as compared with *Samskāras* of earlier lives.

The *Samskāras* are subtle in nature and infinitesimal in form and size. These are like the seeds of a tree which hold the whole tree within them. As these are more subtle than atoms, these can be stored in the *Citta*. There is an assertion by some uninformed quarters that the *Samskāras,* pertaining to innumerous past lives, cannot be contained in a small area of head and heart but this objection can be rebutted with the argument that *Prakriti* is so vast, yet its orb is connected to the head and heart. Being subtle, this orb is inside as well as outside the body. On the same analogy the *Samskāras* can be accommodated in the *Citta* and the intellect which are also small, yet capable of holding these *Samskāras*. At the time of reabsorption of effects in *Prakriti,* when *Citta* merges in causal *Prakriti,* the *Samskāras* contained in the *Citta* are brought back by it at the time of fresh creation. These *Samskāras* once again become the cause for birth and rebirth and once again the cycle of coming and going of *Samskāras* commences its task.

We have explained above, in suitable details, how the *Samskāras* are formed, where these are stored and how these fructify in the presence of some stimulus through memory. This process, is self controlled and automatic and does not require assistance from any agency including God. In the whole process God has not played any role in their fructification. It is our *Citta* that awakens memories and causes fructification of *Karmas*. So long as the mind–stuff is there, the *Samskāras* will continue to flow and cause pleasure and pain. As mentioned earlier, these extend from our body to causal *Prakriti* and so long as our association with *Prakriti* persists, the cycle of birth and re–birth will also exit. Denying any role to God in the dispensation of the fruits of actions, Swami Yogeshwaranand also disputes *Patāñjali's* claim that realisation of self comes on cessation of modifications of *Citta*. He says:

> "I have described seventy kinds of vital airs in my book 'Science of Vital Airs'. This is, as a result, of my own research. *Patāñjali* and Kapil have not mentioned about tendencies (thought waves) arising out of vital airs. Vital air is an entity that subsists all the 24 hours of the day and at no time it suffers any reduction. Life subsists so long as vital air subsists. Thought waves generated by vital airs continue to exist so long as life exists. They can be controlled only when they merge with the mind–stuff. In the mind–stuff, vital airs are present in the form of *Prasupta, Udar, Vichhin* and *Tanu*. *Prasupta* goes into mind–stuff carrying our *Sanskars* with it. After Doom's day, it will reappear with the *Sanskars*. This movement of the mind–stuff alongwith the *Sanskars* and 'thought waves' goes on. I do not know how *Patāñjali* has mentioned about the control of thought waves of mind–stuff. That kind of control automatically comes about on the Doom's day."[17]

In one of the *Sutras, Nyāya Darśana* says, "God is the primary forum for dispensing reward or punishment to men for their actions." In another sutra it is said that when no action is performed, there is no reward or punishment. And with regard to God, this *Shastra* says that no purpose is involved in God's action. Commenting on these mantras, Swami Yogeshwaranand says that if we accept God as the dispenser of fruits of actions, then this job can also be done by a man in authority such as the king or a judge or a highly placed official. He gives a mundane example of the act of setting up of a factory. From concept to execution, or from the beginning to the final completion of the task, the person concerned alone is involved in every activity. The product to be manufactured, the site and location of factory, provision of finance, the engagement of workers, the marketing channels etc., will all be decided by him alone, either directly or in consultation with competent persons. Swami Yogeshwaranand asks whether God has played any part in the entire series of activity. He says that God is redundant in such activities. This is all the result of the entrepreneur's *Karmas,* as he himself would earn profit or suffer loss on account of his venture. He, therefore, affirms that God can never be the arbiter of our worldly actions and, therefore the views expressed by some schools of thought, such as *Nyāya Darśana,* that the result of our actions lies in the hands of God, is totally unfounded. It is, therefore, wrong to blame God for our wrong actions as He never persuaded us to perform those actions. He strongly refutes that God has any role to play either in our actions or their fruits. This gives an apparent impression that Swami Yogeshwaranand is disbeliever in God. To ward off such accusation he says:

> "I know the kind of ideas you have about God. I am not an atheist. My belief in him is stronger than yours. But I do take note of the fact that his major acts are performed by him alone and not by any one else. For example, he causes the movement of the earth. This is beyond us. The sun rises in the East in the morning and sets in the West in the evening. There can be no change in this. Such stupendous acts have to be assigned to God. But when you bring in God to do your domestic work and regard him as your private servant, I have to part company from you."[18]

It will appear from what is stated above that Swami Yogeshwaranand firmly believes that God can never be the dispenser of the fruits of *Karmas*. Most of us hold the mistaken belief that He dispenses such fruits but this happens because of our ignorance of true nature of the Absolute. In reality, both God and soul are perfectly free from actions as well as from dispensation of the fruits of actions.

KNOWLEDGE REVEALED BY GOD

The doctrine that quite early at the time of creation of the world, God revealed knowledge to *Agni* and other *Ṛṣis*, has very wide acceptance. It is mentioned in *Satpatha Brahman* (xi,4,2,3) that in the beginning, God revealed the four *Vedas* namely *Rick, Sāma, Yujur* and *Atharva,* to *Agni, Vayu, Aditya* and *Angiras,* respectively.[19] *Mannu* also makes a similar mention in *Mannu Smriti* (1-23) that in the beginning, after human beings had been created, the Supreme Being made *Vedas* known to *Brahman* (the first born) through *Agni* etc. The reason given by many scholars, including Swami Dayanand Saraswati, is that these four *Ṛṣis* were the purest in heart and, therefore, God revealed the true knowledge only to them in the beginning of creation. The evidence advanced by these scholars, to support their contention that the *Vedas* are of Divine origin, is that the book which has described God as Holy, Omniscient, Pure, Just Merciful etc., which is opposed to neither the law of nature, nor of direct cognition nor even the teachings of *Āptas* (the learned teachers), cannot be other than the book of Divine revelation. Since *Vedas* alone fulfil all these conditions, these are certainly the books revealed by God and are not manmade. Men by themselves cannot gain this subtle knowledge. Savages like Bhils, who reside in deep forests, have never become enlightened even till this day as there is no one to teach them. Even *Patāñjali* has said in one of his *Sutras* that, as in the present time we become enlightened only after being taught by our teachers, so were in the beginning of the world, *Agni* and others taught by the greatest of the teacher, namely God.[20] It is said that the knowledge of the *Vedas* was imparted to the said *Ṛṣis* because their *Cittas* were completely purified and they had attained perfection in *Samādhi*, thereby becoming entitled to gain that knowledge. *Veda* is the collection of Mantras but the exposition of those Mantras, given by the *Ṛṣis*, is contained in the *Brahmānas*. These expositions are also called *Shākhas* and there are eleven hundred and twenty seven such *Shākhas* in the *Vedas*. *Brahmanās* contain biographies of those *Ṛṣis* and because the biography of a person can be written only after his birth, the *Brahmānas* cannot be considered as eternal books. But the *Vedas* donot contain any such biography nor do these mention any proper names or narrate stories relating to a person or an event. On this basis, some orthodox schools of philosophy accept *Vedas* as eternal and ascribe their authorship to God. It is said that due to tremendous compassion towards human beings, the Supreme Lord revealed the *Vedas* to them by whose study, men are rid of every type of ignorance and attain true knowledge of self, God and the universe. Because God is eternal, therefore, the knowledge imparted by Him and the attributes pertaining to Him, must also be eternal. *Sāmkhya* believes in *Satkārayavāda* according to which the effect pre exists in the cause. All causes are of three types, namely present, past and future. If the effect was not existent in its cause before it was produced, then this division of causes would be impossible. *Vacaspati Miśra* advances elaborate arguments in his work *Tattva–Kaumudi* in support of *Sāmkhya* theory of *Satkāryavāda* and defends vigorously against neo–*Nyāya* forms. For this reason, it is said that the nature and attributes of a substance cannot be different from the substance. On the basis of this and similar arguments, an attempt has been made to establish the truth about the doctrine that God revealed the knowledge about reality to a few *Ṛṣis* who propagated this knowledge to other human–beings who further disseminated it to others, generation after generation.

The above doctrine has been taken up by Swami Yogeshwaranand for a critical examination who finally came to the conclusion that the said notion is untenable. He says that the concept that God composed the *Vedas* and revealed the knowledge, contained therein, to certain *Ṛṣis,* is impossible to believe. We have repeatedly said earlier in this work that God is actionless and that action relates to *Prakriti*. If that is so how can God be accepted as having done the work of composing or revealing *Vedas*? That would involve an action and, consequently, He would be perceived as doer of acts. We, human–beings, are also doers and if God is also treated as doer of some acts then no difference will be left between Him and us and He will become finite like us. In that case, He will be devoid of His Omnipresence and Omniscience. In our day to day observation, we have often found that knowledge is passed through the communication of teacher to the student and, that too, over a period of time. There has been no occasion when knowledge is imparted at one go by a teacher or it is acquired by a person immediately on his birth. There is no other agency, including God, which can bestow knowledge to any person in the manner in which *Vedas* conveyed the subtle knowledge to the *Ṛṣis*. It is true that certain individuals exhibit extra–ordinary brilliance even from childhood, as compared with others of their ilk. But that could be because of the accumulated *Samskāras* of previous births, which they carried with them in the present birth. It is not unlikely that when the world was newly created, some highly realised seers appeared on the scene with the store–house of knowledge acquired in earlier births. Such *Ṛṣis* might have brought some knowledge from earlier life but some was developed by them in the current life through inductive and deductive learning. Later on, the total knowledge was consolidated by *Agni, Vayu, Aditya* and *Angiras* in the body of the four *Vedas*. This knowledge was then transferred orally, from generation to generation, till it was finally reduced to the script of the *Vedas*. It seems quite improbable that the knowledge was given to the seers at one time and that, immediately thereafter, they started chanting the *Mantras* no sooner than they were born. It must have taken a long time for the *Vedic* language to develop its idiom and perfect its style. We can see for ourselves that the language of *Rik Veda*, which is believed to be the first written book, is crude and unpolished as compared with the language of later scriptures. In early Sanskrit works, we find a repeated mention of *Rik, Yajuh* and *Sāma Vedas* which shows that *Atharvaveda* was written much later. So, it must be over some period of time that the *Vedas* must have come into being. In view of this, it cannot be gainsaid that all the *Vedas* were revealed at one time by God to His chosen few *Ṛṣis*. Before it reached the status of *Vedic* language, Sanskrit must have been given special grooming so as to be fit to compose the *Mantras* of the *Vedas*.

The doctrine under discussion can give rise to two distinct interpretations. The first interpretation relates to the names of certain *Ṛṣis* at the beginning of the *Mantras*. There is a reason why these *Ṛṣis* were associated with those *Mantras*. Swami Yogeshwaranand gives the following reason for the said association:

> "The *Ṛṣis* whose names appear at the head of a certain *Mantra* or *Mantras*, a *Sukta*, or canto, in a *Veda*, for the first time led the way in having a revealing insight into the essential meanings of those mantras which came to be associated with their names; and after having made their central spirit and ingrained truths on a scientific basis an exclusive subject of their inner experience and

> intense realisation, propagated them for others' benefit by expanding their scope of influence as well as their range of practical application in life."[21]

The name of certain *Devatas* has also been mentioned in the mantras. A *Devata* is one who gives, benefits or blesses and since, *Agni, Indra, Prithvi, Vāyu, Jala* etc. all qualify as benefactors, they have been mentioned along side each mantra. Invocation of these benefactors is relevant to the field of knowledge pertaining to them. The metre and accent of the *Mantras* ensure correct pronounciation and elicit true sense and meanings thereof. There can be no other purpose of the form, text and arrangement of these *Mantras*. The Vedic language was never developed over night but it grew into its full shape first and only then the composition of *Vedas* took place. Early Sanskrit was indeed, very rudimentary but, in course of time, it acquired the respectable status of *Vedic* language superscripting the *Devatas*, the *Ṛṣis*, the metre and the accent. Still later, after the lapse of many centuries, Sanskrit grammar was developed and as the time passed it blossomed into the language in which Upanishads, *Brahman Sutras* and *Śaddarśanas* were rendered. This point can be forcefully established if we compare the language in which works of *Kalidāsa, Bhāsa* and *Amru* were written, with the language of the *Vedas*. The language must have covered a long distance in time to achieve the finnese, sophistication and glamour reflected in the *Puranas*, the epics and the *Mahakāvyas*.

Discussing the other interpretation of the aforesaid doctrine, it is a common refrain that the mantras, which are associated with the *Ṛṣis,* were realised by them intuitively in *Samādhi* and were subsequently compiled in the form of *Vedas*. Each of the four *Ṛṣis,* namely *Agni, Vāyu, Aditya* and *Angiras,* compiled one *Veda* each, on the basis of their inner experience in *Samādhi,* when they first realised the relevant mantras and, accordingly, one *Veda* each came to be known after them. *Brahman,* the leader of the trinity of *Brahman,* Visnu and Mahesa, was the first to be taught the knowledge of *Vedas* and, thereafter, commenced the practice of transferring this secret knowledge through oral tradition, till *Mahrishi Vyāsa* brought out this knowledge in written script.

The *Rik Veda* consists of 10,552 *Mantras,* the *Sama Veda* of 1,875, the *Yajur Veda* of 1,975 and *Atharva Veda* of 5,987. In all, the four *Vedas* comprise of 20,389 *Mantras* which include some repetitions of some *Rik Veda Mantras.* Thus, the four *Vedas* taken together have many thousand *mantras* and it does not appeal to reason that the *Ṛṣis* could have conceived or composed so many mantras at one time. Due to the difference in the style of language of different *Vedas,* one is forced to believe that the four *Vedas* were written at different points of time and, therefore, the four *Ṛṣis* also lived and flourished at different times. In view of this, it is quite likely that the *mantras* associated with their names were collected and compiled much later and their names were thus mentioned at the head of each *mantra*. As already mentioned, certain *mantras* of a particular *Veda* are repeated in other *Vedas* but the name of the same *Ṛṣis* appears wherever the *mantra* appears. It is evident from this that the four *Vedas* were compiled at different times but the concerned *Ṛṣis* included in his collection, if any, mantra from other *Vedas,* that attracted him. The word पूर्वे: ऋषिभि: which is often met with in the *Vedas* and which means the earlier *Ṛṣis,* obviously, relates to different periods of the same cycle of existence. This also indicates that the *Rsis* lived at different times.

According to *Sāmkhya,* at the time of *Pralaya,* every effect of matter merges in its cause and the matter reverts to its original form of *Alinga Prakriti* (non-manifest matter). In such an event even *Vedas* will not survive nor will the knowledge contained therein. Taking the converse of it, the creation of universe has taken billions of years in its movement from primordial matter to the fullfledged material universe. It may not be unreasonable to believe that during the vast span of billions of years, there must have existed other seers and sages prior to the four *Ṛṣis* who were authors of the *Vedas*. Following in the footsteps of those earlier *Ṛṣis* , the compilers of the *Vedas* might have crystalised that knowledge into the sublime knowledge of the *Vedas*. One cannot rule out the possibility of many other *Ṛṣis* living prior to or side by side with the four *Ṛṣis* of the *Vedas*. We know for certain that the *Atharva Veda* was written only after the other three *Vedas* came into existence. It is because the language of *Atharva Veda* is far different from the language of other *Vedas*. Moreover, a large number of *mantras* in the *Sāma Veda* are the same as those occurring in the *Rig Veda,* which shows that those *mantras* were repeated by the *Riṣi* of the later *Veda*. All this is enough proof of the fact that God did not author the *Vedas* nor did he reveal the secret knowledge thereof early in the beginning of creation by evolution of *Prakriti*.

In their overenthusiasm to prove that the above named four *Ṛṣis* were the first to have got inscripted on their pure *Citta* the divine knowledge of *Vedas,* some scholars deliberately interpret the phrase 'earlier seers' which appears again and again in the *Vedas,* to mean the seers belonging to the cycle of creation prior to the present one. This view is belied by the *Yajur Veda* itself.[22] This *Mantra* gives a clear impression that there were other *Ṛṣis* even prior to *Yajurveda*. It is from those *Ṛṣis* that *Vāyu,* one of the four above-mentioned *Ṛṣis*, learnt the precious knowledge of *Vedas*. This proves, beyond doubt that the four *Ṛṣis* of the *Vedas* and the 'earlier *Ṛṣis*' referred to therein, all belonged to and existed in the same cycle of creation and the view that the latter belonged to the earlier cycle, is very far fetched. Those who wanted to prove on the basis of this interpretation that the *Vedas* are eternal and the four *Ṛṣis* were the first recipients of the secret knowledge, have failed to make any valid point. This also fails to prove that God alone authored or revealed the knowledge of the *Vedas* to his chosen seers. The only proposition which may be found acceptable to a discerning scholar is that *Ṛṣis* existed prior to the said four *Ṛṣis* who must have collected the knowledge of *Mantras* and must have compiled the *mantras* composed by earlier *Ṛṣis*, and the four *Ṛṣis* must have made copious use of that knowledge and of those mantras, to create the four *Vedas*. It has already been stated that the words "*Purvaih Rishibhih*" have found repeated mention in the *Vedas*. These words clearly mean that *Ṛṣis* lived prior to the four *Ṛṣis* of the *Vedas* who were acquainted with the mysterious knowledge of the *Vedas*. The views of Swami Yogeshwaranand on this point are expressed below:

> "These four, in a sense, were the pioneer compilers, or even half-way authors, quite admittedly. The four *Vedas*, and similary the religious books of other doctrinaire creeds, which believe them to be a Heavenly Revelation, all these may be said to be a paltry portion of that vast Unending Ocean of knowledge, which sits and sways over all conceivable science and arts inherent in the Grand Creational Process emanating from it, and includes, without exception, everything relating to the Supreme Being, the mysterious finite soul, and Nature, from whose universal womb issue forth not only this drama of life and death but also the picturesque panorama of objects both beauteous and sublime."[23]

He says that the greatest misfortune of the posterity lies in being satisfied with even small knowledge when there appears to be no end to creative vastness of infinite matter nor to the infinite all–pervasive consciousness. No one will ever know these infinite entities nor has any one done so in the past nor will he do it in future. Human faculty of understanding is limited but the subject entities are unlimited. In view of this it is futile to say that God revealed the *Vedas* and that the said view is sacrosanct. Knowledge is a ceaseless endeavour and a sustained and vigorous enquiry in the nature of things and there is no last word on the ascertainment of truth. Therefore, the search for truth in the matter of inert *Prakriti* and conscious Super Soul, must not stop till such time as an inner satisfaction arises in the super–conscious state of *Samādhi*.

The truth about the *Devatas,* whose names are mentioned in the mantras, also does not pose any problem. Every *Devata* implies a subject inherent in him which he expounds in the body of that *Mantra*. Therefore, even in the matter of *mantras* or deities, specified therein, no role is assigned to God nor is He connected to it.

The question whether God is the efficient cause or the material cause of the world, has been fraught with a serious controversy. *Sāmkhya Darśana* treats God only as the efficient cause and matter as the material cause. In fact God is neither effective efficient cause nor effective material cause of any thing but the quality of knowledge and creation is superimposed on Him because of His close proximity to matter. However, *Yajur Veda* contains a large number of *mantras* which euologies the qualities of God and which suggest that God is both the efficient cause and the material cause of the world. God has been spoken of as possessed of innumerous heads, eyes, arms and legs.[24] That God abides in our hearts, cannot be called to question because it is mentioned in the scriptures and also realised by seers in the supreme state of super–consciousness. In the same heart of the *Ṛṣis,* where knowledge of *Vedas* was being revealed, God was also present. In the frenzy of their devotion to Him for the revelation of knowledge, the whole process was attributed to God as superimposition, due to his close proximity. He is viewed as the inspiration and cause of truth and beauty with which the heart was pulsating. In reality God did not do any such thing as He is neither active efficient cause nor active material cause. He just pervades *Prakriti* and, because of his pervasion, *Prakriti* goes on evolving to create the world efficiently and intelligently. Knowledge is acquired and colated through our inner organs of inspiration. But since the internal organs are products of matter, these are liable to change and transformation. Thus, knowledge rests in these changeable organs which are the true source of generation of that knowledge. God and individual soul are not the causes or sources of knowledge because, unlike our internal organs, both these entities are immutable, unchangeable and eternal. Therefore, all knowledge, whether *Vedic*, secular or scientific, is a product of the heart of a person and the hearts are so designed that these can carry forward this knowledge cycle after cycle of creation. This happens because all knowledge is reduced to seed impressions or *Samskāras* and, at the time of *Pralaya*, the balance seed impressions are deposited in nascent *Prakriti* and later on recovered from it when one is borne again. So, therefore, in accordance with the ancient tradition of knowledge, it is carried forward from generation to generation. In the light of this process of passing on knowledge, God's intervention is not required in the whole process of acquisition, accumulation and transference, from one generation to the other. Lest any one should label him as disbeliever in *Vedas* for holding such redical views, Swami Yogeshwaranand, clarifies his position as under:

> "There need be no misgiving about our faith in the sacred lore of the *Vedas*. Undoubtedly we have the same regard for it, perhaps, as others; but the

> way of our evaluation of it as also its justification to others is, of course, different. It is also not true that we deny the existence of God or the individual finite soul; but there, too, the truth is that our mode of understanding these Ultimate Realities and interpreting them to others, as well as a closely critical attitude towards them, is different from that of others, who rather appear to find it somewhat strange, uncommon, and disquieting to their beaten, incoherent beliefs, of which fact we have all along been aware on our part in the course of our preceding investigations. But our mode of uncovering the truth and its exposition are bound to be above the commonplace, because every justification of the endlessness of knowledge would necessarily demand a practical difference of thought and attitude among the advancing seekers of Truth and Reality."[25]

As already stated in the foregoing paras, knowledge is incomprehensible and its scope endless. Then, it will be foolish of us to believe that what we know is the entire knowledge and there is nothing beyond it. It is impossible to compress any knowledge within the bounds of a few books, even if these books are the sacred scriptures of any religion. Books only represent the tips of the iceberg and there is much more beneath it. Since the books of the religions contain only a meagre knowledge, even the seers propagate such meagre knowledge. True and complete knowledge can be acquired only in *Samādhi*. It is only in *Samādhi* that all the three subtle entities namely *Prakriti*, *Puruṣa* and *Brahman* or the matter, the finite individual soul and the infinite Supreme Soul, become the subject matter of intuitive experience of the practitioner.

From the above, one can easily infer that knowledge of any kind has a reference to the inner organs like the hearts and minds of the men and seers and of the teachers. Like any other product of matter, even books, including *Vedas* will perish at the arrival of doom. Only the seed impressions of the knowledge will survive and will be preserved and revived in the hearts of the human beings. The tradition of knowledge goes on in this manner from cycle to cycle and from generation to generation and no other agency, be it God, is necessary to impart knowledge to others at any stage. Hence, the doctrine that God revealed knowledge to certain *Ṛṣis* in the beginning of creation, is not susceptible to any valid proof.

By his unorthodox views, Swami Yogeshwaranand has broken the barriers between myth and reality by questioning the authority of scriptures relating to the acquisition and delegation of knowledge of the Vedas and has opened a serious debate on this issue. However, going by the logic of his arguments, he has made out a good case in his favour. Men of the current age need a convincing reason for every thing and what Swami Yogeshwaranand has concluded is surely based on such a reason.

INCARNATION (AVATĀRA)

In Geeta, Lord Krishna says that whenever there is decay of righteousness, and rise of unrighteousness, then to protect what is right, to destroy what is wicked and to establish righteousness, he takes birth again and again in every age.[26] When Krishna himself makes this assertion, then the common people who believe Krishna to be the Supreme Personality of Godhead, are led to accept the concept of incarnation which means that God incarnates on earth in human form to achieve certain objectives. In the case of Krishna, the objective was to kill Kamsa and to destroy the kula of Kauravas. Similarly, Sri Ramachandra was born as incarnation of Vishnu to kill Rāvana. The scriptures inform us that God appears on earth in some such form to achieve the aforesaid and other similar objectives. Going by the inadequacy of the objectives mentioned above, it seems absurd that God who is Omnipotent and can achieve these objectives by a small unmanifest act, should need to take birth to kill a single demon for the benefit of some persons. Duryodhana was a very popular prince with his people and was also highly attached to his sister, brothers and parents. He was also very respectful to his Gurus and cared well for his friends. His only fault was that he was inimical towards Pandavas. To punish Kauravas, God considered it necessary to be born as Krishna. This does not appear logical because God is unbiased and impartial and, therefore, he should not have taken sides with Pandavas who would have been allowed to fight their own battle to recover their lost territory. Being all powerful and all prevalent, God need not have taken birth for such petty causes.

Swami Yogeshwaranand does not subscribe to the concept of incarnation of God and raises many pertinent questions in this behalf. He asks if God is all pervasive and impartible whole, then which portion of his all pervasive whole, resulted in His incarnation? Because He is an impartible whole, it is not possible to divide Himself into parts and allow a portion of Him to be incarnated. Even if we assume that a portion of Him does become an *Avatāra,* then He becomes subject to change and mutation on account of the relationship of the part and the whole. Since God is eternal and unchanging this relationship does not apply to Him. Even if it is said that God incarnates to give salvation to His devotees, the proposition remains unacceptable for the reason that salvation will be attained by a person only if he conducts himself virtuously in accordance with the rules laid down by our *Dharmaśastras*. There is no other way to obtain *Mokṣa.* We may say as Swami Yogeshwaranand would have us say, that in the process of evolution when *Prakriti* reached the stage of cosmic *Citta*, the divinity which was already pervading it, came to be known as *Iśvara* or overlord. But this is true of individual souls and not of God because there is no evidence, even in the *Vedas,* to show that change has taken place in God. He remained immutable, unchanging and impartible whole as ever and, therefore, to call Him overlord or *Iśvara* (incarnation) is without reason because, God does not pass from one state to another. He remains *Brahman,* the Absolute at all times and, therefore, it is out of question for Him to assume the position of incarnation as *Iśvara. Prakriti* is infinite and because *Brahman* pervades it, He is also infinite. If *Brahman* is presumed to be finite, then he must be abiding in a specific portion of infinite *Prakriti.* In that case He will be a regional Lord who will be incapable of governing the limitless universe. A doubt will also arise as to who will govern motion and activity in the regions where God is absent. The all–pervading, indivisible, Omnipotent *Brahman,* who is subtler than the most subtle and far greater than *Prakriti*, will have to accept the inferior role of *Iśvara* or incarnation. But incarnation is said to exist because we have been told of many *Avatāras* such as Rama, Krishna, Buddha, Mahavira, Christ etc. Swami Yogeshwaranand does not agree that these were incarnations of God. He says:

> "All these superhuman personages of the past, had their natural births at some time or the other. They were married and had their children. They, likewise, underwent the afflictions of childhood, youth, old age, birth and death in their life time. They waged wars, and faced feuds, strifes, and different other conflicts among their customary worldly occupations. These hard facts of their lives generally tend to show that, although somewhat superior in virtues to us mortals, they also were human beings, after all; inasmuch as they took their births of human parents, in human

> homes; and none of them is living today, having mortally left this accursed globe. Now, will it speak of our differential rationality or wisdom, if we were to designate certain blessed mortals, simply because of their greater degree of virtuosity or other talents in comparison to others, as divine embodiments or incarnations of the Almighty, or think that He chose to come down to Earth in their unique form? It does not stand to reason. And the answer to these two questions is simple and straight. If it is admitted that their births took place under the roofs of human habitation, then the candid conclusion must be that *human beings are born to human beings*, and that all these great personages were mortal men at their best."[27]

According to him, only human beings are born of human beings and, consequently, all these persons were also human beings with the difference that because of good deeds done by them in the past, they became highly elevated and evolved souls. We find in our daily life that some persons are in possession of extraordinary qualities while others have common place traits. But persons belonging to both the categories are subject to the same laws of nature, involving birth, suffering and death. The distinction lies in the acquisition of qualities by them. Those who possess extraordinary qualities are addressed by us as *Avatāras*. We do this out of our faith in or affection for them but not for any scientific reason or logic. God who is indivisible, all pervasive and Omnipotent whole, cannot be made subject to the law of birth and death. Swami Dayanand Saraswati rejects the Geeta verse in which Krishna says that he will incarnate on earth in every Yuga whenever there is destruction of Dharma. He rejects it on the ground that *Yajur Veda* mentions that He is unborn. He is pure, is never born and never takes a human form. According to him, Krishna could never be God. He says that people who do not have knowledge of *Vedas,* are easily led astray by the sectarians who being themselves ignorant, believe in and propagate such false things to them. He who is born must necessarily die one day and, accordingly, the so called incarnates must also die. And while they live, they undergo the same process of pleasure and pain as other human beings do. The Supreme Being, who is possessed of infinite power, attributes and activity is not required to take human form and become subject to birth and death. Division of God into incarnations, cannot be supported by reason because, like ether, He is impartible whole. Ether being infinite and Omnipresent, can neither go in or come out. Similarly, God being Omnipresent and infinite, remains the whole and like ether can never go in or come out.

There is no mention of *Iśvara* in the *Sāmkhya* system but *Yoga* accepts *Iśvara* as an entity which has been thus defined in one of *Yoga Satras*. "*Iśvara*, the over-lord of the universe, is without the following earthly *Kleśas* namely: *Avidya* (ignorance), *Asmita*(ego), *Rāga*(attachment), *Dveṣa* (aversion) and *Abhiniveṣa* (clinging to life). He is also free from *karma, Vipāka* and *Āṣaya*."[28] We have already mentioned afflictions as *Avidya. Karmas* are good or bad actions and their fruits are called *Vipāka* which appear in the form of *Jāti, Ayus, Bhoga* etc. The subliminal impressions, which correspond to the fruits of actions, are called *Āśayas*. Thus *Iśvara* of the *Sāmkhya* is a special *Puruṣa* who is untouched by *Klesa, Karma, Vipāka,* and *Āśaya*. If God has to incarnate as *Avatāra,* He will become subject to all these faults and He will cease to qualify as God as per definition given in the above Sutra. When *Karma* is not attributed to God, He will not be required to bear its fruits. As already mentioned *Āśayas* are the seed impressions of the fruits of actions. Since God does not perform any actions, there are no fruits to be borne and, hence, no *Samskāras* are generated. As a result, there will be no impulse which could be responsible for fructification of any *Samskāra*. The characteristics of God, enunciated in the above Sutra, do not fit well on any of the great souls like Rama, Krishna, Buddha, Mahavira etc. and, therefore, they can not be called as incarnations of God. Indeed they were great souls of the highest order and, for this reason, we may call them by whatever name we may like but they can never be regarded as *Avatāras*.

It is also a common belief that God takes the form of "*Jivā*" in the individual. Like all concepts mentioned so far, this concept is also baseless and falls flat. Going by this concept God will become liable to change when He transforms to "*Jivā*" and as such like all other members of the class of "*Jivās*" He will be bound by bondage and emancipation. If it is argued that the said change is only a passing phase of His original state, even then His existence will become transient and changeable. In any case His attributes of being eternal, unchanging and indivisible, will be seriously effected. He will, then, be involved in all the activity and be treated as the doer and reaper of the fruits. As such, He will acquire all the flaws and shortcomings which every human being has. Further, if '*Jiva*' is taken as a fragment of the Supreme consciousness, even then the Supreme Consciousness cannot escape the charge of divisibility. Thereby, His Omnipresence, and His being an indivisible whole, will become meaningless. Thus, the '*Jiva*' or the individual soul cannot be a part or spark of the Universal Consciousness called God. The individual souls cannot be born out of Him because He is eternally changeless and cannot be divided into finite souls. Swami Yogeshwaranand says :

> "The appearance of *Brahman* as '*Jiva*' on earth, whether it is accepted as a transient phase of reality, or a part of the Whole, or on Cause–and–Effect and transition basis, or still on the

> Universal Illusion theory, is altogether a natural as well as a logical impossibility."[29]

The characteristics of *Brahman*, as stated in the scriptures, are that He is all–pervading, actionless, without limbs or organs, immutable and changeless, everlasting and eternal etc. Although He is mentioned as formless, yet no entity can exist without having a form. Therefore, He too has a form but He cannot be compared with any other object of the world. He shines with every object and, therefore, every form is His form. In one of the mantras of *Kaivalya* Upanishad, the word used for Him is '*Anantarupam*'[30] which means innumerous forms. This lends ample support to the above view. Even elsewhere in the Upanishads, it is said, *"Rupam Pratirupo Babhuva"* which means that, being fully associated with the shape and size of every object, He shines with the shape and form of that object. Swami Yogeshwaranand explains this subtle point as under:

> "If we view Him as the Embodiment of pure knowledge, and knowledge is essentially inclusive of karma as well, then He is beheld by us as Embodiment of Knowledge–cum–Karma both. If on the other hand, we conceive of Him as a Fountain of Pure Consciousness, in that case from the root, '*Citi–Samjnāne,*' according to which Consciousness also implies the seat or embodiment of Wisdom, He appears to us as Living Wisdom, or Knowledge Enlivened. Until to-day, His real form has never been ascertained as to what or what–like Form He may be determined to have with certainty, after all. That He has an Entity in Existence is not in the least questionable. None but He can be the Primary Cause of motion in the dead and inert Vastness of Matter. True, indeed, that He is the source of all motion in

> '*Prakriti*; but He must be something with a visage, of course. In actuality, it is extremely difficult, if not next to impossible, to determine with certainty what form He really does have; for does have; for does not He ("*Rupam Rúpam Pratirupo Babhuva*") elusively assume the form of the very mirror through which He is supposed to be reflected?[31]

As He reflects the form of the object, through which we decide to realise Him, many people make the mistake of taking Him as possessed of many forms. He is subtler than the subtlest and for that reason, He pervades every thing. Also being extremely subtle, an ordinary person is unable to grasp Him. His subtleness or extreme fineness has been expressed in Kathopanishad which states that the Universal Spirit is subtly permeating all living beings and is mysteriously hidden behind the veil of *Prakriti* so that only a selected few who have essentially sharp vision, can realise Him.[32]

On the question whether *Brahman* adopts the form of *Iśvara* and incarnates on earth as an individual, Swami Yogeshwaranand has devoted long years in quiet contemplation and in intuitive absorption, to ascertain the reality of *Brahman* and the individual soul but he frankly admits that he has been unable to see any change or attribute in Him. To him *Brahman* has never appeared as giving birth to individuals nor has He appeared as divided into fractions. On this account, and also on the basis of logic and reason, he rejects the doctrine that *Brahman* incarnates or appears as *Avatāra*. There is no doubt that the Upanishads do speak of God multiplying Himself into diverse forms. How these forms are caused has been suitably explained by Swami Yogeshwaranand. According to him when *Prakriti* transforms into various results and reaches the stage of *Citta*, then the Divinity which was already present due to its pervasion in *Prakriti* in its primordial form, comes to be known as individual soul.

During all this process of evolution, nothing new was created nor was any created thing destroyed. The Supreme consciousness or the Absolute *Brahman* was already present in the individual *Citta*. All that we did is that we chose to call that divine presence as '*Jīvātman*' or finite soul. The functions of that living being were guided or directed by the said finite soul, so called by us. This concept resolves all doubts and maintains the immanence or Omnipresence of God. At the same time, it does not require Him to create any separate souls for individuals. Under this concept, the soul is the regional presence of the all pervasive Supreme soul. Swami Yogeshwaranand says that 'no question of bringing in or bringing out anything from anywhere arises under this stipulation.' This makes it abundantly clear and proves beyond any doubt that *Brahman* does not change into multiple forms nor does He stand in need of incarnating on earth. His presence in countless *Cittas* resolves the controversy about plurality of souls because an individual soul is required to perform living functions of a human body which can be performed by the presence of Universal soul in the *Citta* of individual body. He, therefore, concludes that the Supreme Being does neither assume the role of *Iśvara* nor of the subsidiary state of '*Jivas*' for individual human beings. While *Prakriti* transforms from stage to stage, He remains everlastingly unchangeable, ever the same. Discussing Vyasa's commentary on the concept of *Iśvara* mentioned in Yoga Sutra 1-24, *Vijñāna Bhikṣu* says that in order to refute the *Sāmkhya* theory that there is no *Iśvara* other than *Pradhāna, Vyāsa* explains that *Jīvātman* when associated with the adjuncts like *Buddhi* and so on, is called *Puruṣa*–so when these limitations are removed, the *Jīva* itself can be called *Iśvara*. We may say that this comment of *Vyāsa* is a harbinger of the theory that *Jīvātman* is nothing but divinity trapped in *Citta* which is the special feature of the philosophy of Swami Yogeshwaranand. However, the purport of *Vyāsas'* commentary is different from the purport of the theory propounded by Swami Yogeshwaranand. According to *Vyāsas'* the *Jiva,* before liberation, was tainted by the *Kleṣas* and, therefore, cannot be *Iśvara* who is never so tainted. On the other hand, he (Yogeshwaranand) considers the same untainted Divinity as *Jiva* when it is caged in *Prakriti.*

In so far as human beings are concerned, they are governed by the law of *karma* according to which we must reap the corresponding fruit of every action and since one life span is not enough to work out and exhaust all the *karmas,* we take birth after birth. Our actions leave behind their seed impressions in subliminal form which are called *Samskāras*. Under favourable conditions these *Samskāras* sprout and yield fruit in good time. Since in each life we perform more karmas than we exhaust, the balance *Samskāras* are carried to the next birth which the soul must necessarily take to reap their fruit. This is true of *'Jīvātmas'* of all beings because all of them perform actions by mind, deed and speech. But God is on a different footing all together. He is actionless and, therefore, no *karmas* are formed in His case. He is unborn and, therefore, He is beyond life and death. Because He is all pervasive, there is no need for Him to move from one place to another. He does every thing through *Prakriti* by pervading it and, therefore, actions are attributable to *Prakriti* and not to God. Thus, there is no need for God nor does He ever do, to take birth and, hence, the doctrine of incarnation cannot be sustained.

Some say that He incarnates to engage in His Leela (Sport). No reason is given in support of this view. It is difficult to accept the concept of Leela because the manifestation of the vast universe, the creation of sun, moon and stars, the milky way etc are enough to prove His Leela and His might and it is not necessary that He should take human form to show His Leela. Swami

Dayanand Saraswati has mentioned in his famous book, 'Light of Truth' as under:

> "The *Vedas* declare God to be unborn, indivisible, formless etc. and, therefore, not subject to birth and death and the necessity of incarnation. The doctrine of the incarnation of God cannot stand the test of reasoning for He, who pervades the universe like ether, is infinite, invisible, and is not susceptible to pleasure and pain, and cannot be contained in a drop of semen or in the uterus or in a bodily tenement."[33]

Swami Dayanand further says that being all–pervading, He cannot be imagined to exist in any particular object only. He thus emphasizes that true faith consists in believing things what they actually are; believing that fire is fire and water is water. Any contrary view is the very apposite of true faith and this is so in the case of incarnation as well. Swami Yogeshwaranand fully subscribes to these views which are based not only on pure logic but also on his direct perception gained in his intuitive vision in deep *Samādhi*. This will help in discarding certain age–old false beliefs which are fed to credulous humanity, generation after generation.

BRAHMAN – WHETHER WITH FORM AND ATTRIBUTES

One of the *Sutras* of *Bādrayan's Brahman Sutras* say that *Brahman* is only formless to be sure for that is the dominant note of the teachings of Upanishads.[34] Upanishads like *Brhadārankya*, *Chāndogya*, *Mundaka* etc. uphold this view. In the sentences of these Upanishads, *Brahman* has been accepted only as formless. But there are other texts which speak of *Brahman* with form. Commenting on *Brahman Sutras*, with regard to form of *Brahman*, *Śankaracharya* says that so long as they do not lead to some contradiction, their apparent meaning should be accepted. But when they involve some contradiction, the principle to be followed for deciding in favour of one or the other is, that those that have the formless *Brahman* as their main purport, are more authoritative than others which do not have that as their main purport. He, therefore, says that it is according to this that one is driven to the conclusion that *Brahman* is formless and not its opposite, though texts having both the purports are in evidence. In the very next *Sutra, Bādrayan* affirms that *Brahman* can have appearances but such an appearance is like light. The light assumes the form of the figure it contacts and it appears like straight or bent as the case of the figure may be. Similarly *Brahman* also seems to have the forms of earth, planets, stars, etc. when in contact with those things. Thus the scriptures accept the duality of *Brahman* being with and without form and attributes.

Swami Yogeshwaranand disagrees with the scriptures and denies the above mentioned duality of *Brahman*. According to him the two properties are mutually contradictory and, therefore, cannot co–exist. If a thing or an entity has attributes, it will remain in possession of those attributes at all times, whether in the past, present or future. He quotes the example of *Prakriti* (matter) whose inherent qualities are *Sattva*, *Rajas* and *Tamas*. These qualities will ever abide in *Prakriti* and will not depart from it at any time. These qualities existed when *Prakriti* was in its primordial form, persisted during its intermediary evolution and remained with it when *Prakriti* evolved itself into its present form of the vast universe. There was never a time, nor there ever will be, when *Prakriti* is devoid of any of these qualities. Similarly, *Brahman* has always been absolutely and essentially colourless. He was always without attributes and shall remain so at all times. If attributes are assigned to Him, He will be brought to the level of matter which is inert and, consequently, changeable. In that case the absolute consciousness of *Brahman* will be liable to alteration and change. Swami Yogeshwaranand says that the scholars who have given credence to *Brahman* being with and without attributes, have done so without any sound logic. People accept the traditional view about God, without question and allow such views to take firm roots in their minds. Any denial of the traditional views that God is so and so is deemed as blasphemy which may bring untold misery on them. But we should not forget that pleasure and pain result from our own actions and not from assigning attributes to God. We reap the fruits of our actions and it is too trivial a matter for God to watch our actions and assess them for reward or punishment. Being actionless, He does not intervene either in the performance of our actions or with harvesting of their fruits. If He acquires a form He will become changeable like *Prakriti.*

The universe is endless like *Brahman* and therefore, the knowledge with regard to these two, has also to be endless. To attain full knowledge about both is nearly impossible and dependence on the version of sages and seers, based on knowledge gleaned from religious books, is not free from risk. Swami Yogeshwaranand, therefore, states:

> "Accordingly, in regard to a determination of our sense of confidence and satisfaction in the field of these mystic spheres of knowledge, we shall be called upon–on the basis of the '*Sthali Pulaka*' maxim that 'perception is always our surest guide' in determining the sources of our knowledge–to take our firm stand on the limited and perceptive part of our experiences, namely, inductive process of understanding, and then draw rational and logical inferences relating to the extra–perceptive portion of our knowledge,

> that is, through a priori or deductive mode of reasoning."[35]

Sh. J. Krishnamurti who is highly acclaimed as "an artist both in vision and in analysis" recommends that man should be absolutely and unconditionally free to reach beyond himself and beyond material welfare and to achieve that objective, he should seek freedom from the age–old concepts which are spoon–fed to him for centuries by his teachers, his saints and their books.[36] This lends support to the view expressed by Swami Yogeshwaranand who also says that we unnecessarily accept the preachings of our teachers, elders and Gurus as sacrosanct and avoid realising the truth through fair reasoning and sound logic. He, therefore, says that the two qualities of *Brahman,* namely being with and without attributes, are self contradictory and cannot exist simultaneously just as fire and water cannot exist in an object at the same time. Although He is free from any attributes, He is able to constantly generate motion and activity in matter (*Prakriti*) by His mere presence. This motion and activity is induced by Him not only in matter but also in all its modifications. It is because of His pervasion in matter that the creation, maintenance and destruction of the world is attributed to Him. *Brahman* is super-conscious, all pervasive and timeless but these are not His attributes. In fact, these are inherent traits of existence. From these, it is not meant that *Brahman* has many facets because He has only one facet namely His being Super-conscious. All other nomenclatures such as Omnipresence, Omniscience, extreme subtlety etc. are not attributes but mere traits of 'a particular form of existence'. On this point Swami Yogeshwaranand expresses his views as under:

> "Such synonymous terms are indifferently used for our own understanding, or for the assimilation of others in an exposition of His

> inherent characteristics. And, instead of understanding His real form, through ignorant and incorrect attitude of the mind, we misconceive Him because of the different qualifying synonyms used for Him as though He had many facets upon His Unitary Reality. As a result of the foregoing argument, the Supreme Being can be justifiably determined as an Absolutely Colourless BEING."[37]

God pervades *Prakriti* fully and thoroughly–within and without. There is no place in *Prakriti* where God is not present, whether *Prakriti* is in its gross form or subtle form. It is by His presence and prompting that *Prakriti* engages itself in creation. *Brahman* is not required to nor does He involve Himself in the process of creation. However, by mistaken belief people consider *Brahman* as the creator, maintainer and destroyer of the creation. The whole process of creation and destruction is carried on by *Prakriti* alone. *Prakriti* is composite by nature, being constituted of its three *Gunas,* namely *Sattva, Rajas* and *Tamas* and, therefore, it is liable to change. By its evolution from its ab–original stage, it goes on changing and passes from various stages till it assumes the grossest form of the world as is visible to us. As it changes, it manifests many qualities which we superimpose on *Brahman,* in our ignorance.

Brahman remains without attributes at all times and in all circumstances. It is only *Prakriti* which undergoes constant change. *Prakriti* comprises of three *Gunas* namely *Sattva, Rajas* and *Tamas* and every transformation of *Prakriti* invariable possesses all these three *Gunas* because the qualities of the cause are inherited by the effect which is affirmed by *Satkāryavāda* of *Sāmkhya*. If God had transformed in the manner of *Prakriti,* then His qualities must also have been reflected in the resultant effects. Because God is Supreme Conscious Being, his product must also be conscious. But we don't see any conscious effect of God's mutation. The first crop of God becomes the last crop also because we do not see any further creation of conscious species by individual souls. God can never transform or else He will become like *Prakriti* only. By this pervasion, if God prompts *Prakriti* to create, then who will prompt God to create? And if God becomes the material cause, then there will be no one to inspire *Prakriti*. If the conscious being like God and inert matter like *Prakriti*, both become the material cause of things and objects, both will be similar and liable to change. In the process of evolution, *Prakriti* commences its transformation from the invisible form of *Alinga Prakriti*, moves to *Mahat*, then at some stage, it attains the status of five great elements. Evolving further it creates the earth the living beings etc. and finally it destroys the entire creation and returns to its original, invisible form of *Alinga Prakriti.* If God mutates like *Prakriti,* He should also return to His original state after reaching the culmination of His transformation. But we do not see this happening in the case of God. Many such faults will creep in if we consider God as the material cause of things. We save all this bother for God if we do not assign any attributes to Him. Thus, God has always been changeless, actionless, without attributes, invisible and ever colourless but, none the less, the Lord of all creation.

Swami Yogeshwaranand has tried to ascertain, in his deep contemplation in super-conscious state, whether God is possessed of any qualities and what he realised is extracted below:

> "Depending on our own experience, we may modestly aver that *Brahman* is responsible only for the creation of motion and successive activity in Matter or lifeless '*Prakriti*'. Matter is inert. In a lifeless substance, there is no automatic, or self–born, urge of doing anything, or movement, or speed, unless it comes in contact with, and is

> charged by, another conscious object so that this Eternal conscious contact of the Efficient Principle with matter should always be existent in the world. Real and Ultimate Existence, in fact, is shared only by two Entities of Inert and Conscious nature, respectively. The Inert is prone to goaded activity; while the Conscious is completely without the self–propagatory propensity to action. Because this conscious Entity is intransigently Attributeless, It remains everlastingly Colourless and absolutely Free from any discrepancy. '*Prakriti*', or Matter, due to the Other's incessant conjunction and itself being a mutable entity, gets charged with activity and carries on the entire course of productivity through its different processes. And, so, the Triple Action of Creation, Sustenance, and Disintegration goes on in its due and orderly procedure. For a whole longtime without beginning, this endless process of the Eternal Stream has been going on, and shall continue to go on forever. This leads the argument to its inevitable conclusion that the Supreme Being or *Brahman* is altogether Flawlessly Without Attributes."[38]

When we consider *Brahman* as devoid of any attributes, an argument can be advanced that, if we do not conceive of Him as possessed of attributes, the multiplicity of results, taking place in matter as a result of His prompting or inspiration, should be similar and should not bear difference of any sorts. Our answer is that the multiplicity of results taking place in matter, are caused by transformation which is a native trait of *Prakriti*. A transformation implies change of an earlier position to the present position or a change from cause to the effect. If such a transformation did not occur, how could one distinguish between the cause and the effect? Take the case of earth. We make a variety of objects from the ores and minerals as well as other material taken from earth. If the objects thus produced are not different from their causes, how could we say that a change has taken place giving rise to the product or the effect. But all these changes are affected only in *Prakriti*. A similar change does not take place in God who is, therefore, free from all attributes.

The qualities present in the cause are transferred to the effect. If some quality is not possessed by the cause, it cannot be passed on to its effect. We generally observe in the world that the degree of knowledge, intelligence and skill, possessed by a man, is visible in the objects made by him. If this is so, then it is logical to expect that the innumerous objects of the world, which are supposed to have been created by God, should manifest extreme intelligence because God is supposed to have the highest degree of intelligence and knowledge. In this sense of the matter, there is no doubt that knowledge possessed by God is far higher than that of man. Man's knowledge is always waxing and waning and is liable to change but intelligence of God remains firm and does not change at all. The universe is not only massive but intelligent too which could not have been created by millions of individuals by pooling together their effort and intelligence. The same is the case with earth, sun, moon and stars and other heavenly bodies which are believed to have been created by God and which manifest His extra ordinary skill and prowess. These creations are perfect in all respects and one does not come across any defect or shortcoming in these creations. On the other hand we see many shortcomings in things which are made by man. It, therefore, proves that man, the cause of these objects, is also imperfect and wanting in many respects. Gods' works have no defects or failings. Let us look at the unique factor in respect of God that is His Omnipresence and Omniscience. It is His Omnipresence which is responsible for transformation in *Prakriti* from stage to stage. It has nothing to do with His attributes or with His being an active agency in creation. If some shortcomings are observed in the works of God, such as failure of rains or floods, earthquake, pestilence or epidemics, these are really not divine lapses. All these are caused by the five gross elements and, therefore, these elements alone are responsible for such maladies. There are material reasons for all these happenings. Swami Yogeshwaranand says that in such happenings, the elements go their own ways overstepping their co-ordinated functions. God has no role to play in this. No doubt, there is in existence, the close proximity of God with the material elements which keeps the elements ever engaged in action but He is not involved with *Prakriti* beyond that. He is not in need of any attributes because if He had attributes, He would be bound like individual soul and would become finite. For these reasons, Swami Yogeshwaranand has come to the conclusion that *Brahman,* who is the Supreme Being, is absolutely without attributes.

By proclaiming God as without attributes, Swami Yogeshwaranand has introduced certain changes in the concept of *Brahman* which has prevailed so far, and by doing so, he has definitely enriched the spiritual philosophy. This concept spells a marked improvement over the *Sāmkhya* philosophy by limiting the role of *Brahman* to only pervasion in *Prakriti* to energise it and cause its evolution.

ABODE OF BRAHMAN

The doctrine that has been taken for discussion here is that *Brahman* is enthroned in heaven from where He governs the world. According to this doctrine, God is believed to be living in heaven from where He rules the world. The idea of heaven being His abode creates problems and gives rise to many doubts which need to be resolved. First of all if He is confined to a particular region, He would be limited and finite and in that case, being restricted to a 'specific place', He would not be able to govern the vast universe. There are innumerous heavenly bodies and only an all–pervading entity can have access to all these bodies to govern them properly. For this reason, God's confinement to a particular region is unconceivable. If He is confined to heaven, then one will like to enquire, whether He has a body like ours. If so, He will be similarly subject to pleasure and pain, knowledge and ignorance, righteous and unrighteous and good and evil? Is His body also made of five *Mahabhutas* like our body or is it produced by some other elements? One would like to know the material cause of His body. Another question that needs to be answered is whether there is a ground like our earth on which He lives or whether He floats in the firmament of the sky. If He stays in the sky, He must be having a particular support to live high up in the ethereal abode. Then to manage the world, while sitting in the aforesaid secluded area, He will need proper manpower and infrastructure. He will need a team of various types of officers of appropriate categories to implement His orders and instructions to be able to govern this vast universe. But we do not find any such thing happening in the sky. Presuming that the said system is functioning unobserved by us, and it will come to our observation at some time or the other, then what is the difference between heaven and the world of ours? This does not respond well to the idea of God residing in the heaven and administering this massive universe from there. Reason does not approve of this concept and, therefore, it seems to be unintelligible.

Upanishads do mention about the existence of heaven but these do not mention about its exact location. It is also not said, how far above the earth, this heaven is located nor is it mentioned whether a man enters the said heaven in the same material body or some other body which is to be acquired to gain access to it. If the heaven is a solid mass like earth, it must have an axis to rotate around and must have some characteristics of its own. A question also may be asked whether God lives there alone or with His subjects and what are the special objects found there. Is there a sky like ours over the heaven and also does God move about in heaven or keeps sitting at one place? These and many other related questions come to every thinking being who wants a logical and satisfactory explanation.

Swami Yogeshwaranand who has endeavoured to verify the truth of every spiritual belief, in the super–conscious state of deep *Samādhi*, has perceived no such characteristics about God. He did not notice the entity called God, sitting in a fixed place called heaven and ruling His enormous creation from there. He has also not observed any special favours being showered on men, saints, incarnations in heaven, which are denied to men in our world. His observations on this subject are as under:

> "By now, my own devotional practices have been carried on for quite many long years; but I have not come across any vision or experience of a heavenly '*svarga*', as the abode of God, wherefrom He may have been found to direct His control and governance of this world or any other; or where He might have established Himself as a ruler. Nor does it appear that men, gods, saints, prophets, or incarnations, who deserve to go there, may be blessed with special delicacies of joy or happiness belonging to that blessed Divine Paradise (*svarga*), which might exclusively be its privilege of distinction and may not be found on earth here. During these constructive years of my '*Sadhana*', I have not been able to know a

> Supreme Being, who, while staying in one particular region may be controlling all other regions of the Universe. Intuitive experience does not corroborate God's vision in one form in this world, and of quite another in the paradise. Were it so that God lived in certain region of His own liking, it might be possible to think of a special Paradise for him. In the Universe, there is no end to different heavenly bodies. All these bodies should have their own respective Gods. The stipulation of 'as many Gods, as many bodies' will surely turn Paradise into one of the worlds having its God like this Earth having its own. On the Earthly Globe also there are many countries, where their respective rulers, monarchs, or parliaments control and manage their affairs. Amongst all these states, controversies, conflicts, enmity and friendship go on taking shapes, as usual. Amongst all these multiple paradises also similar conflicts, strifes, controversies, enmity and friendship will find ample room for their natural growth. Such a paradise, too, will not be very much different from our own world on the surface of the Earth."[39]

When asked that if there is no such thing as heaven or paradise, then it will be fruitless to do deeds for attainment of the said heaven, Swami Yogeshwaranand explains that the fruits of good actions, performed in accordance with the scriptures, are never lost. But such fruits are not realised in the type of heaven visualised by sages and seers. Since the Supreme Being is all–pervasive, there is no need to seek Him in an unknown region called heaven when we can find Him here on earth itself. We should remember that being Omnipresent, *Brahman* is pervasive everywhere and, therefore, He can be realised here on earth. In such a case, it is idle to seek an imaginary region, called heaven, to reap the fruits of good and noble deeds.

There are some special experiences termed as divine experiences. The mystics refer frequently to such experiences. These are the experiences which one gains in the subtle world while enjoying subtle elements. Swami Yogeshwaranand also mentions that, out of *Rajas* predominating *Tanmantras,* are created subtle objects which offer enjoyment to subtle bodies.[40] Granted that certain divine experiences are gained when subtle body enjoys subtle objects, yet it is not necessary, for reasons already stated, to gain these experiences in the so called heaven. Such experiences arise even in this world but one can realise these experiences by intuitive vision. It is, therefore, not possible to have these experiences except in *Samādhi*. In the subtle body are present the subtle objects, the *Pancatanmātras* as well as God owing to His all–pervasiveness. If that is so, then there is no reason why we cannot enjoy the said super–natural experiences even in our own world. All these ingredients are here which are necessary for causing a divine experience. It is, therefore, unnecessary to search an unseen and unexperienced heaven to reap the fruits of noble deeds.

It is also not necessary to go to heaven to realise *Brahman* because by His quality of all pervasiveness, He is present everywhere, here on earth, as well as in the so called heaven. It is not that He will bless us only in heaven. He can do so here as He is present very much on earth. For this reason, there is no need to go to any other region after emancipation. Swami Yogeshwaranand does not deny the existence of heaven in so many words. All that he says is that in his long practice of meditation, he has not realised God sitting in a separate area called heaven. However, those who want to seek God in heaven, may do so of their own choice but they will find God the same in heaven as on earth. There is a saying worth following that when honey is available next to our house, why go all the way to a distant hill for the same purpose.[41] *Brahman* pervades *Prakriti*, thereby intelligently energising it to create. It is by His mere presence in its womb that *Prakriti* has produced this wonderful universe which baffles imagination. First of all the earth itself is a unique creation which provides substratum to the rest of creation comprising of all sentient and insentient things, such as living beings, hills and dales, flora and fauna etc. Then there are numberless heavenly bodies which function skillfully and flawlessly. There are heavenly bodies which revolve around their own axis and also around other bodies in a fixed orbit. The sun rises under a prescribed pattern and sets, appears and disappears under a divine law. There has been not a single instance of their colliding with one another. This flawless working of the cosmic system is due to the presence of *Brahman* in *Prakriti* and due to his prompting. Millions of human beings together cannot create even one mountain, let alone the whole universe. He is the Supreme Being and He alone can undertake such mighty tasks of massive dimensions. If such be His vastness, prowess and acumen, how can man who is like a drop in the ocean, know fully about God. It is because of God's presence in matter that every thing functions under a pre–determined system and with perfect harmony. The point, that is projected here, is that when the Supreme Being, who is the greatest of all and due to whose Omnipresence the solar and other systems function with supreme efficiency, it is absolutely unnecessary for us to search Him elsewhere or seek His company in heaven. God does not move from one place to another nor does He need to make any efforts to fulfil any objective. His all pervasiveness takes care of all actions of *Prakriti* which go on endlessly. Human systems might some time fail or succumb to some flaw, but God's system remains ever perfect and free from any lacuna of any kind.

The job of soul is to lend motion and activity to the body it occupies. Similarly the Supreme Being, gives movement and action to the whole universe.

How do we know that the aforesaid conscious entities cause motion and activity in their respective domains *viz.* human body for the soul and the universe for God? The answer is that it is only in the presence of soul that the body functions. If we do not believe in the existence of soul, then a living body and a dead body should be the same. But it is not so. In the same way, the heavenly bodies and this beautiful world is active because of the prevalence of the Supreme Spirit. Without the presence of the Universal Spirit, every activity in the universe will come to a dead stop. God is the efficient cause of the world and it is due to His intelligence, imparted to the objects of the world, that the world order is functioning flawlessly. God's contact with *Prakriti* is eternal and God and *Prakriti,* being the efficient and material causes respectively, the totality of the creation performs its functions in perfect order. And this function will go on forever. Swami Yogeshwaranand accords this orderly working of the universe to the Omnipresence of God for if we deem Him as finite, there was always a possibility of an imperfect disposition or some sort of distortion in the functioning of cosmos. He, therefore, says:

> "The impact of this Divine Order, as is felt here on earth, is exactly the same that may be found in the Paradise or Heaven itself, because it is everywhere the same. Hence, without the least ambiguity on our part, it may, conclusively, be affirmed that God's Orderly Array of the Universe obtains identically the same everywhere; in all countries, and the diverse spheres of its vast expanse. It is only in case of planning and organisation by men who are ever limited and

> imperfect in their knowledge that lacunas are left, and the resultant disturbances arise. It is certain that in the Providence and Disposition of a Perfect and All–Knowing Supreme Being no Lapse or retraction would ever be possible."[42]

The concept of heaven is more relevant for *Mimāmsa* than for any other school because the highest good in *Mimâmsa* conception, is the attainment of heaven. And heaven is attained by performing Vedic rituals. He who performs rituals, not for any personal motive but as a duty enjoined by the *Vedas*, gets entitled to a place in heaven where he abides till the fruits of such good *Karmas* are exhausted. The soul, according to *Mimāmsa*, is an eternal, infinite substance which is related to a material body and which survives death to be able to reap the consequences of its actions as prescribed by the *Vedas*. *Mimāmsa* believes in the theory of potential energy, which implies that there is a power in every cause. An important application of the theory of potency is to suggest a solution to the problem as to how a sacrifice performed now, bears fruit after the current life, in heaven when the action has ceased. The explanation given by *Mimāmsa* is that the a ritual performed here, generates in soul of the performer an unperceived potency called *Apurva*, which remains in the soul and bears fruit under favourable circumstances. However, while *Mimāmsa* recommends the performance of ritualistic sacrifices for securing a place in heaven, it does not give any intelligible description, of heaven. The mention of heaven is more detailed in *Purānas* than in any of the six orthodox systems of Indian Philosophy. But *Purānas* are mere historical books as these record such events as a dialogue between sage *Yajnavalkaya*, and many other such dialogues. *Swami Dayanand Saraswati*, the greatest follower of *Vedas*, thoroughly condemns the study of *Purānas.*[43] He says that there may be some good points in *Purānas* in as much as they help in understanding the true meanings of *Veda Mantras,* but, otherwise, they are not spiritual texts like Upanishads and intend to mislead the people in order to project the image of the concerned deity.

We have already mentioned that even to realise *Brahman,* one does not have to proceed to some other region because *Brahman* is everywhere, being Omnipresent. Therefore, it is entirely possible to enjoy His bliss even here in this world. Thus, viewed from any angle or based on any valid argument, the existence of heaven of God, or the so called paradise, belies any rational proof and is, therefore, untenable. This breaks the myth of a cherished abode called heaven where the souls are supposed to live after emancipation and enjoy the bliss of *Brahman.* This again is an exceptional contribution to philosophy, made by Swami Yogeshwaranand.

PRAYERS, WORSHIP AND DEVOTION

Worship of God comprises glorification of Him, prayer to Him and communion with Him. Glorification is of two types, namely positive and negative. We glorify Him positively when we extol Him for possessing positive qualities as in *Rig Veda Mantra* XXX, 8, in which it is said that the Supreme Being Overspreads all; He is all powerful, Pure, Omniscient, Immortal and Uncreated etc. Negative glorification consists in praising God as free from undesirable qualities like passion, malice and also as being never embodied, impartible, and free from pleasure and pain and from ignorance etc. It is said, that the objective of glorification is to reform one's nature, attributes and character, in accordance with the nature, attributes and character of God. If God is just and merciful, we should also acquire these traits and that will serve the objective of glorification. In pursuance of the version of *Yajur Veda Mantras* (XX–9 XXX–14), a prayer is to be addressed to God to "bestow wisdom on us for which the sages and yogis have prayed, be merciful and shed that light in our heart, endow us with unfailing energy, strength and power; you are not moved either by praise or censure, so make us like that." There is no dearth of *Mantras* in the *Vedas* in which prayers have been addressed to God to bestow on us all good things of life. Like glorification, prayer is also said to be positive or negative according as the deity is looked upon as possessed of good traits or as free from bad traits. Communion is *Upāsanā* which literally means to come close to. It means that we should do all that is required to be done in order to come close to God by the practice of yoga. In Sutras 30-32 of *Sādhnapada*, Mahrishi *Patāñjali* lays emphasis on *Yamas* and *Niyamas*, the first two limbs of his *Aṣṭānga Yoga*. In pursuance of this, Swami Dayanand Saraswati has laid great emphasis on the discipline provided in *Yamas* and *Niyamas,* as absolutely necessary for *Upāsanā*.[44] *Upāsanā* is positive when God is contemplated as possessed of positive traits such as Omnipresence, Omniscience etc. and it is negative when he is contemplated as free from negative traits as malice, hatred, ill–will etc. *Upāsanā* is believed to rid a person of all impurities, dualities, grief and sorrow. By coming close to God one gets the type of relief which one gets by coming close to fire when he is shivering with cold. For the above reasons, the sages recommend that we should worship God which means we should praise Him, pray to Him and commune with Him.

As against what is stated above, Swami Yogeshwaranand says that God is totally indifferent to praise and censure and, therefore, there is no question of his being pleased or displeased through devotion or worship.[45] He is not subject to any instinctive infirmities and is far above pleasure and pain and also beyond all human emotions. If these emotions are attributed to Him, He will have to come down to the level of human beings.

In fact all such attributes pertain to *Citta* which is a product of matter. God is beyond matter and is a Super-Conscious Being who is not embodied, has no limbs, is eternal and everlasting. Since praise and censure do not effect Him, He is not moved by worship or devotion. We sing His praises because we super–impose on Him certain attributes which really don't belong to Him, but He remains unimpressed by it. However, we have observed in our personal experience that he rewards our prayers when prayers are honestly made. Swami Yogeshwaranand does not agree that God ever grants or denies if any prayer is made to him for bestowal of some benefit or for elimination of some suffering. According to him, apparent fulfillment of a prayer is the result of a change in our own fundamental disposition and our psychic attitude. What has come about is not the result of worship of God but the fruit of our own change of attitude. God has nothing to do with the success or failure of our endeavour which is always based on the fruits of our *Karmas*. Swami Yogeshwaranand gives his own explanation of the outcome of worship and of our personal effort. He says:

> "We offer Him our worship and our act of worshipping Him bears (must bear) its inevitable fruit. Now, that is nothing but the result of our action that we perform in worshipping the Almighty; not that His Pleasure has brought us something as His casual charity and beneficence. He never says to anybody, 'offer me your worship and adoration, and I'll be pleased to grant you gift and boons.' In fact, it purely relates to our own minds that we fill them with pious thoughts of worship and experience a becalming shadow of peace therein. In the light of our cherished values or ideology and habitually developed personal virtues, whatever acts we perform in life are always done according to our respective

> inclinations. With a view to making these acts proper and thrive, we bring to bear upon them the necessary force of due situation, suitability of time and occasion, means and appropriate material. Then those well-regulated and disciplined acts of ours become capable of yielding the desired and expected results. Although we are pleased to say that it is the good return of our worship and devotion and that God has been kind and Munificent in rewarding our labours, yet, the bare truth is that the quality and substance of the effort or action governs the fruit in the offing primarily and solely in direct proportion to itself."[46]

That God answers the prayers, bestows favours or dispenses the fruits of actions, are traditional views, held from times immemorial and handed over to us generation after generation. No proof, however, is available that He does so. The Supreme Being is actionless, without limbs and free from human emotions like greed and avarice, pleasure and pain, praise and condemnation etc. Such an entity can be neither pleased nor displeased by any means. Hence, it cannot be said that He grants our prayers and supplications. In our own wisdom, being imbued with his tremendous might and Omnipotence, we ascribe such qualities and attributes which really don't belong to him. It is purely due to our fondness for Him. It is again due to our fondness for Him that we instal an idol made of stone, put faith in it, treat it as God and address our prayers to that idol. Now the stone is made of matter and is inert and lifeless. So also is the idol. Such an idol cannot grant any favours or answer our prayers, howsoever we may cry or prostrate before it. The fact, however, is that people still make offerings to it and beg for fulfillment of their desires. Their attitude towards God is similar. The truth of the matter is that neither the stone idol nor the Supreme Being gave anything to anybody but there is a human tendency based on erroneous perception, to believe that God and the stone idol do have the power to bestow favours or dispense the fruits of our actions. Swami Yogeshwaranand has his special views on this subject. He says that worship does bring reward to the devotee but achievement is essentially the fruit of devotee's own personal effort. He emphasizes that such an achievement, or failure thereof, is nothing but a pure return of the fruit of action resulting from human industry. It is sheer ignorance to assign the achievement to the grace and benevolence of God who did not play any role at all in the whole process.

We do experience in life that saints and sages, who worship God over a time, do acquire the qualities similar to those of God. On this basis, can one not say that worship and devotion do have desirable influence on the devotee, atleast for some time when the mind is withdrawn from sense objects? In this connection, it may be said that the scriptures prescribe that we should develop a spirit of devotion to God in accordance with the following attitude and meaning:

1. God is impeccably pure, I should also be pure;
2. As He is stainlessly free from all types of influences; I too should remain unaffected by my surroundings;
3. As He is unattached, so I too should remain unattached to gross, subtle and causal bodies;
4. As God is actionless, I should also surrender fruits of all my actions to Him;
5. As God is above all sense enjoyments, I too should have dispassion towards such enjoyments;

If one engages oneself in devotion with the above and other similar ennobling sentiments, one will naturally reap the fruits of one's actions which accord with his pious nature. It is exactly as per the age old adage which says, "as you sow, so shall you reap". It is futile to attribute any part of the result of one's own action to God who has done nothing in this case. Similar is the case of *Dhyāna* or meditation. Since God has neither form, shape or any other marks of identification, it is not possible to perceive Him in *Dhyāna* (meditation). Even by the sharpest vision in meditation, no one can visualise Him by an intuitive eye. When *Dhārna* is intensified, a state arises when one is aware neither of time nor space nor causation. He is aware only of the object of meditation and nothing else. In *Patāñjali Sutras* meditation has been defined in *Pada* 3 *Sutra*–1, according to which the mind that is fixed on the object of meditation should not falter even for a moment and should continue its identity with the object in one continuous stream.[47] Yoga philosophy terms this continuity of flow as meditation. *Sāmkhya* philosophy defines meditation almost similarly. According to this philosophy, when mind is pure and free from any *Vritti's* and is concentrated only on the object of meditation, it is said to be in the state of meditation. Even if we enter upon such a state of meditation, the success is to be ascribed to one's own persistent effort. A continued flow of concentration of mind in meditation, will yield a prolonged experience of peace and harmony. This experience is the result of the man's own effort in which he concentrated his mind in meditation. God is neither responsible for bringing about the state of meditation nor was any vision of God available in that state, which gave so much of peace and bliss to the practitioner. On the basis of above discussions, it can be clearly said that worship of or meditation on God does not bring any rewards from God though fruits of one's personal effort can certainly be realised in accordance with the law of *Karma*.

This brings us to a very peculiar situation. If devotion and meditation are unable to yield any significant advantage for the aspirant, then why should one engage in these wasteful practices? Swami Yogeshwaranand recommends that in spite of what is stated above, one must persevere with the duties cast on him by his *Ashrama* (*Brahmacarya, Grahasta* etc.) and by his *Varuna* (*Brahmana, Kshatriya* etc.) because a faithful performance of such duties acts as a means to inculcate piety, righteousness, dharma etc. Respect for these actions has already been ingrained in our psyche through tradition and, therefore, such noble deeds will, indeed, give us bliss and happiness. "*Anukulam Vedaniyam Sukham*" is a well known aphorism which means that things which accord with your nature always bring joy and happiness. For this reason, all these actions which are enjoined upon us to perform according to our *Ashrama* or *Varuna,* will surely become the source of peace and happiness. Therefore, Swami Yogeshwaranand says:

> "You should, therefore, discharge and gladly perform all the allotted responsibilities and obligations of the place you occupy in your life and the society you belong to. To be sure, they will be the vehicles of your well-being and the happiness of your life. Nobody can escape doing things in life, whether he happens to be a wise sage or a mere bundle of clotted nonsense. Without resorting to action, life itself will become impossible. When actions are indispensable and must be done, why not, then, do the best of them?"[48]

If worship of God is purposeless, then is there any use in chanting *Veda Mantras* like *Gayatri* and the like? Swami Yogeshwaranand says that chanting of *Mantras* is not a wasteful activity because a *Mantra–Jāpa* acts like a whetstone to sharpen the mind (*Manas*) and intellect (*Buddhi*). As a result of repeated chanting of *Mantras,* intellect becomes sharper like a razor which is stropped or whetted on a stone. The experience shows that the practice of *Mantra–Jāpa* stops the distortion caused in the mind by the memories of uncharitable past events and also prevents the mind from wreckless waxing and waning. While chanting the *Mantra*, mind gets fixed on the *Mantra* and becomes more amenable to personal control. It is through *Mantra* that one attains to the highest stage of *Samādhi* in which one is able, by the sharp intuitive vision, to distinguish between truth and non–truth. These and many such benefits accrue from the *Mantra–Jāpa* but, in no case, can one perceive God either through chanting of *Mantrās* or in the firm state of *Samādhi* or accredit Him with these attainments. It is a pure and simple result of our own industry through which we carried on persistent devotion, meditation and *Mantra–Jāpa*. Since man enjoys freedom of action, he is also responsible for the fruits of his actions which are brought about by the combination of certain factors such as personal effort, situation, opportunity, determination and the instrumental material necessary to accomplish the desired result. Once we do a deed we have to bear its consequences ourselves. Award of the fruit is not dependent on the will of God. If God was to decide and award the reward and punishment for our actions, then we could not be personally held responsible for our own deeds. In such situations, God will become answerable for our actions. We can, thus, conclude that a man is free throughout his life to do things and reap the corresponding fruits and in the whole process God remains unconcerned and un-involved.

Presuming that worship and devotion to God does bring the fulfillment of our desires, then why does it happen quite often in our lives that in spite of doing good and noble deeds, a man suffers from a chain of miseries? All his prayers, his worship of God and his total devotion and dedication to Him, prove to be of no avail. The answer to this question is that the deeds, whether good or bad, do not bear immediate fruits. The seeds of *karmas* (actions) remain embedded in the *Citta* till some stimulus arises which prompts the seed to sprout and bear fruit in good time. It is, therefore, not necessary that our good or bad deeds, should yield immediate results. Some actions give rise to the result immediately, some after some time and some others in a later birth or births. If I scold a person and he slaps me, the action has borne fruit immediately. In a second case, I appeared for the examination now but the result will arrive after two months which means that the action will bear fruits after some time. In yet another case, a man commits murder but goes scot free for want of proper evidence. He will be punished in a latter birth or births. As already mentioned in an earlier chapter, the *Karmās* bear fruit only under required conditions and, till all the requisite circumstances have appeared, the action will remain fruitless. The fruit may appear late but no action goes without fructifying. Hence, a delayed fruit does not at all mean that the action has become barren and incapable of yielding the fruit. Activity arises due to the association of the soul with the body and, accordingly, we ceaselessly perform actions through out our life. If this is so, then wisdom demands that we should do good deeds so that we obtain pleasure as a result of such actions. As long as the soul abides in the body, the desire to do things remains alive. The duality of desire and aversion lasts till life. Birth and death are also caused by desires. It is, therefore, evident that negation of desire is not possible except at the time of *Pralaya* when the organs of mind, intellect, ego and *Citta*, merge in their causes and there is neither body, nor senses nor objects to give rise to desires. Desire does not leave anybody, be he a commoner or a self–realised man. The urges like thirst and hunger, movement and rest and evacuation of excreta etc. are common to both. Wishing and desiring is a natural attribute of the *Antahkarna*. Even aspiring for knowledge of truth and detachment from sense objects, entails desire. Just as *Samskāras* of *karmas* cannot be totally eliminated, the desires also cannot be totally eradicated or banished from *Antahkarana*. In the matter of desires, a yogi may be compared to a patient who being ill, has no appetite for food and for other enjoyments of life. A yogi too does not find any attraction towards the sense objects and remains detached from the world. The difference lies in the fact that a yogi is drawn away from the enjoyments of the world by cultivating the truth bearing knowledge of the futility of such enjoyment, as it causes mental agitation which distracts him from *Samādhi*, while the patient is compelled by his physical debility and by the malfunctioning of his organs of enjoyment. There is a voluntary disbandonment on the part of the yogi, while the sick man is compelled by his physical failure. If one is unable to discard trivial desires like hunger and thirst etc, it is only befitting that one should perform the types of actions which are ordained by the scriptures. Gita says that every man should regularly perform *Yajna* and sacrifices, share with others the highest gifts earned by him and must continually promote his enquiry into the truth with a spirit of renunciation. It is, therefore, necessary and enjoined on every human being to pursue the aforesaid vows. And these observances should not be meant only for our own welfare but for the good of others as well. Swami Yogeshwaranand has expressed his own views on the subject as under:

> "So long as life is there, the body has to be supported with action. And, in doing things, even the enlightened self realised man cannot be an exception to having some slight desire or inclination, at least, if not a keen one; for without it no action is ever possible. The body itself is an effect and metamorphic result of perversity of mind; as such, even during the period of 'Jivan–Mukti' or the yogi's state of blessed care–freeness

> from the entanglements of life, some vestiges of that causal perversity do linger on."[49]

In the scriptures, desire has been viewed as mental perversion (*Mahopanishad* 4-1-16) and the Yoga system corroborates it. It says that the perversity of mind (*Avidya*) plays the chief role in the soul's contact with the objects of the world which contact must be stoutly discarded.[50] As long as the body remains in touch with soul which means that as long as the three bodies namely gross, subtle and causal bodies are alive, the suspension of desires and their resulting woes is not possible. It is only during the final disintegration of the world that dissociation of these bodies takes place and one gets rid of the woes caused by desires. It implies with sound logic that *Mokṣa* is possible only during the period of doom and not at any other time. This course of discussions leads us to the obvious conclusion that acts and duties ordained by the scriptures must be performed for their own sake and not for appeasement of God and that we must carry, on during the tenure of life, all such acts dispassionately and without attachment to the fruits till the time of doom, when *Mokṣa* will materialise on its own.

Through imparting instructions on worship, meditation and adoration of God, Swami Yogeshwaranand has brought in an entirely new concept of this philosophy. He says that worship etc. is necessary but it does not appease God because He is impervious to praise or censure. Worship brings fruits to the practitioner in the form of peace, bliss and contentment, in pursuance of the law of *karma* according to which good karmas give happiness and bad *Karmās* give pain.

The view of Swami Yogeshwaranand that worship of God bears fruits only in the form of bestowing peace, bliss and contentment, goes against not only the age–old belief in God but also against the verdict of *Vedas*. *Rig Veda* (x,48) says, "1,o men, lived before the whole universe came into being. I am the giver of wealth. Let all men look to me alone as children do to their parents," Elsewhere in the same *Mantra* 48(5), it is said:

> "I am God Almighty, I am the Light of the world like the sun. Neither defeat, nor death, can ever approach me. I am the controller of the universe, know me alone as the Creator of all. Strive ye diligently for the acquisition of power and wealth such (as true knowledge). Ask ye of me. May ye never lose my friendship. I give true knowledge, which is real wealth, unto men who are truthful. I am the revealer of *Vedas* that I advance the knowledge of all. I am the prompter of the good and true. I reward those who devote themselves to the good of humanity. I am the cause, I am the support of all that exists in this universe. May ye never turn away from me. May ye never accept another God in my place, nor worship him."

The above and many more *Mantras* in *Rig Veda* and *Yajur Veda* glorify God as giver of every thing. In *Rig Veda Mantra* (VIII 79-2) it is said as under:

"He clothes all that is naked ;

He doctors all that is sick;

Through Him the blind man sees, the cripple

Goes about."

Here the Divine benevolence is described in the above manner which is not compatible with what Swami Yogeshwaranand says. We find many metaphors in Vedas such as "instruct me as parents instruct the son," or "stimulate our mental power" or "send us a good and happy mind". Again there is a prayer in Rig Veda (82-5:y) which says, "O God, send far away all evil: send us what is good." The *Vedic* seers have spoken of God as all–

powerful who makes men what they are and who, out of His grace, gives to those who ask. He is considered as brightener of mind, forgiver of sins, inspirer and purifier. In this view of God, as propounded by the Vedas, it is difficult to concede what Swami Yogeshwaranand says about worship of God. He says that God is indifferent to both worship and insult and that pleasure and pain result only from the *karmas* and are not awarded by God. The doubt arising from this version about God, has been clarified to some extent by Swami Dayanand Saraswati who says in his famous book *Satyartha Prakaṣa* (Light of Truth) as under:

> "*Stuti* (Glorification) consists in praising Divine attributes and powers or in hearing them being praised, with the view to fix them in our mind and realise their meaning. Among other things it inspires us with love towards God".

"*Prarthana* (Prayer) is praying to God, after one has done his utmost, for the gift of highest knowledge and similar (other blessings) which result from union with Him. It creates humility, etc (in the mind of devotee)".

" *Upasana* (Communion) consits in conforming ourselves, as far as possible, in purity and holiness to the Divine Spirit, and in feeling the presence of the Deity in our heart by the realisation of His All–pervading nature through the practice of Yoga which enables one to have direct cognition of God. *Upasana* serves to extend the bounds of our knowledge"

"*Sagun Stuti* consists in praising God as possessed of specific attributes which are inherent in Him; while *Nirgun Stuti* consists in praising God as devoid of attributes which are foreign to His nature".

"*Sagun Prarthana* consists in praying to God for the attainment of virtuous qualities; while *Nirgun Prarthana* consists in imploring the Deity to rid us of all our faults".

"*Sagun Upasana* consists in resigning oneself to God and His will realizing Him as possessed of attributes that are in harmony with His nature; while *Nirgun Upasana* consists in resigning oneself to God and his will, realising Him as devoid of attributes that are foreign to his nature."[51]

From the above, one may draw a reasonable conclusion that what is meant by the Omnipotence of God is that He can do His job of creation of the universe without any external assistance. Similarly He bestows all boons on human beings, if they worship Him, in order to acquire all noble attributes of God such as mercy, compassion, charity, knowledge, wisdom etc., and inculcate all that is good so that they perform only good deeds which bring fruits in the form of happiness by way of peace, bliss and contentment. It seems that Swami Yogeshwaranand has tried to approach the subject of prayer and worship from the point of view of Swami Dayanand who, even otherwise, had cast tremendous influence on him.

REFERENCES

(1) Essential Colourlessness of the Absolute (p. 3-4)
(2) *नास्ति सांख्यसमं ज्ञानं नास्ति योगसमं बल्म!*
(Mahabharata Śantiparva – 304.2)
(3) Yoga Sutra (1-23)
(4) Chāndogya Upanishad (III-14-1)
(5) Essential Colourlessness of the Absolute (p. 9)
(6) Vaiśeṣika Darśana (1-1-7)
(7) Vaiśeṣika Sutras (1-16)
(8) Essential Colourlessness of the Absolute (p. 14)
(9) Essential Colourlessness of the Absolute (p. xiii)
(10) Śvetaṣvatara Upanishad (pp. 6-8)
(11) Essential Colourlessness of the Absolute (pp. 15-22)
(12) Yajur Veda Adh.40 Mant.8.

स पर्य्येगाच्छुक्रमकायमव्रणामस्नाविर शुद्धमपापविद्धम् !
कविर्मनीषी परिभू रू स्वयम्भूर्याथातथ्यतोऽर्थान
व्यदधाच्छाश्रतीभ्यरू सर्माभ्य:

(13) Essential Colourlessness of the Absolute (p. 22).
(14) Essential Colourlessness of the Absolute (p. 23)
(15) Science of soul (p. 153)
(16) Science of Vital Force (p. 117)
(17) Beads of Sermons (Pt - II p. 133)
(18) Beads of Sermons (Pt - II p. 138)
(19) Light of Truth (p. 237)
(20) Light of Truth (p. 238)
(21) Essential Colourlessness of the Absolute (p. 27)
(22) Essential Colourlessness of the Absolute (p. 30)
(23) Essential Colourlessness of the Absolute (p. 31)
(24) Essential Colourlessness of the Absolute (p. 32)
(25) Essential Colourlessness of the Absolute (p. 33)
(26) Geeta 4 - 7 यदा यदा हि धर्मस्य ग्लानिर्भवति भारत। अभ्युत्थानमधर्मस्य तदात्मानं सृजाम्यहम्
(27) Essential Colourlessness of the Absolute (pp. 45-46)
(28) Yoga Sutra (1-24)
(29) Essential Colourlessness of the Absolute (p. 48)
(30) Kaivalya Upanishad- (pt-1, man 6)
(31) Essential Colourlessness of the Absolute. (p. 48)
(32) Essential Colourlessness of the Absolute. (p. 49)
(33) Light of Truth (Ch.XI p. 373)
(34) Brahman Sutra (III-II-14) अरूपवदेव हि तत्प्रधानत्वात्
(35) Essential Colourlessness of the Absolute. (pp. 36-37)
(36) Freedom from the known(p. 10)
(37) Essential Colourlessness of the Absolute (pp. 36-37)
(38) Essential Colourlessness of the Absolute (p. 40)
(39) Essential Colourlessness of the Absolute (p. 72)
(40) Science of soul (p. 124)
(41) Arke cenmadhu vindet, kimar tham parvate urajet?

(42) Essential Colourlessness of the Absolute (pp. 77-78)
(43) Light of Truth (Appendix)
(44) Light of Truth (p. 215)
(45) Essential Colourlessness of the Absolute (p. 100)
(46) Essential Colourlessness of the Absolute (pp. 101-102)
(47) Yoga Sutra (3-2)
(48) Essential Colourlessness of the Absolute (p. 105)
(49) Essential Colourlessness of the Absolute (p. 111)
(50) Yoga Sutra (3-2)
(51) Light of Truth (pp. 731-732)

4

Realisation of Self

REALISATION OF INDIVIDUAL SELF

The seat of Soul is stated to be the *Citta* or the Sub-conscious mind-stuff (so called by Swami Yogeshwaranand) which is located in the region of the Heart. In the same *Citta*, there exist millions of *Samskāras*. When a certain *Samskāra* is ripe to yield fruit, it is taken to the intellect by the ego where it is converted to its gross form and conveyed to the senses through the medium of mind *(Manas)* which perform the action resulting in pleasure or pain caused by that *Samskāra*. This process goes on endlessly every moment. In such a big mass of *Samskāras* which are in motion between the intellect *(Buddhi)* and the *Citta*, the individual soul, which is said to be small in size, is also mixed up and has to be searched in that *Citta*. The *Samskāras* are inert and lifeless but the soul is lively and conscious. Finding soul in such a massive jumble of lifeless *Samskāras* in the *Citta*, which is constantly throbbing and moving, is like searching for a needle in the hay stack. It is extremely uncommon for a common man to be able to envision soul in the wilderness of the *Citta*. No one can ever achieve the objective of envisioning soul without first gaining total knowledge of it. There may be some seers who gained access to the soul through deep meditation, but none of them has left any account of his experiences in *Samādhi* which could act as a lamp post or mile stone, for the new comers. Swami

Yogeshwaranand is, perhaps, the only one *Yogi* who recorded his experiences in a book, kept for that purpose, which record he went on updating, as and when new experiences arose, necessitating amendment of the truth recorded earlier. His method of realisation of self is not a repetition of age old versions but he has verified the truth of his experiences in his super–conscious state. The scriptures claim that the soul is of the size of an atom or of rice etc. which shows the subtlety of its form. To realise such a minute entity is not an easy job. Swami Yogeshwaranand himself admits that "in spite of having spent years to master meditation, I still feel that I have yet much to accomplish."[1] Being so subtle, no ordinary person can gain knowledge thereof.

In order to reach the soul we must enter our gross body first, which encloses two other bodies, namely the subtle body and the causal body. Amongst themselves, the three bodies share the five *Koshas* (sheaths) which function individually as well as in consonance with one another. It is necessary to gain complete knowledge of these bodies and sheaths before we reach the soul. However, to enter the gross body, one must acquire total control over mind and should be able to firmly concentrate on one single object. But mind has the quality of restlessness and, therefore, it can be controlled only by fixing the mind on a particular thing. With practice, mind must be trained to obey our orders and stop running after the sense objects. The object of concentration could be our body or any of the five elements or the soul or God. Since our objective is to realise the soul, it is better if we choose the soul as the object of concentration. Having acquired some control over the mind, we should sit quietly alone in some secluded place and then concentrate on the chosen object. We will find that there are vibrations in mind which give rise to thoughts constantly. Swami Yogeshwaranand says that what is necessary is to keep wiping off these layers of thoughts. Ultimately we will reach the source of thoughts where we will come to know the electrifying power at the source of these thoughts. We could stop these vibrations by the force of our concentration. Then we will be able to sight the mind and the intellect which will appear as inert objects. About the power, generated by concentration of mind, Swami Yogeshwaranand's experience is quite revealing. He says:

> "For the first five minutes you practise focussing of your vision. You will feel some tremor emanating from your body. It may be in the form of waves or in the form of vital air, or in the form of rays, or in the form of light, or in the form of feeling. In short, it may be any kind of nexus and this will enable you to communicate with a person living in a foreign country. You will also know the location of the source of these thoughts. Every moment such vibrations occur. It is as if they are surveying the orb of the sky. In this way, the rays from our mind establish contact with the minds of others. To illustrate, this luminous bulb in my room lights all parts of the room by means of its rays. I try to control my senses and mind by establishing nexus between them. If you understand all this, you will perhaps understand the relationship between the mind and intelligence in the brain."[2]

Before sitting for *Samādhi*, we should purify the body by the austerities, contained in the first four limbs of *Ashtānga Yoga,* namely *Yama, Niyama, Āsana,* and *Prānayāma*. Then we should sit in any comfortable posture. We should renounce all thoughts and imaginations of mind and make it still. Then we should practice *Unmani Mudara* by half closing the eyes and fixing the mind at a spot between the eyebrows. A big effort should be made to visualise a light at that spot. Continue to visualise the said light in the forehead for some time. We should sit in a relaxed mood because the pressure used in the effort to focus gaze between the eyebrows, tires the brain which causes the mind to wander. Therefore, visualisation of light in the *Brahmarandhra* (forehead) should be relaxed by each interval of about a few minutes. But we should continue to relax while sitting in the *Āsana.* Swami Yogeshwaranand says that for proper practice of *Samādhi,* we require a realised preceptor to guide us but, if no such teacher is available, we should pray to God for guidance and, in the case of really devoted aspirants, a *Guru* may manifest in the form of inner guidance. He says that faith, purity and perseverance will always bring divine grace in the form of Guru, either as a qualified teacher or as inner revelation.[3]

The light arising in the middle of the eyebrows will become visible slowly by regular practice. The light will be dim in the beginning but, if practice is continued, it will appear like a flame, a glow–worm, an electric light or sun shine, depending on the perfection attained in practice.[4] The duration of this stage depends on the mental temperament of the person and also on the strength of his practice. While suspending all functions of the mind and, with further effort in concentration of mind, the image of that light will become more and more clear. One should hold on to this light from the moment it appears, and make it more and more steady. Swami Yogeshwaranand calls it divine eye or subtle eye (*Divya Chakṣu*). This light has to be grabbed by the aspirant who should attain full control over it. Then he will be able to use it as a torch in the darkness and move it to any region of the body to see the subtle characteristics of the food sheath (*Annamaya Kosha*). As he progresses in meditation, he will see a bright light emanating from the earth as if there is a miniature sun in the earth giving out that light. With further concentration, he will see a small moon emitting blue and white light.

Later on, he will see a pale blood coloured small object like sun, different from the sun as seen earlier. This sun will appear as the orb of intellect *(Buddhi)*. He will also be able to see consciousness close by which will also appear bright like the sun. Some more steps will be required to be taken by him to reach the stage when he can first envision the soul and then God.

The above is the result of the experience gained by Swami Yogeshwaranand himself in deep *Samādhi.* As already mentioned by him, when we fix our gaze in the forehead between the eyebrows, we acquire a divine light. It is by this divine light that one can see the inside of the gross body including the mind and intellect. When the aspirant enters the gross body, with the help of this light, and explores the *Brahmarandhra,* he will see the ten subtle centers of our senses, five *Tanmatras,* mind and intellect. In this region there are two *Koshas* (sheaths) namely *Annamaya kosha* and *Prānamaya kosha.* While *Annamaya kosha* is the modification five great elements (*Panchamahabhútas*), the *Prānamaya kosha* is constituted of ten *Prānas* of which five are the main *Prānas* and five are sub *Prānas*. These *Prānas* dwell in different parts of the body and perform different functions. How Swami Yogeshwaranand visualised the colour, form and abode of these *Prānas* is shown in *Illustration No. 5.* The illustration shows that the area of the body occupied by *Apāna* is between the navel and the feet. From heart to navel is the seat of *Samāna* while from heart to throat is the seat of *Prāna.* From throat to the crown of the head is the seat of *Udāna Prāna*. *Vyāna Prāna* pervades the whole body. Since each *Prāna* operates and functions in the area of its occupation, *Vyāna* being all pervasive in the body, functions in the whole body. The sub–*Prānas* are situated in the mouth, nose and eyes which is also their area of operation. *Prānamaya Kosha,* being subtler than *Annamaya Kosha,* encases *Manomaya Kosha* and *Ānandmaya kosha.*

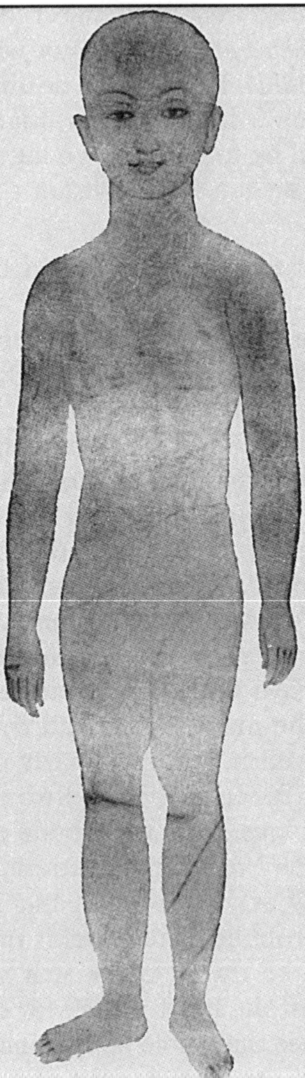

Illustration No. 5
Pranamaya Kosha
प्राणमय कोश का स्वरूप

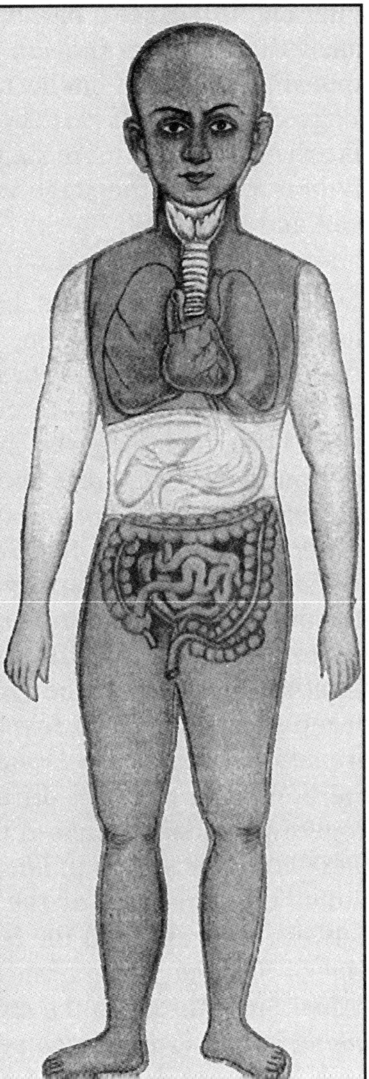

Illustration No. 5
Parts of Prāṇamaya Kosha
प्राणमयकोश के विभागशः कर्म

Illustration No. 5: *Pranamaya Kosha*

The soul which abides in the *Ānandmaya Kosha*, identifies itself with the modifications of *Prānamāya Kosha* which covers it and treats itself as the doer and enjoyer. Swami Yogeshwaranand says that *Prānamāya Kosha* can be mastered by the practice of *Prātyahara* and *Dhārana*. *Prānamāya Kosha* exists in the body of all living beings and pervades the gross body. It is, therefore, of the size of gross body which is confirmed by *Taittiriya Upanishad*.[5] Swami Yogeshwaranand affirms that his own experience in *Samādhi*, tallies with the version of the *Upanishad*. According to him, the five sheaths are of the form of a physical body which they pervade, and when viewed by firm concentration the aggregate of the five sheaths, it appears like a white cloudy image (*Chhāya Puruṣa*) of light colour. If *Sattva* predominates, it appears as if transparent but luminous and when *Rajas* predominates, it is golden in colour. When *Tamas* predominates it is smoky in colour. An aspirant can have clear visualisation of *Prānamaya Kosha* in *Samādhi* with the help of divine eye. He has also to understand the relationship between the subtle and causal bodies with *Prānamaya Kosha*. Swami Yogeshwaranand experienced this relationship in *Samādhi* which is shown in details in *Illustration No. 6*. The illustration expresses how the *Prānamaya Kosha* has pervaded *Annamaya Kosha* and *Anandmāya Kosha* with its luminous rays. With regard to this mutual relationship of the *Koshas*, Swami Yogeshwaranand differs with our ancient texts which accept only five sheaths (*Koshas*). He treats even water-sheath, fire–sheath and air–sheath also as *Koshas*.[6]

In an earlier chapter, we have explained in detail the limbs of *Antahkarna* along with their forms, colours and functions. *Antahkarna* is the internal organ which is responsible for all our inner and outer experiences. *Jīvātman* or the individual soul, is a conscious principle. But consciousness arises only when the soul comes into

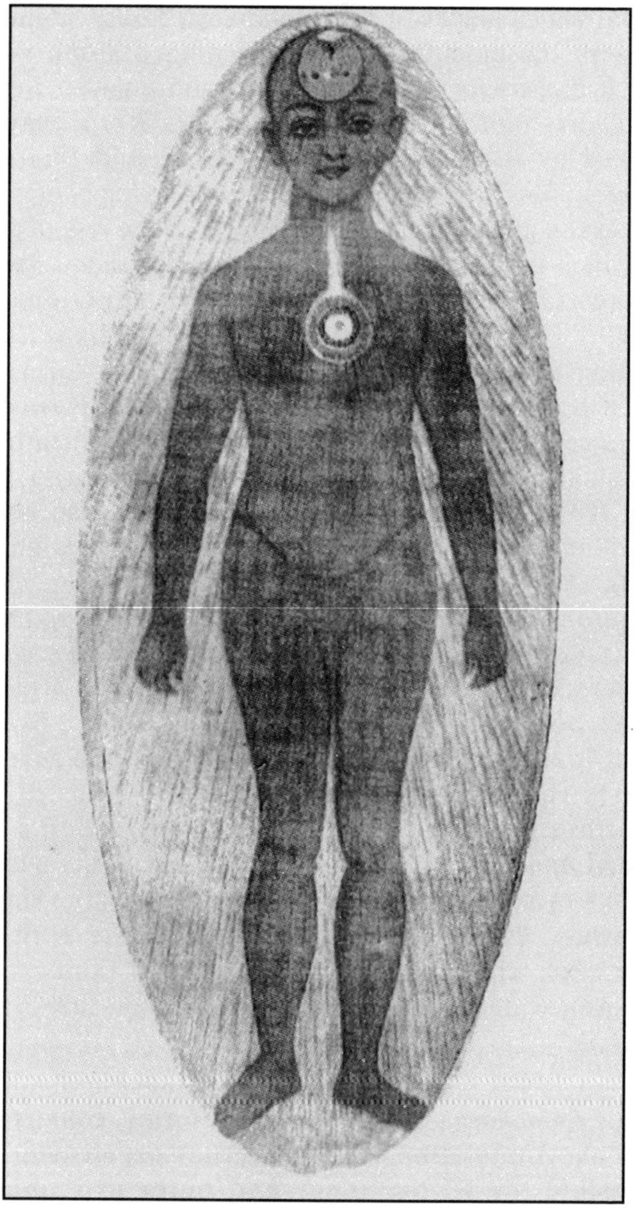

Illustration No.6: *The relationship of subtle and causal bodies with the* Prānamaya Kosha *[Science of Soul (p. 112)]*

contact with inert but luminous *Antahkarna*. It is this combination which creates action and this action, when it associates with knowledge which is the very potency of the soul, converts the *Antahkarna* into a conscious principle. In *Anandmaya Kosha*, this combination of action and knowledge, manifests as subtle *Prąna* in which there is luminosity of the consciousness which belongs to knowledge and there is also fickleness which belongs to action. The principles of knowledge and action combine to give rise to the life force which first arises in the heart wherefrom it is transmitted to all parts of the body in the form of vapours, like a current of luminous rays. This current of fine vapours which appear like luminous rays, is sent towards the *Brahmarandhra* in an unbroken succession. It is through these rays that both *Vijñānamaya Kosha* and *Manomaya Kosha* get energised and the mind spreads this life force to the physical body and makes it alive. Based on his own experience, Swami Yogeshwaranand explains the function of life force as under:

> "Contact of conscious *Jivātman* with inert and luminous *Antahkarna* creates action (*Kriya*). This action coupled with knowledge, which is the very potency of the *Puruṣa* (soul), converts the *Antahkarna* into a conscious principle and revives the entire *Anandmaya Kosha,* wherein it becomes subtle *Prāna.* In the subtle *Prāna* the luminosity of consciousness is of knowledge, and fickleness belongs to action. These two having united, assume the form of life-force. The heart sends the life-force, in the form of luminous vapour or of a current formed from luminous rays, towards *Brahmarandhra* continuously in unbroken succession."[7]

The life force, mentioned above, arises due to the

contact of the soul with body and sustains the three bodies and five sheaths throughout life. Now what happens when the soul departs from body? Swami Yogeshwaranand says that at the time of death the astral body and the causal body, confined in the orb of five *Tanmatras,* assume the form of luminous *Śiva Pinda* (auspicious form) and leaves the gross body. The forms of such bodies of *Yogis,* who have conquered the elements, are similar to their physical bodies. The astral bodies of various persons are different and are in accordance with the presence of *Gunas*. *Sattva* predominating bodies are beautiful and luminous like the moon; *Rajas* predominating bodies are tall, of golden colour, lustrous but slightly thin and *Tamas* predominating bodies are brown or smoky in colour. These are smaller in size, broad and not so pleasant.

It is necessary to understand the energies of *Jñāna* and *Kriya,* or knowledge and action, which arise in the form of *Suksham Prāna* (subtle air) when "*Ātman*" takes its abode in the *Citta*. *Kriya,* unlike inert activity, is the energy which is seen in the *Citta* in the same manner as electric energy is seen when a bulb is lighted. It is *Ātmik* energy of the nature of a mere potency. When a bulb is lighted, we observe that its mid-centre is illuminated first and the light pervades the whole bulb, and illuminates all objects around it. In like manner, the portion of the *Citta* which first comes into contact with soul, becomes conscious. Hereafter, the entire process, in which the consciousness pervades the entire *Citta* and then the whole of *Antahkarna,* is called *Kriya*. It is because of this *Kriya* that the *Antahkarna* appears conscious and performs all the internal and external functions of the body. Swami Yogeshwaranand says that one can see this process in *Samādhi,* as he did. One can also see in *Samādhi* how the *Antahkarna* offers all types of enjoyments *(bhoga)* to the *Puruṣa* (soul). That which observes the above process is called *Jñāna* or knowledge. *Citta* is inert by itself but when the soul bestows consciousness on *Citta*, it performs the function of knowing. The two energies of the soul, namely knowledge and activity, emerge from the *Citta* in the form of vapours. *Ahamkāra* or ego is the limb of *Antahkarna,* which perceives and guides the *Kriya* and it is *Citta*, another limb of the *Antahkarna,* which depicts knowledge. *Citta* has a duel flow namely inward flow and outward flow. When *Citta* is full of *Sattva Guna* (quality of purity) and *Rajas* and *Tamas* appear only as auxiliary as if absent, then its flow is inward. Such a *Citta,* when it becomes free from all *Samskāras* and gets absorbed in *Vivekakhyati* (discriminative knowledge), becomes helpful in gaining the knowledge of *Puruṣa* and *Prakriti.* The realisation of self, or *Ātma-Sākṣātakāra,* is achieved in *Samādhi* when *Citta* is engaged in inward flow. This *Samādhi* leads to the clouds of virtue called *Dharma–Megha,* which aid the soul in resting in its essential nature *(Swarúpa Sthiti*). Even after coming out of a *Samādhi (vyuthāna*), the *Samskāras* of supreme dispassion *(Param–vairagya*) enable the soul to abide in its essential nature. The next step is to realise the bliss of *Brahman*, the Supreme Being which leads one to the door steps to *Mokṣa*. When *Citta* is engaged in the outward flow, the mind becomes fickle and the senses run after the sense–objects and take one away from realisation of self by not allowing him to go into *Samādhi*.

Citta and *Ātman* are two distinct entities and it is very necessary to understand the difference, or else, we may confuse one with the other and fail to have the vision of the soul. How do we obtain the knowledge of the object that we perceive? It is obtained by the reflection of that object either in the intellect or in *Citta*. Without being coloured by an object, neither *Buddhi* nor *Citta* can give us any knowledge. We receive knowledge of only those objects which are reflected in the intellect or the *Citta*. We cannot have knowledge of any other object. *Mahrishi Patāñjali* also says the same thing in *Yoga Sutras*. He says that the object is either known or not known by *Citta,* depending upon whether it is coloured or not by that object.[8] As mentioned earlier, *Vrittis* belong to *Buddhi* and *Samskāras* belong to *Citta* and both, these limbs of *Antahkarna,* reflect by their own light, every object, along with its form and colour, in the fraction of a moment. *Paruṣa,* as a conscious being and also as owner of both *Buddhi* and *Citta,* goes on watching the modifications occurring in the two. Therefore, *Puruṣa* is always aware of every change or movement of *Buddhi* and *Citta.* Since *Citta* is ever changing and *Puruṣa* is unchanging, no action of *Citta* goes unnoticed by *Puruṣa. Citta* abides in the casual body and *Buddhi* abides in the subtle body. Since both are confined to only one place each, they can perform only one action at a time. But they perform their actions so rapidly that one feels as if they are doing so many actions simultaneously. *Citta* has its own light but when it comes into contact with *Jīvātman,* it becomes bright like an ocean of light. Since *Ātman* is so subtle that it cannot be easily known, many people take *Citta* as *Ātman* and by realising *Citta,* they think that they have realised the self. About the illusion caused by the brilliance of *Citta* in association with soul, Swami Yogeshwaranand says as under:

> "Unable to realise the subtlest *Ātman,* more subtle than minute atomic particles, some have taken *Citta* itself to be *Atman,* because the *Puruṣa* seems to be invisible, being immersed in the luminous myraid–rayed ocean of *Citta-Sattva.* This is the hard knot of *Asmita* (ego), an invisible obstacle which is neither easy to visualise nor easy to untie. This small *Citta* becomes so luminous, so bright due to luminosity of *Ātman,* and becomes so coloured by the idea of ego, that although it is not impossible, it is certainly difficult to separate — to pick out the minute subtle *Atman*–in this ego

> coloured luminous *Citta*. There is no doubt that among the principles concerning self and non-self this search is the most difficult in the world."[9]

Of all the schools of thought, *Yoga* gives an authentic method of realisation of self by acquiring *Ritambhara Prajna* (truth bearing knowledge). The term is used by *Raja Yoga* or *Ashtānga Yoga* and represents the power of that intellect which grasps only the truth. It does not know even a trace of untruth. *Patāñjali* says that, by mastering the eight limbs of *Yoga* and with destruction of impurities of body and *Antahkarna*, the light of knowledge shines more and more, till finally, there arises the discrimination between *Puruṣa* and *Prakriti*. With perfection of *Nirvichara Samādhi,* there arises the light of *Adhyâtma Prasada* (the clouds of virtue). An intellect, brightened by *Adhyātma Prasāda,* becomes capable of directly perceiving the hidden internal forms of the objects. Such a perception is more direct than the perception acquired through senses or through inference or testimony. Once this truth bearing knowledge is obtained, one realises the subtle knowledge of the difference between *Puruṣa* and *Prakriti*. This discriminative knowledge is known as *Viveka Khyāti.* This knowledge has one more quality. It is that the evil *Samskāras* do not arise in *Samādhi* in the form of memory nor can the *Samskāras* enter *Citta*. This light of knowledge attenuates the dormant *Samskāras*, overpowers them and inhibits them from sprouting. It is mentioned in *Geeta*[10] that the *Samskāras* are burnt up by the knowledge mentioned above and prevented from acting. Swami Yogeshwaranand says that the *Samskāras* of *Karma* return to *Prakriti* and remain dormant because matter can change form but can never be destroyed.

The *Sāmkhya* theory that the world is constituted by *Prakriti* which comprises of three *Gunas*, has found favour with Swami Yogeshwaranand but, even in the theory of *Prakriti*, he has a difference of opinion with *Sāmkhya* and

Yoga schools. *Sāmkhya* and *Yoga* accept *Antahkarna* as having three limbs namely mind, ego and *Citta*. For them *Citta* is included in *Buddhi* and *vice–versa*. Therefore, they believe that in the process of creation of the world, the triad of mind, intellect and ego alone have played the part of the *Antahkarna,* with the understanding that *Citta* is included in *Buddhi.* But Swami Yogeshwaranand differs and says that *Citta* is an independent organ of *Antahkarna* and, if is treated as included in Buddhi, it will become difficult to explain the phenomena of *Samskāras.*

Swami Yogeshwaranand describes in detail, how *Jīvātman,* the lord of the five sheaths, abides in Linga *Ṣrira* or *Ānandmaya* Kosha situated in the space of the heart. Inside the heart, there is small hollow space of the size of a small grape. Within this hollow of the size of a grape, is the Bliss Sheath which shines like a golden egg. The Bliss Sheath is an aggregate of six orbs, one enveloping the other like the pillow cover. The innermost orb is that of the soul and to reach that orb, one has to pierce the other five orbs as experienced with the divine vision in firm *Samādhi*. On the basis of the vision of the six orbs gained by Swami Yogeshwaranand, the six orbs are explained as follows:

Orb of *Brahman*: Of the six orbs, the orb of *Brahman* is the outermost. We may ask that, when *Brahman* is all pervasive, how can he be confined only to a small orb? The answer is that, while ether is all–pervasive, it is still spoken of as ether of the jar or ether of the room. In the same way, the all-pervasive *Brahman* is said to be in the ether of the heart in the form of orb of *Brahman* to facilitate easy understanding. Those who desire to realise *Brahman* as Absolute, Indivisible, All Pervading, must first realise him in the said orb. It is necessary to do so for the reasons that the region of the perception is circular in form and also that the *Prakriti* has endowed the facility of realising *Brahman* in the heart. *Chāndogya Upanishad* lends support to this concept by saying that the ether in the region of the heart is no different from the outside ether.[11] The outer ether appears to be void but actually it is filled with *Brahman*. The ether inside the heart is also similarly filled. Just as the reflection of sun falls on the rock and on the lake but it is only the lake that reflects the sun, in the same way, we can have a vision of the soul and *Brahman* in the orb situated in the heart.

The orb of *Brahman* encompasses all other orbs and holds them in its womb. This orb is extremely white in the manner of speaking or else it is un–manifest and its colour is indescribable. The aspirant realises this orb only after realising all the other five orbs. Swami Yogeshwaranand contends that until *Samayama (Dhārna, Dhyāna and Samādhi)* is fully mastered by an aspirant, he will not be able to have the vision of this orb even by entering the heart in *Samādhi*.

Orb of *Prakriti*: The orb of *Prakriti* lies, sequentially, next to the orb of *Brahman* and is a fraction of the infinite non–manifest *Prakriti*. It is light yellow in colour and it is the real causal body of the soul to which the soul is eternally related. This is the relationship which is caused by ignorance. Because the orb is quite subtle, it is not so easy to have its vision. However, this orb maintains the aggregate of all other orbs within it.

Orb of *Prāna*: This orb lies inside the orb of *Prakriti*. Swami Yogeshwaranand says that when an aspirant enters the region of the heart through intense *Samādhi*, the first vision that he gets, is that of the orb of *Prāna*. Its colour is like that of luminous vapours or of shining rain drops. However, its colour is effected by the three *Gunas* and changes in accordance with the predominance of the particular *Guna*. It is said that the orb of *Prāna* is the gross effect of the contact between the soul and the *Citta* which manifests in the form of *Prānas*.

Orb of *Ahamkāra*: The orb of *Ahamkāra*, the ego principle, is the gross form of *Asmita*, the principle of "I–ness". This orb also changes in accordance with the dominance of *Sattva, Rajas,* or *Tamas*. Its colour is that of the peacock's neck as if a bluish green glass shade is placed on a white luminous light. This orb lies in the lap of the orb of *Prāna* and can be realised by a sharp divine vision acquired in *Samādhi*.

Orb of *Citta*: Inside the orb of *Ahamkāra* is the orb of *Citta*. It is said that the orb of *Citta* is the residence, or the palace of the soul. It is extremely luminous and white so as to appear nearly transparent. *Vrittis,* in the form of ripples, constantly arise in the same way as waves arise in the ocean. These waves awaken the dormant *Samskāras* abiding in the *Citta* which move to the intellect for fructification. This orb is also similarly influenced by the three *Gunas* of *Prakriti*, as the other orbs.

Orb of *Ātman*: The orb of *Ātman* is smaller in size than even an atom but it is almost as subtle as *Brahman*. It is the only of its type and, therefore, it is incomparable with any other object. Because of its association with *Citta*, it assumes the colour and form of the *Citta*, otherwise it is colourless. According to Swami Yogeshwaranand, the soul exists as an extremely subtle point or a dot in the orb of *Citta*.

The six orbs mentioned above exist as an aggregate and appear as if forming a *Jyotir Linga* or a mass of light. The aggregate which comprises of subtle *Prāna, Ahamkāra, Citta* and the soul and belong to the Bliss Sheath, is organised by subtle *Prāna*. *Prakriti*, being a part of the universal non–manifest *Prakriti*, remains outside this aggregate and beyond the sphere of the orb of *Prāna*. The contents of *Brahmarandhra,* and those of the heart, are all luminous and are in the forms of orbs. The only difference is that the orbs in *Brahmarandhra* are more luminous and brighter than the orbs abiding in the cave of the heart. The lights in the heart are gentle, milky white, tranquil and pleasant but the orbs in the heart are much smaller in size than those abiding in *Brahmarandhra*. There are lights and lights in the astral and causal bodies and it becomes difficult for the practitioner to find the light of soul in the mass of all these lights. Even, if an aspirant has practiced for a long time, if he takes any light, arising from the body, as the light of the soul, he will never attain the necessary discriminative knowledge. He should test his knowledge of their lights through *Prajna Loka* or the light obtained through intuition. If he acquires the knowledge by this method, it will be then free from all misconceptions, doubts and illusions. These misconceptions can be removed only through the said intuitional light. When a light of *Sattva* prevails, one acquires the knowledge of the objects which cannot be perceived by the senses. The realisation arising in the state of *Samādhi,* solves every doubt relating to the entire creation, *Antahkarna*, the soul and *Brahman*. Perfect wisdom accrues only in *Samādhi*. By perfecting *Nirvicāra Samādhi,* one acquires *Adhyātma Prasāda,* which is also known as *Ritambhara Prajna,* and which is truth bearing knowledge. *Mahirishi Vyasa Deva,* while commenting on the *Yoga Sutras*, has described the speciality of this light.[12] He says that *Prajna* arises in all the different *Samprajnata Samādhis,* but it is only the *Prajna* in the *Nirvicara Samādhi,* that reveals the ultimate truth regarding *Puruṣa* and *Prakriti*. Thus, *Ritambhara Prajna* which, ariṣes in the state of *Samādhi,* gives direct knowledge of everything. Hence, the sequence of reaching the *Swarupa Sthiti,* or self–realisation, is that first *Ritambhara* arises by the practice of *Nirvicara Samādhi,* then *Viveka Khyati,* the discriminative understanding arises. *Patañjali* has also stated that, when a yogi develops distaste towards even the continuous flow of discriminative knowledge, then there arises a divine light in the form of *Para Vairagya* or extreme dispassion. The state of *Para Vairagya* brings *dharma megha,* the clouds of virtue, which check all *Samskāras* except the *Samskāras* of *Para Vairagya* which remain in the *Citta*. *Patañjali* describes this state by saying that "when all the remaining *Samskāras* are converted into the state of burnt up seeds and thus disappear, then the conscious soul attains establishment in its essential nature."[13] The sequence of the stages for self-realisation and the knowledge thereof, is non susceptible to any oral description because these are beyond the reach of senses and can be perceived personally by the aspirant. Swami Yogeshwaranand has described this state as under:

> "All these states are acquired by supreme self–effort and the grace of God. That is why the knowers of *Brahman* and the realised sages have not given definite words pertaining to knowledge and wisdom. The state of *Dharma–Megha Samādhi*, the cloud of virtue free from *Samskāras*, is an absolutely delusionless state. This is the state of *Sthita–Prajna* or steady vision. In this very state, *Dharma* is realised in the form of divine grace."[14]

Now what is *Bhoga* or enjoyment of the Soul? *Sāmkhya* says that, the state which results from the experiences of the desirable and the undesirable, is known as *Bhoga* which culminates in *Citta.*[15] Swami Yogeshwaranand says that *Bhoga* does not culminate in *Citta* alone because *Citta* is inert and unconscious. It cannot enjoy *Bhoga*. *Purusa*, though not the actor, is endowed with the capacity to enjoy. He says that *Puruṣa,* in conjunction with *Citta,* is the support of enjoyment. *Puruṣa* alone is not the support. This view is broadly approved by *Sāmkhya.*[16] It says that just as food is produced by the subjects and is eaten and enjoyed by the King, who is the lord of the subjects, in the same way, enjoyments which pertain to the functions of the intellect, are super-imposed on the conscious *Puruṣa*. Let us give another example. The victory or defeat in the battle-field, is caused by the army and its commander, but it is attributed to the king. Therefore, enjoyment is not for the soul and for the *Citta* and is attributed to soul. The absence of all instruments of *Bhoga,* and the establishment of the soul in its essential nature, is called *Apavarga* or release which is generally known as *Mokṣa*. The state of essential nature or *Swarúpa Sthiti,* is the peaceful state of the *Citta* which is free from *Samskāras* and which appears like a field of clear moonlight without any form or size. *Citta,* when it is absolutely free from any impurities, reflects the soul in its true existence. But when one rises from this state, one sees an enchanting realm of pure light, like the light of moon in which one envelops his individual consciousness and experiences the feeling of *Asmi,* 'I am'. If the flow of *Sattva* continues, he can re–enter the state of his essential nature and enjoy the bliss. If, however, he does not enter that state, then he experiences the feeling of *Aham Asmi* (I am) in the level of ego–principle and not *Citta*. One is flabbergasted by this experience in *Swarupa Sthiti* which Swami Yogeshwaranand has explained as under:

> "If the *Sāḍhaka* is keenly attentive he sees the waves of the ego–principle arising with the contraction and expansion of *Citta*. Then his experience is as if someone is swinging. The individual soul experiences the joy of swinging due to waves of perception of *Aham Asmi* pertaining to the ego–principle. This is the state of *Ananda* or joy. At times, in a particularly *Sattvik* and peaceful state, one's experience is as if clear sparkling water is flowing from a fountain and moving onwards with gentle and merry ripples playing on it. The very vision of it fills the heart with joy. Around this place one sees clouds hovering. They are a little thicker than vapour, devoid of water and are light, like white clouds but shining as if from the rays of the sun; they

> appear very beautiful in their shadowy forms. The orb of subtle *Prāna* shines in this form also. Here, *Ahamkāra* is mixed in the form of shadows."[17]

The experiences of *Ānanda* and the vision of the sparkling water flowing from the fountain, as also of white shining clouds, is unique and very pleasant. But such an experience is *Swayam Veda* or subject to one's personal experience. The soul can be compared only to itself. It is atomic in size, luminous but without limbs, free from modifications and full of knowledge and action. The search for soul is like the search for a pearl in a bottomless sea. *Kathopanishad* also makes a similar mention when it says that only a few heroes alone are able to see innermost soul.[18] *Ātman* is the seer of the self and the experience of seeing takes place when the self is reflected in the *Citta*. The act of seeing the self by *Puruṣa* is certified by *Ahamkāra* (the ego) or else the *Puruṣa* would never know that it has seen the self. *Jīvātman* is the consciousness of the *Citta* and it remains aware of every movement of the *Citta*. In the state of essential nature (*Swarupa Sthiti)* the painful memories of fear, grief and dilusion vanish, and one acquires the peaceful state of *Jivanmukti*, but he cannot discard his gross body till he has exhausted all his *Karmas*. However, in this state, the *Kliṣta Vrittis* like *Avidya, Abhinivesha* etc. become like burnt up seeds and for a yogi to give up this body, is like discarding the old and worn out clothes. Then death ceases to cause any fear for him.

When a Yogi acquires perfection in *Nirvicāra Samādhi*, he also acquires closer proximity with the soul. Then he sees divine lights in the region of the heart where the *Citta* is also located. There he realises the orb of *Prakriti* which is outside the orb of subtle *Prakriti*. Then, one after the other, he realises the orbs of *Prāna*, *Citta* and of the *Jīvātman*. This happens prior to the transcendal state (*Turiya Avastha*) which is the state in which the seer realises the Supreme *Brahman* who has pervaded the entire heart, inside and outside. After the *Ātman* acquires this knowledge pertaining to the Absolute, there is no other knowledge for him to acquire. According to Swami Yogeshwaranand this is the limit of human Knowledge, beyond which no knowledge exists.

REALISATION OF DEATH

We have mentioned earlier that in pursuance of the method of realisation of self, propounded by Swami Yogeshwaranand, when a *Sādhaka* (Practitioner of Yoga) purifies his body through the first four limbs of *Ashtānga* Yoga and engages himself in continuous practice with faith and perseverance, he becomes adept in *Dhārna*. Gradually, he sees light in the middle of the eye–brows which is initially dim but with practice it can be made bright and steady. In Yoga this light is called divine eye or subtle eye (*Divya Chakṣu*). With this light one can see all gross and subtle objects which senses cannot grasp. With the help of this light a Yogi can enter the gross body. There, he should visualise, by this divine eye, the *Annamaya Kosha* and *Prānamaya Kosha*. He will know for himself how all our organs, situated inside the body, are functioning. For example, he will see how the food we eat is digested and assimilated and how the waste is excreted. He will also see how the five main *Prānas* and how five Sub–*Prānas* are performing their functions in different parts of the body. Not finding the soul in the gross body, the Yogi will move to the subtle body in which are located the five *Tanmatras*, five subtle centers of the *Jñāna Indriyas* (senses of perception), five subtle centers of *Karmendriyas* (senses of action), mind (*Manas*) and intellect (*Buddhi*). There, he will visualise how the senses send their perceptions to mind after crossing the barrier of *Tanmatras;* how mind performs its functions of *Ādāna–Pradāna* (giving and taking) by conveying decisions of *Buddhi* to the *Indriyas*. As he fails to find *Ātman*, even in the subtle body, he enters the causal body (*Kārna Śrira*) in which he visualises the functions of *Ahamkāra* and *Citta* with *Samskāras,* abiding in the *Citta*. He will realise the orbs of *Prakriti*, *Prāna*, *Ahamkara*, *Citta* and finally that of *Ātman*. With sharp vision gained in *Samādhi*, he succeeds in seeing his own self by reflection in the mirror of *Citta*. He, therefore, gains complete knowledge of every thing from gross *Prakriti* to extremely subtle *Jīvātman*. All that is left for him to realise is the Absolute *Brahman* which will be discussed later in this work. We now discuss here how to realise death which is no less important than soul. Swami Yogeshwaranand has explained in a simple and easily intelligible manner, the concept of death in Yoga. One hardly comes across this concept being discussed in the books of any other Yogi.

Death is an object of extreme fear. Although death is inevitable, yet every one wishes to postpone it indefinitely. The reason is that we see people experiencing extreme mental and physical pain at the time of death and we do not want that we should suffer similarly. This type of suffering is caused by the fructification of the sinful deeds of the dying person. If there are no sinful deeds committed by the person, there would be no such suffering and death would come to him like the falling of a leaf from the tree–naturally and painlessly. When the knowledge of reality dawns, and the person realises the self and the organs of the body, he renders impotent the *Samskāras* of all sinful deeds. *Abhinivesa Klesa* affliction is the desire to cling to life which causes fear of death. By realising the self, the Yogi also understands the nature of *Abhinivesa Klesa* and then he becomes free from the fear of death. The pain of death is caused by infatuation for physical body which the soul, due to ignorance, starts considering it as its own. The craving for sense enjoyments makes it painful for us to leave the world which is full of physical enjoyments. Even the thought of death sends shivers down the spine of the people who are infatuated with life and its surroundings. But a self-realised person knows the futility of such attachment and, therefore, death causes no fear for him. Those, who have perfected *Samādhi,* can envision the whole process of death, in *Samādhi*. In *Samādhi,* if we make a sustained effort, the consciousness gets more and more focused at the centre in the region of heart. This affects the gross body and we feel, as if, ants were moving in the feet and legs. After some time the feet and legs become heavy, somewhat like when we are about to fall asleep. Initially a new comer in *Samādhi* gets scared of this unusual condition. But after some time, when *Puruṣa* experiences harmony in itself, these symptoms vanish on their own. Therefore, this process does not cause any fear in the mind of the Yogi. Similarly at the time of death, when a Yogi is about to discard his body, he finds no difficulty at all because he brings up this process by the force of will. In the case of common men, the process of death takes place without their knowledge, and therefore, it instills fear in them because they cannot understand the nature of this process. Death is like the flow of a stream. When the flow ceases, the stream dries up. The process of death is exactly similar to it. As we have stated, the life force arises in the *Citta* as soon as the soul takes its abode in the *Citta*. This life force issues out from the *Citta* in the form of subtle *Prāna* comprising of the energies of Knowledge and Action (*Jnāna* and *Kriya*), which energises, first the causal body, then subtle and lastly gross body. Death takes place when the life force stops issuing from the *Citta*. When the heart becomes still suddenly and completely, death is spontaneous but, normally, this process takes some time. The flow of life force gets obstructed and even though the *Prānas* become dull, the flow does not stop completely. First some sort of fainting or unconsciousness will occur in the physical body but one may regain consciousness intermittently. Life force moves through many sheaths before it reaches the physical body. The condition, mentioned above, is caused by obstruction in the flow of *Prāna* in one of the sheaths. The flow becomes dull, in the same way as a dysfunctional pump becomes unable to throw water to the prescribed distance. The flow of life force becomes erratic. It goes up to one sheath or the other and finally, due to its acute debility, it gets confined to the region of the heart. When *Prāna* becomes dull and sluggish, as explained above, the effect is first felt in the physical body because the *Prānas* and Sub–*Prānas* are first withdrawn from that body. The *Prānas* move to the centre or the source which lies in the heart. When this happens the whole of the physical body stops functioning and all its parts become cold. Then the *Manomaya Kosha* and *Vijñānmaya Kosha* also become stagnant and cease functioning. Swami Yogeshwaranand says that, in the said state, the mind, the intellect, and the subtle senses, along with the orbs of five *Tanmātras*, move towards the heart and encircle the causal body.[19] The subtle centres of the senses get fixed in the *Tanmātras*. When the flow of *Prānas* (life–force) withdraws itself in the causal body, step by step from the orb of *Prakriti* to the orb of the soul, then the soul, passes out of the body with the whole mass of light. The aggregate of this mass of light, along with the soul, form a luminous conch shape mass and then pass into the orb of ether. The form and shape of every subtle (astral)body becomes like the form and shape of the body in which it enters, be it the body of a human–being, an animal, a bird, an insect or a worm. Although the astral or subtle body changes according to the form and shape of the new body, the soul remains unchanged. This sums up the nature of death, its concept and scope and also as to how the soul moves from one body to another when it discards one body and adopts the other.

There are three aspects of the illustration which Swami

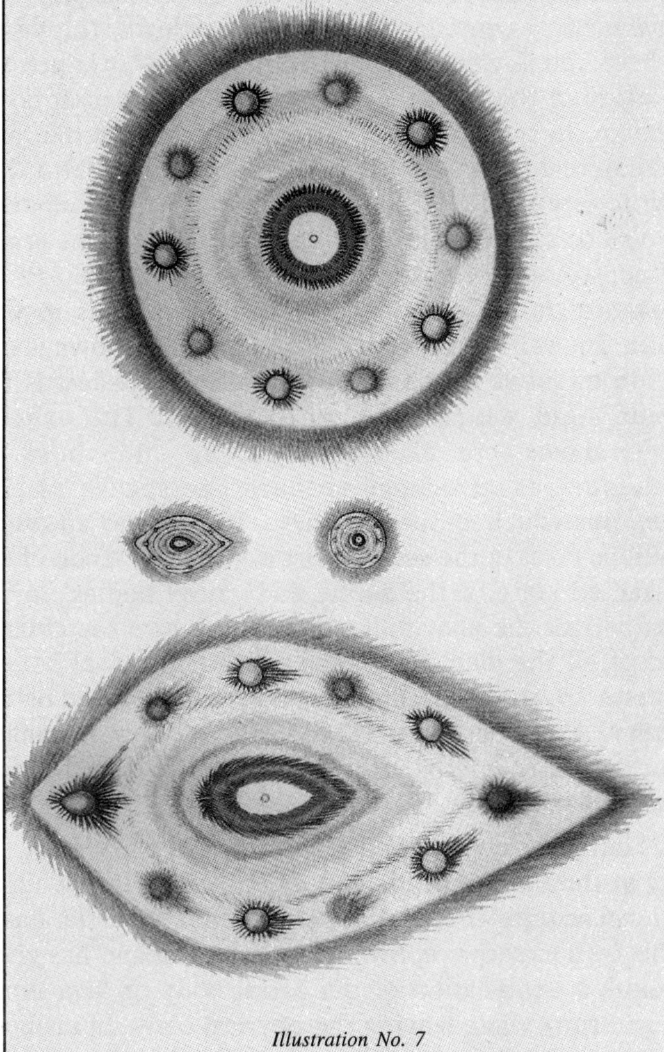

Illustration No. 7

Astral and Causal Bodies after Death

सूक्ष्म तथा कारण शरीरों का संयुक्त हो कर परलोक गमन

Illustration No.7: *Astral and Causal Bodies after Death*

Yogeshwaranand has given of the astral (subtle) and causal bodies as envisioned at the time of death. This vision has been suitably depicted in *Illustration No.7* in which the departure of the astral body associated with causal body, is shown. In the first part *Jīvātman* is shown in the form of a diamond particle in the centre of the Orb of *Citta*. The *Ātma* is very luminous and the *Citta* is of white colour. It can also be seen that, outside the orb of *Citta* is the orb of *Ahamkāra,* which is of blue colour. Outside the orb of *Ahamkāra,* is the orb of subtle *Prāna,* which is rosy in colour. The yellow coloured orb of intellect is shown above the orb of subtle *Prāna.* Above the orb of intellect is the orb of mind which is of white colour. The orbs of *Jñānendriyas* are of bluish colour and those of Karmendriyas of orange colour. The sheath of five *Tanmātras* which encases all these, is shown as an orb of luminous rays. In the second part is given the vision of the contracted state of the subtle and causal bodies. In the third part of the above illustration, is shown the circular form of all the elements of the astral and causal bodies. All these are shown as luminous orbs. This is based on the personal experience, gained by Swami Yogeshwaranand himself, and, it will be interesting to verify it in the state of deep *Samādhi.*

The experience, when Linga Śrira departs from the body at the time of death, is a unique experience which a Yogi can acquire after he has perfected his *Samādhi.* Based on his own experience, Swami Yogeshwaranand has given a detailed explanation of the astral body or Śiva Pinda (Linga Śrira) while leaving the physical body. In his book 'Science of Soul', he has given the following description:

> " At the time of death, Sukshama Sharira (astral body), the principle of Brahmarandhra and the causal body together confined in the orb of five *Tanmātras* and thus in the forms of luminous Śiva–Pinda, leave this physical body. The forms of

> astral bodies of Yogis, who have conquered the gross and subtle elements and who move in the Heavens, are similar to the physical bodies that they have left aside behind. These astral bodies are also seen to be of different types according to the differentiation of three *Gunas*. The *Sattva*–predominating bodies are especially luminous white, shining like the moon and very beautiful. The forms of their bodies are like the well–developed muscular physical bodies of this world and are very pleasing; their faces are ever beaming with happiness. Rajas-predominating bodies are tall, of golden colour, beautiful and lustrous but they are somewhat thin. *Tamas* predominating bodies are of brown or smoky colour, of smaller sizes, broad, and thus not so pleasing; their movements are dull, they exist in the skies of different worlds."[20]

He says that at the time of death, the causal body combines with the astral body and forms an aggregate, which looks like an oval mass, called Śiva Pinda. Then this luminous aggregate moves to the heaven or the so called other worlds of different Lokas. And when the soul returns, after the duration of its liberation, or on recreation of the universe after *Pralaya*, the finite *Ātman*, luminous with knowledge and consciousness, attached to a particular portion of Vyasti *Citta,* which is a part of Samasti *Citta*, once again takes its abode in the gross body, chosen by it, and once again, by its contact with inert *Citta,* the two energies of knowledge and activity arise with which the body performs its actions throughout life.

It is normal for each one of us to have certain expectations of life after death. Generally, the people believe that the departed soul has gone to find its abode in heaven. Different religions define heaven differently, according to their individual concept. In fact, heaven is the realm in which each individual wishes his desires to be fulfilled. The so called heaven, therefore, projects a realm which they seek to achieve. Thus, heaven is a projection of one's thoughts and desires, and is more like a dream than reality. In dreams, the things and objects appear to be real but when we wake up, all is gone. The heaven is, therefore, transitory, if at all it is true. Even our ancient seers conceived of heaven as non–eternal. *Mimāmsa* school is the chief protagonist of heaven but, even according to *Mimāmsa*, one lives in heaven to enjoy the fruits of good *Karmas* and as soon as these *Karmas* are exhausted, the soul must necessarily return to the world and commence another cycle of actions and their fruits. Heaven, or any existence after death, is governed by the law of *Karma* and is determined by our own *Karmas*. We may enjoy the pleasures of heaven as long as our good deeds last but ultimately this stock must get exhausted causing termination of our sojourn in heaven. Every thing that is subject to, or conditioned by time, space and causation, is perishable and so is heaven.

What happens to the soul when it discards the body—its outer garment? The scriptures tell us that the soul continues to exist. It is said that, after death, the soul goes to the realms where it exists without the help and assistance of the physical body or the material universe. As mentioned earlier, there is an intermediary state between life and death. It is the state in which *Prānas* have ceased to function in the gross and subtle bodies but these have not yet departed from the causal body. This is the stage when one should prepare to welcome death. If one does not accept this situation, or is not prepared to face it as a reality, he suffers a great agony or mental torture which he is unable to explain to others. In the aforesaid intermediary stage, those who have not realised the self or who are not otherwise enlightened to experience various temporary realms, which are pleasant or unpleasant, depending upon the quality of our *Karmas,* are extremely disturbed. The Tibetan Book of the Dead[21] and our Garuda *Purāna,* deal extensively with the realms which one passes through after death. When an unrealised soul departs, it lapses into a long and deep sleep. If it is so, then those who claim to communicate with such souls, are either under the spell of hallucination or they are deliberately lying, because it is not possible to communicate with some one who is asleep.

After death one comes across many realms, depending upon whether one has performed good and righteous actions, or whether one was engaged in evil deeds. Swami Rama says that after death, the virtuous souls, can have a clear vision of the Divine Self in higher realms. He says that the realms of Pitriloka and Svargaloka are not real and cannot reveal the highest truth and that liberation cannot be attained in these Lokas but in this life itself.[22]

The theory of rebirth is based on the concept that, he who desires to be born is born and he who does not desire is not born. In other words, the soul is born again and again to reap the fruits of its actions. There is no such thing as eternal retribution in heaven or hell. Our Riṣis, who authored the Upanishads, were also not impressed by this hypothesis. It is illogical, on every ground, to inflict upon the soul, eternal punishment for the faults of a few years. Our scriptures have placed the concept of rebirth on a logical basis by saying that the soul's embodiment is caused by its unfulfilled desires. Swami Rama says that "the length of time the soul must spend in the transition of death before accepting another body, is solely dependent on the intensity of desires and that there is no hard or fast rule set by nature." The embodied soul discards the body after its desires are fulfilled and assumes another body depending upon its tendencies or the nature of *Karmas*. It proves that we ourselves are the architects of our future destiny and it is idle to ascribe the rewards and punishments to God. Considering that the span of life on earth, or the stay in heaven, is of a very transitory nature, the realised souls want to avoid the cycle of birth and death and aspire for *Brahman* Loka where the stay is supposed to be permanent and the soul lives in perpetual bliss and happiness.

The departure of soul from the body is followed by the departure of vital force called *Prāna*. The breath is the vehicle which carries *Prāna* to all the three bodies and five sheaths. Therefore, when *Prāna* departs, death occurs. As already mentioned, the subtle and causal bodies do not die with the gross body and the combination of these bodies accompany the soul when it takes rebirth. *Citta,* which is repository of all the *Karmas,* always remains with soul till the time of *Pralaya* and carries the remaining *Samskāras* with it which start bearing fruit in the next birth. Therefore, life and death undistinguished as these are, are nothing but different names of the same reality. One who goes beyond this differentiation, conquers death and becomes immortal, having parched the remaining Karmas and having freed himself from the bondage of matter.

To a Yogi, many subtle bodies become visible in the state of meditation. Some such bodies are of great souls who appear to be preaching. Even Patanjali makes a similar mention. He says that the Yogi while meditating in the middle of the eyebrows, sees the subtle bodies of the *Siddhas*. Some such Siddhas appear as ice coloured, others as bright coloured, like gold, and yet others as dull blue and dim.[23] The subtle bodies of those who are to be reborn in near future, have colours different from those of the Siddhas. While the bodies of the Siddhas have complete knowledge of the *Tanmātras* and of the subtle enjoyments, the bodies of such souls, as are to be reborn, do not have any such knowledge. Their knowledge is akin to the knowledge of animals and beasts and their motion in the cosmos also appears, as if, directed by some one. Such bodies are still routed in the gross world, unlike those who have obtained liberation through knowledge. The latter bodies move in the cosmos or the region of the *Tanmātras,* as they desire. These bodies are not directed by any one else and also have no obstacles. Swami Yogeshwaranand advises that when a Yogi sees such figures in meditation, he should concentrate more deeply and then decide whether he wants to see these sights or not. He should carefully investigate the activity of the subtle world in which the said bodies exist and apply his subtle eye to it. In that state, he should also see *Brahman* through His proximity to *Prakriti* and feel His all Pervasiveness.

This, in the substance, is the nature of death and the concept of life after death, which is attested by Swami Yogeshwaranand through his deep experience in his super–conscious state.

REALISATION OF BRAHMAN

In his book 'Science of Soul', Swami Yogeshwaranand has explained how the knowledge of self can be acquired by the knowledge of each of the elements on the basis of *Sattva, Rajas and Tamas,* the three *Gunas* of *Prakriti.* According to him, no other teacher has described the knowledge of self in the manner in which he has described this knowledge. He says that the said method of self realisation is the result of his personal research, based on his own experience. Similarly in his book 'Science of Divinity', he has shown, based on his own experience, how every object, while undergoing changes, passes through five stages of evolution, namely *Sthula* (gross), *Swarùpa* (form), *Suksham Rupa* (elementary or subtle form), *Anvaya Rupa* (origin) and *Arthavatta Rupa* (purpose), and also how *Brahman* can be realized at every stage of evolution of the object. He says that even this method of realisation of the Absolute, is the result of his own knowledge gained through his personal experience and that no other teacher, seer or scholar has explained the knowledge of *Brahman* in this manner in the past. If an aspirant has obtained the knowledge of self on the basis of what is mentioned by him in his book 'Science of Soul', it will be easier for him to realise *Brahman* in some time because he has already learnt the method of analyzing his self and has also acquired knowledge of the gross objects. Without gaining this initial knowledge, it will not be possible for him to have knowledge of the Supreme Self. As *Brahman* pervades *Prakriti,* we must realise the process of evolution of subtle *Prakriti* into various elements and understand how during the whole process of evolution, each element was associated with God. The entire process of creation can be comprehended through *Dhārna, Dhyāna* and *Samādhi*. This method also helps in comprehending the nature of *Prakriti,* its activity, *Ātman* and *Brahman*. According to Swami Yogeshwaranand, it is the best method for realisation of *Paramātman*.

The yoga system describes *Dhārna* as a concentration of *Citta* on a particular object, but Yoga treats *Citta* and *Buddhi* as one and the same thing.[24] The method of *Dhārna* is to sit errect in a comfortable posture with eyes open or closed. Swami Yogeshwaranand directs one to control the mind and sense organs and with the help of intellect, through the vision of subtle eye, look into the earth as far as possible and fix the gaze on the final point reached in the earth. Impressions of any objects should not arise. The attention be continually fixed on that predetermined object. This is called *Dhārna*. *Sāmkhya* corroborates this concept of *Dhārna* and says that *Dhārna* is a continuous and unbroken concentration on an object when even the idea of the object is absent.[25] When *Dhārna* has lasted for a reasonable time, one enters the state of *Dhyāna* and when *Dhyāna* has lasted for a long time, which could be as much as six hours, one enters the state of *Samādhi*.

Dhyāna is the state of self–forgetfulness in which one visualises only the object of concentration and nothing else. If this state continues for nearly ten hours, then the state of *Sāmadhi* manifests. *Sāmadhi* is of two types namely *Samprajnāta* and *Asamprajnāta* which are also called *Sabija* (with seeds) and *Nirbija* (without seeds) *Samādhis*. *Sāmprajnata Sāmadhi* is further divided into four types of *Sāmadhis* namely (1) *Savitarka*, (2) *Nirvitarka*, (3) *Savicāra* and (4) *Nirvicāra Samādhis*. These *Samādhis* are explained as under:

(1) *Savitarka*: In this *Samādhi* the word meaning and knowledge are mixed and the aspirant is in doubt about the object on which his vision is fixed. For example, if concentration is fixed on earth element, the aspirant will be confused as to whether it is sound or meaning or knowledge whereas earth is neither sound nor meaning nor knowledge. The clarity with regard to the object of concentration comes in *Nirvitārka Samādhi*. But the knowledge gained even in this *Samādhi* is rather mixed up and the aspirant will find himself unable to accurately determine the nature of the earth on which he has fixed his vision.

(2) *Nirvitārka*: In this *Samādhi*, the word, meaning and knowledge of the object of concentration becomes much clear to the aspirant. He is enabled to experience the nature of the element of his concentration but this knowledge is restricted to only the five elements.

(3) *Savicāra*: This is the *Samādhi* in which the realisation of self takes place. In this *Samādhi*, the aspirant perceives the subtle elements which include five *Tanmātras*, five subtle organs of perception, five subtle organs of action, mind, intellect, *Ahamkāra, Citta, Tamas, Rajas, Sattva,*

time, direction, space and subtle or unmanifest *Prakriti,* which are all products of matter. He can also perceive what forms are assumed by these elements in the process of evolution. Self is always in association with *Citta* and, therefore, the self cannot be realised in isolation. In *Samādhi,* when the self discards the support of *Citta* and wants to establish in its own essential nature, then at the stage of realisation of *Citta*, one has a feeling of 'I exist'. This can be realised in this *Samādhi.*

(4) *Nirvicāra*: This is an improvement over *Savicāra Samādhi*. Even in this *Samādhi*, the aspirant perceives all the above mentioned elements without their causes, reason or time. After perfecting the four types of *Samprajñāt Samādhis* mentioned earlier, the aspirant takes up practice of *Assamprajñāt Samādhi*. In this *Samādhi*, impressions of the objects are completely stopped and one attains complete detachment from the world and its objects. After the aspirant is fully established in total renunciation, he attains the state of salvation through this *Samādhi*.

Yoga system mentions only the above *Samādhis* although some scholars divide the four *Samprajñāt Samādhis* into six while some others make it into eight *Samādhis*. Swami Yogeshwaranand mentions the aforesaid four *Samprajñāta Samādhis* together with one more *Samādhi* which he calls *Śúnya Samādhi*. This *Śúnya Samādhi* is not found in the yoga system of philosophy. Narrating his own experience of this *Samādhi*, he states:

> "I may give my own experiences. When an aspirant gives up Jap, contemplation and meditation, and engages himself in extinguishing the doubts and distracting ideas which arise in him, and has no other aim or target to be achieved

through *Samādhi,* and for a long time keeps himself occupied only with one single idea, then his body, sense organs and internal organs feel stiff and cease to be active. This state may last for several hours and even for several days. When the aspirant rises, he feels that during the time of his *Samādhi* he felt or thought nothing and his body and *Antahkarna* were absolutely inactive. The organs and *Prāna* had stopped working and his body becomes pale and the face looks depressed. He cannot open his mouth and the eyes become closed. He does not hear any sound and his posture becomes absolutely steady and this state lasts till he gets up.

When he begins to get up, he feels some sensation in his *Brahmarandhra*. He does not hear if somebody talks to him. When he tries to open his eyes he finds that he cannot. He cannot even stretch his legs because they have become stiff. If he is massaged by somebody, he regains the movements. If he has sat in *Samādhi* only for ten or twelve hours, then he takes only a few minutes in regaining his former state, but if he was in *Samādhi* for several days, then he might take even two hours before he is able to get up.

After he has risen he can have no idea at all of trouble or joy in that state. This shows that he did not experience these feelings in *Samādhi*. If he had, then he could have told something about it. We cannot say that his self steadied in itself, because when he sat in the *Samādhi* his target was not the self. His aim was to annihilate distracting thoughts and doubts. How could he then steady his self in self? May be, that without any object in view, the self of the Yogi became steady in self but we cannot say anything about it."[26]

Thus *Śúnya Samādhi* can arise when one does not have any particular object of knowledge as the main aim of concentration. So, this *Samādhi* provides neither knowledge nor ignorance because the sole aim of the aspirant was to extinguish distracting thoughts, doubts and apprehensions and knowledge was not his objective.

Reverting to the philosophy of realisation of *Brahman,* expounded by Swami Yogeshwaranand and contained in his book "Science of Divinity", it is observed that he has dealt with 34 objects of which *Brahman, Ātman and Prakriti* are eternal and the rest are non–eternal. Even *Prakriti* is eternal only as cause but it is non–eternal as effect. *Prakriti* is eternally associated with *Brahman* which is the efficient cause of the products of *Prakriti*. It is this association which gives rise to knowledge and activity in *Prakriti*. In the first part of his book, Swami Yogeshwaranand has explained the five stages of the five gross elements, namely earth, water, fire, air and the space and how *Brahman* can be realised through all of them. He has also explained how these elements are associated with *Brahman* and how, because of this association, *Brahman*, being the efficient cause, causes movement in them. He has shown that each element has five states and that *Brahman* can be perceived in each state. In the second part of the book, he has given the description of five *Tanmātras,* five organs of action, five organs of perception, the mind and the *Ahamkāra* (ego principle). He has given a detailed explanation of how these are produced and how *Brahman* can be perceived in each of them. Third part of the book deals with the creation of *Sattva, Rajas* and *Tamas Ahamkara* as also cosmic mind and intellect. He has given suitable explanation of the three *Gunas* of *Prakriti* which are the material causes of the creation in totality. He has also explained how *Brahman* is associated with these elements and how this causes motion in *Prakriti*. Here also he has shown how *Brahman* can be realised through the aforesaid creation. The Fourth part of the book deals with the *Alinga Prakriti* or *Prakriti* in its absolute equilibrium. He has explained how the initial six objects namely, the time, direction and space and *Sattva*, *Rajas* and *Tamas*, came into existence and how *Brahman* is associated with *Prakriti* in its cause and effect forms. It is also explained how *Brahman* can be realised through it. In the fifth part, Swami Yogeshwaranand has explained the state of release or liberation (*Mokṣa*). This part deals with the nature of release and how it is attained by the self. After discussing many theories, brought out by other systems of thought, he has tried to establish that *Ātman* and *Brahman* are non transformable. It is also discussed whether the release is permanent or it has a fixed duration. We have mentioned, on the authority of Swami Yogeshwaranand, that *Brahman* can be realised at each stage of transformation of *Prakriti* into five great elements namely earth, water, fire air and space. He says that the gross earth is the final form of subtle earth element. Prior to the creation of earth element, the other four elements had already been created. For creation of earth, the subtle smell *Tanmātra* started to transform itself and when it came into contact with water, the contact brought the five elements also into reckoning. Till then the earth and water were only in the form of smell and taste but when these came into contact with fire, they acquired a visible form. Due to the presence of *Brahman*, other elements combined with earth, water and fire and the sensation of touch manifested. Before it reached the final stage of creation, earth developed eleven qualities which are:

(1) Form;

(2) Firmness;

(3) Weight ;

(4) Hardness;
(5) Crust;
(6) Cracking;
(7) Dryness;
(8) Contraction;
(9) Support;
(10) Forebearance;
(11) Sarvabhogyatva (provider of enjoyment);

When the earth developed the above eleven qualities, at each stage of development, it was the presence of *Brahman* which motivated the development. According to Swami Yogeshwaranand, when earth assumed the form of a substratum to support life, vegetation appeared first of all. Then came the birds and animals. Thereafter came the great souls which had to return to the world on termination of their duration of salvation, along with those who strayed from their path of Yoga. The creation of these souls was asexual. The creation of beings through contact of man and woman started only after that. In all this the directing power was *Brahman*, because inanimate objects, by themselves, cannot proceed intelligently and systematically. A Yogi, in his state of *Samādhi*, can acquire the knowledge of how these *Mahabhutas* (the great elements) are created and can visualise the entire process of creation. It is for this reason that Swami Yogeshwaranand commenced with earth in cosmic form through which to realise *Brahman*. The Yogi who wants to gain knowledge of *Brahman* must fully realise the five stages of transformation of earth element. The knowledge of these five stages of transformation of earth will lead him to detachment as he will realise that his bondage is caused by earth. *Brahman* pervades the earth element in and out and, therefore, one can realise *Brahman* through this *Mahabhuta*. Having realised the cosmic earth element, the aspirant also realises objects. But *Brahman* is subtler than the subtlest and, therefore, the aspirant has to sharpen his vision in *Samādhi* and move on to water element which has five forms and which forms he must necessarily perceive in deeper *Samādhi* to have the feel of *Brahman's* presence.

The five forms of water are exactly like the five forms of earth which we have already mentioned. While earth has been stated to have eleven properties, water has ten properties which are as under:

(1) Suksamata or thinness;
(2) Snighata or oiliness;
(3) Mriduta or softness;
(4) Heaviness
(5) Prabha or brilliance;
(6) Śuklata or whiteness;
(7) Śheetata or coldness;
(8) Sammelan or combination;
(9) Pavitrata or purifying property;
(10) Protection;

The purpose of mentioning these details is that the Yogi should know and realise how the above transformations have taken place in the presence of *Brahman*. The visible form of earth and water clearly indicates that their creator is *Brahman* and it is due to this that water is worshipped by followers of all religions. The Hindus worship water and take a dip in Ganga and in the sea. The Parsis also worship sea. Even Muslims in Egypt have a special adoration for the waters of river Nile. The various forms of worship of *Brahman* at different stages of transformation of water are indicated to realise the presence of *Brahman* at each stage. These transformations act as means of acquiring knowledge of *Brahman* which knowledge leads to salvation.

The yogi should now move to the next element fire. Fire is subtler than water which we have just now discussed. He should perceive the five forms of fire in the same way as he perceived the five forms of earth and water and also feel the presence of *Brahman* in it. He should make his *Samādhi* firm and his concentration very penetrating. This concentration should be acquired through *Dhārna, Dhyāna* and *Samādhi*. Fire has eight properties and it transforms into these properties only due to the proximity of *Brahman*. These properties are:

(1) Lightness;
(2) Upwardness;
(3) Brilliance;
(4) Ripening;
(5) Purification;
(6) Power or Ojasvita;
(7) Burning or Dahakata;
(8) Destructiveness.

The material cause of fire is its corresponding *Tanmātra* but the efficient cause is *Brahman* who is also the efficient cause of the total creation. Therefore, the yogi must realise the proximity of *Brahman* in each transformation of the fire element and, once he realises *Brahman's* presence in one object, he can easily realise it in every object. It is mentioned in *Vaiśeṣika Sutras* that the self and the mind, taken together, can realise the self in the self itself and once it is done, *Brahman* can also be realised.[27] *Atharva Veda* says that the Sanyasi can know Him.[28] It all tantamounts to the fact that it is the realisation of the soul that leads to the realisation of *Brahman*.

The eight attributes of fire are not apart from fire because the object and its attributes inhere in each other and are the same. Similarly *Brahman* is all pervasive and, therefore, *Brahman* cannot be considered as separate from pervasiveness. Fire pervades water because it is subtler than water and *Brahman,* being subtler than all, is capable of pervading every thing. A yogi can see in *Samādhi,* with his deep vision and sharp intellect, all the transformations of fire and, at the same time, he can also experience the presence of *Brahman* at each stage of transformation for He is the efficient cause of the whole process of transformation. Fire abides in the bodies of all beings and also pervades the space. It pervades all the animate and inanimate things and it is for this reason that fire is worshipped all over the world. And in this all pervading fire, the Yogi should realise in the *Samādhi,* the all pervasive *Brahman*. But, as already stated, to know *Brahman*, one must first know the self with which one can compare *Brahman*. Swami Yogeshwaranand says that you can perceive *Brahman* in the cosmic fire if you have already perceived your soul. If soul is not first realised, one will stop only at the knowledge of fire and the knowledge of *Brahman* will evade him.

The next element is air. When touch *Tanmātra* transforms, it evolves into air element. Space, which is already present, helps the air element to undergo transformation by providing space which is necessary for creation of air element. As compared with air, fire, water and earth are grosser in content and, therefore, these are visible to the naked eye. Because it is subtle, air is invisible. While water and earth are the objects of taste and smell *Tanmātra* respectively, air is the object of touch *Tanmātra*. Air can be experienced only through touch and through no other means. The Yogi can realise in *Samādhi* how the touch *Tanmātra* undergoes various transformations in the presence of *Brahman*. Air has the following eight properties:

(1) Tremulousness;

(2) Slanting Movement;

(3) Constant Movement;
(4) Dryness;
(5) Purification;
(6) Coverlessness;
(7) Force;
(8) Shock (Akshepa)

All the above transformations take place due to the proximity of *Brahman* and the Yogi must visualise not only the transformations but also feel the presence of *Brahman*.

Prakriti is constituted of three Gunas namely *Sattva*, *Rajas* and *Tamas* and because, air is also a product of *Prakriti*, these Gunas are necessarily present in air. Because of *Rajas*, it is always in motion. The *Sattva* and *Tamas* also exist in it but these are present only as auxiliary, in a small quantity. Its quality of purification and of coverlessness indicate the presence of *Sattva Guna* in it. It sustains all living beings which also shows that *Sattva* is present in it. In its *Tamasic* form it moves inside the heavenly bodies and helps in their movement. At the time of *Pralaya*, when fire consumes the whole universe, air acts as its main helper. Swami Yogeshwaranand says that air is the mobile form of *Brahman* and is, therefore, worthy of worship. The Upanishadic view also lends support to what is said by him, when it says that *Brahman* resides in the air but the air does not know Him. The air is His body which He moves from inside.[29] When the Upanishad says that air is the body of *Brahman*, it only makes a symbolic mention because *Brahman* does not have a body. He only pervades the air and wherever there is air, *Brahman* is also present. While the air moves, *Brahman* does not move because He is all pervasive and is present every where. One must visualise the transformations of air and realise the presence of *Brahman*.

It may be noted that all through in his works, Swami

Yogeshwaranand has been talking only of the feel of *Brahman* and not of the experience of any physical visualisation of Him. According to Him no one can fully know *Brahman*. Even Keno–upanishad says, "if you think that you have known Him correctly, then certainly you do not know Him. One who claims that he has known Him, in reality does not know Him."[30] Swami Yogeshwaranand expresses himself on this point as under:

> "In the name of the *Brahman* many religions have been founded. Every religion has tried to know him and has known him to a certain extent. In our opinion the wise man is he who does not claim that he alone has known the whole of the *Brahman*, while others have not known him. The Keno–upanishad says, 'If you think that you have known him correctly, then certainly you do not know him or have known very little of him.' What you have known or others have known should be meditated on. This is how I understand. In fact one who claims that he has known Him does not know Him. If *Brahman* had been fully known to one individual, then it would have been limited and localised. That very little of *Brahman* is known to a Jiva, shows that the knowledge of *Brahman* is limitless. A knower, then, should never claim that he knows *Brahman* in entirety."[31]

He says that as an easy way, we can perceive God through a medium which could be light or *Prāna,* which abide within our body. He, however, says that if you want to see and understand God in His purest form, then you should not make light or *Prāna* as the medium but cast your vision directly on him. And if you do so, a stage will come when your intellect will have direct nexus with the Supreme Consciousness, but such an experience cannot be expressed in words. When you fix your gaze on it, you see consciousness only in one form and no matter when you see it, it will appear in the same form which you will be unable to recollect or define later on, but you will have the satisfaction of having comprehended consciousness in its true form.[32]

The last element through which *Brahman* can be realised is the space *Mahabhuta* which, although formless like air, is subtler than it and is also invisible. While air can be experienced through touch of the skin, ether can be realised through ear. Space *Tanmātra* or sound *Tanmātra,* and the modifications of ether can be experienced only through ear. *Samādhi* for realising space *Tanmātra* has to be a specially deep *Samādhi* so that the vision could penetrate the orb of space *Tanmātra* and lead to primordial *Prakriti* where one may realise *Brahman,* being in close proximity to space element, and try to realise its efficient cause. Just as in the formless air elements, formless *Brahman* was realised, the Yogi should now realise the space element as also its transformations and feel the presence of *Brahman* therein. Like all other elements, space also has five forms. It has only three qualities which are as under:

(1) All–pervasiveness (Sarvatragati);

(2) Dispersiveness (Avyuha)

(3) Availability.

Like *Brahman,* space or *Ākāsha* is also considered as all-pervasive but the pervasiveness of the two is different. It is regarded as pervasive in comparison with the other four elements and not in comparison with *Brahman* who is subtlest of all. It consists of only the particles of sound *Tanmatras*. Just as *Brahman* is everywhere, *Ākāsha* is also everywhere and this makes it easier to realise *Brahman* in it. Swami Yogeshwaranand gives the following method of realising *Brahman* in *Ākāsha*:

"Control the activities of your *Buddhi* by becoming

> calm and quiet and let your yogic eye penetrate the subtlety of *Ākāsha*, and, therein, realise the intelligence of *Brahman*. You will feel a subtle tremulousness, which exists in a very slight and subtle form in the *Ākāsha* itself. Then penetrate deeper and deeper. You will feel that it comes from *Brahman*, in whom there is intelligence. There cannot be an absence of activity where there is an association of *Brahman*. In every object the subtle activity exists. The activity exists in every object according to the affect of *Dharma*, *Sādhana* and *Avastha*. It may be more or less according to the nature of an object. *Brahman* urges general activity. The sun gives equal light to all but a diseased eye feels it differently. The sun rays are equally warm but when passed through a sun glass, they become extremely hot and produce fire. When passing through an ordinary glass the rays do not become so hot. Besides, the rays do not pass through iron, copper and wood. Similarly the light of *Brahman* moves to every object equally but the difference in the nature of objects, causes different perceptions. There is no region in the *Ākāsha* where some particles, called Dwenuka, Trasrenu, Chatasrenu or Pancharenu, do not move. They always pervade it. Your eye must penetrate through them and reach the region where they are absolutely absent, and what exists is only the space. There you should realise the pervasiveness of *Brahman*."[33]

Those who worship formless *Brahman*, for them the best media is *Ākāsha* because *Ākāsha* is also formless and all pervasive like *Brahman*. But because *Brahman* is subtler than *Ākāsha*, He pervades it. On this account, *Ākāsha* is gross as compared with *Brahman* which pervades it. It is, therefore, in *Ākāsha* only that *Brahman* can be realised and the pervader pervaded relationship understood.

We have so far discussed and described the knowledge of five subtle elements, their relationship with *Brahman* as their efficient cause and the presence of Brahman in all their transformations. We have also mentioned how to realise Brahman in all these transformations. Swami Yogeshwaranand says that just as one can have knowledge of transformation of the five elements into their gross form, and can also realise *Brahman*, in the same way one can obtain knowledge of five *Tanmātras* and also gain realisation of *Brahman*. While *Bhutas* are gross elements, *Tanmātras* are subtle or cosmic elements. The five *Tanmātras* are sound, touch, form, taste and smell. These *Tanmātras* are extremely subtle and correspond to the five gross elements. In *Sāmkhya* these are called *Tanmātras* but in yoga these are called subtle *Bhutas*. In *Nyāya* and *Vaiśeṣika* these are called atomic particles but considered as eternal, whereas in *Sāmkhya* and yoga, these are considered as non–eternal because these are created by cosmic *Tamas Ahamkāra* and what is created is always destroyed. The *Tanmātras* are the final form of cosmic *Ahamkāra* with a combination of *Sattva, Rajas* and *Tamas* which are present in all the transformations. By themselves, the *Tanmātras* have no life because these are created by inanimate matter but it is due to proximity of *Brahman* that they appear to be intelligent and transform themselves into gross forms to provide pleasure and pain to the living beings. Because of His proximity, the Yogi can realise *Brahman* in the *Tanmātras* and their transformations. We, however, do not intend to go into the detailed method of realisation of *Brahman* in *Tanmātras* because it is similar to realisation of *Brahman* in five *Mahabhutas.*

In addition to the five *Mahabhutas* and five subtle *Tanmātras,* Swami Yogeshwaranand also mentions three other elements through which *Ātman* and *Brahman* can be realised. These three are *Prāna* (the vital Force), *Divya Śabda* (Divine Sound) and Divine Lights, all of which are valuable for realising the soul and *Brahman*. He has written three books, one each pertaining to *vital air,* sound and lights. In his book "Science of Vital Force" he has described in detail, seventy types of *Prānas* and explained how realisation of soul, *Brahman* and *Prakriti* can take place through touch of *Prāna*. This is based on his own personal experience in *Samādhi*. He says that realisation of self and *Brahman,* through *Prāna,* has not been known to any other scholar in the past although many techniques of self-realisation, by means of light, have been mentioned. According to him, the distinctive feature of his book is that by following the given instructions, the aspirants will be able to directly experience all the inert and conscious objects by the touch of *Prāna*. He has recorded the existence of thirty types of *Prānas* in the gross body, thirty types of *Prānas* in the cosmic objects and has proved that all these *Prānas* and their relationship with *Brahman,* can be realised in *Samādhi*. He has also described the origination of *Prāna* in the balanced state of *Prakriti,* its awakening due to contact of *Brahman* with *Prakriti*, the discrimination between *Puruṣa* and *Prakriti* as also the means of attaining liberation.

In his book "Science of Divine Sound", he has explained the existence of 108 sounds and given various techniques of realisation of self and *Brahman* through these sounds. He says that sound first originated in the balanced (quiescent) state of *Prakriti.* He has also mentioned that the gross world and gross bodies were created millions of years after the creation of the world of subtle and causal bodies. Knowledge has manifested in the human heart in a communicable form as sound which embodied meaning and knowledge and which is peculiar to only human beings. It is only human beings who can expand and develop sound, meaning and knowledge. In other living beings it exists only as common variety. He has given 108 techniques of realisation of *Brahman*. These techniques relate to sounds of which thirty sounds exist in gross body, thirty in subtle body, twelve in causal and thirty six in macrocausal bodies. He says that on realising self and *Brahman* by means of these 108 types of sounds, one attains dispassion which leads to final emancipation.

In his book "Science of Divine Lights" he has described 155 lights with the last light being that of *Brahman*. All these lights are illuminated by the light of *Brahman* who imparts movement to all the other 154 lights. The book consists of four chapters of which the first chapter deals with sixty nine types of divine lights operating in the gross body and gross elements. He has explained the realisation of self and *Brahman* through all these lights. Second chapter deals with six types of divine lights in the region of astral world and astral body and also deals with the methods of realisation of self and God through these lights. In the third chapter, he has discussed six types of Divine lights and given many methods for realisation of *Brahman*. In the fourth chapter thirteen types of macrocosmic entities are mentioned and the presence of *Brahman* in twelve of them has been explained. He has also given a detailed explanation of how to realise *Brahman* through the said entities. In the final paras he has explained the essential nature of the soul and its stay in *Mokṣa*.

With this we bring to the final conclusion our discussion on the philosophy of self-realisation of Swami Yogeshwaranand which is not only different in most part, from the philosophy known to us so far, but throws a flood of light of fresh information on the most subtle subject of soul and God. This information is the result of many decades of research and verification of its truth in the super–conscious state of his deep *Samādhi* and can be appreciated only by some one who has done similar research and verification in *Samādhi*. While discarding some age old beliefs on the subject and deviating from the views of such acharyas as Kapil and *Patāñjali*, he has thrown open many avenues for further study and research in matters which have been considered sacrosanct so far and amenable to no discussion. This indeed is his contribution to the field of spiritual philosophy.

REFERENCES

(1) Beads of Sermons (Part IV p. 74)
(2) Beads of Sermons (Part IV pp. 79-80)
(3) Science of Soul (p. 67)
(4) Science of Soul (p. 67)
(5) Taittriya Upanishad (Brah. Vathi, Sec. 2, Mantras 1-2)
(6) Science of Soul (p. 115)
(7) Science of Soul (p. 152).
(8) Yoga Sutra (IV-17)
तदुपरागापेक्षित्वाच्चित्तस्य वस्तु ज्ञाताज्ञातम्
(9) Science of Soul (p. 328)
(10) Geeta 4-37 *ज्ञानाग्निः सर्वकर्माणि भस्मसात् कुरूते तथा*
(11) Chāndogya Upanishad (3-12-9)
(12) Yoga Varttika (Part 1, p. 245)
(13) Yoga Sutra (1-3) *तदा द्रष्टुः स्वरूपेरवस्थानम्*
(14) Science of Soul (pp. 307-308)
(15) Sāmkhya Sutra (1-104)
(16) Sāmkhya Sutra (1-105)
(17) Science of Soul (pp. 309-310)
(18) Kathopanishad (2-4-1) *कश्चिद्धीरः प्रव्यगात्मानमैक्षत!*
(19) Science of Soul (p. 321)
(20) Science of Soul (p. 153)
(21) The Tibetan Book of the Dead (p. 155)
(22) Sacred Journey (pp. 94-95)
(23) Yoga Sutra (3-32)
(24) Yoga Sutra 3 – 1 *देशबन्धश्चित्तस्य धारणा*

(25) Ṡāmkhya Sutra 3-30 ध्यानं निर्विषयं मन:
(26) Science of Divinity (pp. 8-9)
(27) Vaiṣeśika Sutra 9-1-11
आत्मन्यात्मनसो: संयोगविशेषादात्मप्रत्यक्षम्
(28) Atharva 9-3-6-1 योविघात् ब्रहम प्रत्यक्षम्
(29) Brahd Upanishad (3-7-7)
(30) Kenopanishad (2-1)
(31) Science of Divinity (pp. 98-99)
(32) Beads of Sermons (Part II p. 25)
(33) Science of Divinity (p. 108)

Bibliography

(1) Dasgupta, S. N., A History of Indian Philosophy (Vol. 1), Delhi, Motilal Banarsidass, 1997.

(2) Chatergee, S. C. and Dutta, D.M., An Introduction to Indian Philosophy, Calcutta, Published by themselves.

(3) Yogeshwaranand Saraswati, Swami, Beads of Sermons (Vol. 1-6), New Delhi, 1995.

(4) Vireswarananda, Swami, (Tr.), Brahman-Sutras (Śankara Bhāshya) Advaita Ashrama, Calcutta, 1978.

(5) Swahananda, Swami, (Tr.), Chāndogya Upanishad with Commentary of Śankaracārya, Rama Krishna Math, Mylapore, Madras-4.

(6) Pelletier, Kenneth R., and Garfield Charles, Consciousness East and West, London, Harper and Row Publishers, 1976.

(7) Yogeshwaranand Saraswati, Swami, Tr. by Mumuksu and Saraswati, Abhyudayanand Swami, Essential Colourlessness of the: Absolute (Nirgun Brahman), Rishikesh, Yoga Niketan Trust, First Edition, 1976.

(8) Larson, Gerald James and Bhattachrya, R. S., Encylopedia of Indian Philosophies (Vol .IV) Sāmkhya:, Delhi, Motilal Banarsidass.

(9) Krishnamurti, J., Freedom from the Known:, London, Victor Gollanez Ltd., 1985.

(10) Munshiram, Manoharlal, Gaudapada Karika, New Delhi.

(11) Yogeshwarnand Saraswati, Swami, Himalaya Ka Yogi, Tr. by Dr. M. L. Sharma and Abhyudayanand Saraswati, Part I and II, New Delhi Yoga Niketan Trust, 1978.

(12) Radhakrishnan, Dr. S., Indian Philosophy (Vol. I), New Delhi, Oxford University Press.

(13) Williams, R., Jaina Yoga, Delhi, Motilal Banarsidass.

(14) Chinmayananda, Swami, Kaivalya Upanishad, Bombay, Central Chinmaya Mission Trust.

(15) Chinmayananda, Swami, Kathopanishad, Mumbai, Central Chinmaya Mission Trust-1989.

(16) Dayanand Saraswati, Swami, Light of Truth:(Satyartha Prakasha), Tr. by Dr. Chiranjiva Bhardwaja. Sarvadeshik Arya, Pratinidhi Sabha, New Delhi, 1984.

(17) Ranade, R.D., Mysticism in Maharashtra, Delhi, Motilal Banarsidass, 1988.

(18) Chinmayananda, Swami, Mandukya Upanishad: With Karika, Mumbai, Central Chinmaya Mission Trust.

(19) Jayanta Munshiram Manoharlal, Nyāyamanjari, New Delhi.

(20) Śivananda, Swami, Practice of Yoga, Rishikesh, The Divine life Society, 1979.

(21) Yogeshwaranand Saraswati, Swami, Science of Soul: (Atma-Vijñāna), Tr. by Swami Jyotirmayananda, Yoga Niketan Trust, 1997.

(22) Yogeshwaranand Saraswati, Swami, Science of Divinity: (Brahma Vijñāna), Rishikesh, Tr. by Dr. M. L. Sharma, Yoga Niketan Trust, 1973.

(23) Yogeshwaranand Saraswati, Swami, Science of Vital Force: (Prāna Vijñāna), Tr. by Swami Muktananda Saraswati, New Delhi, Yoga Niketan Trust, 1980.

(24) Yogeshwaranand Saraswati, Swami, Science of Divine Lights: (Divya Jyoti Vijñāna), Rishikesh, Tr. by Devendra Kumar Kapoor, Rishikesh, Yoga Niketan Trust, 1991.

(25) Yogeshwaranand Saraswati, Swami, Science of Divine Sound: (Divya Shabad Vijñāna), Tr. by Swami Muktanand Saraswati, Rishikesh, Yoga Niketan Trust, 1984.

(26) Shastri, Acharya Udayveer, Sāmkhya Siddhānta, Delhi, Vijaykumar Govindram Hassanand, 2000.

(27) Rama, Swami, Sacred Journey, New Delhi, Himalayan International Institute of Yoga Science and Philosophy, 1996

(28) Virupkashanand, Swami, (Tr.) Sāmkha Karika of: Íśvara krṣna, Chennai, Ramkrishna Math, 1995.

(29) Gambhirananda, Swami, (Tr.) Śvetaśvatāra Upanishad, Calcutta, Advaita Ashrama, 1995.

(30) Chinamayananda, Swami, The Holy Geeta, Mumbai, Central Chinmaya Mission Trust, 1989.

(31) Ballanture, James R., The Samkhya Aphorisms: of Kapila, New Delhi, Munshiram Manoharlal.

(32) Chinmayananda, Swami, (Commentary), Taittriya Upanishad, Bombay, Central Chinmaya Mission Trust, 1992.

(33) Sinha, Nanda Lal, The Nyāya Sútras of Gotama, Delhi, Tr. by M. M. Satish Chandra Vidyābhúsana, Motilal Banarsidass.

(34) Evans-Wentz, W.Y., The Tibetan Book of the Dead, London, Oxford University Press, 1960.

(35) Desai, M.R., (Commentary) The Yoga Sutras of Patāñjali, Kolhapur, Desai Publication Trust, 1972.

(36) Aranya, Hariharanand, Swami, Yoga Philosophy of Patāñjali: With Bhāsvati, Tr. by P.N. Mukherji, University of Calcutta, Calcutta 2000.

(37) Rukmani, T.S.(Tr.), Yogavarttika of Vijñāna Bhikṣu, New Delhi, Munshiram Manoharlal.

(38) Gupta, Munilal (Tr.), Shri Vishnu Purana: (In Hindi), Gorakhpur, Geeta Press.